We Will Rise in Our Might

Documents in American Social History
Edited by Nicholas A. Salvatore

We Will Rise in Our Might

WORKINGWOMEN'S VOICES FROM
NINETEENTH-CENTURY NEW ENGLAND

Mary H. Blewett

Cornell University Press

Ithaca and London

First published 1991 by Cornell University Press.
First printing, Cornell Paperbacks, 1991.
Second printing 1994.

International Standard Book Number (cloth) 0-8014-2246-9
International Standard Book Number (paper) 0-8014-9537-7
Library of Congress Catalog Card Number 91-55077
Printed in the United States of America
*Librarians: Library of Congress cataloging information
appears on the last page of the book.*

♾ The paper in this book meets the minimum requirements
of the American National Standard for Information Sciences—
Permanence of Paper for Printed Library Materials, ANSI Z39.48-1984.

To the memory of my grandmother,
Nora Beatrice Drinkard Dykeman, a vamper,
and to the memory of my mother,
Eunice Violet Dykeman Hedge, a backstayer.

Contents

Contents

Illustrations

Acknowledgments

Three people helped me in different ways to complete this book. Carole Turbin, a colleague and friend, drew me with her warmth and intelligence into a circle of historians and sociologists interested in exploring the worlds of working-class women. Thomas Dublin shared an intense interest in the sources and the experiences of New England shoeworkers and sustained this work with his long-term support and helpful criticism. When Alice Kessler-Harris became crucially involved in the Sears case, she was forced to put aside her editorial duties on the completed manuscript of my book *Men, Women, and Work* and thus unwittingly placed me in a position of creative frustration that prompted the writing of a first draft.

I also thank my undergraduate class in Women in American History, who with patience and courage read the first draft and suggested changes. Others whose advice and criticism contributed to the final shape of the work include Maurine Greenwald, Patricia Sterling, Nick Salvatore, and Kerby Miller.

Many institutions and individuals helped me to assemble this collection by affording me access to photographs and illustrations and permission to quote from documents. I am grateful to Baker Library, Harvard Business School; Old Sturbridge Village; the Beverly Historical Society; Boston Public Library; Margaret Conrad, Acadia University; Barbara Ward, Essex Institute; Haverhill Public Library; Ronald Karr, Reference Librarian, University of Lowell; Caroline Singer, Haverhill Historical Society; Kenneth Turino, Lynn Historical Society; the Manchester Historic Association; Clare Sheridan, Museum of American Textile Histo-

[xi]

ry; Ruth J. Morton; United Food & Commercial Workers International Union, AFL-CIO, for the papers of the Boot and Shoe Workers' Union at the Wisconsin State Historical Society.

MARY H. BLEWETT

Lowell, Massachusetts

We Will Rise in Our Might

INTRODUCTION

The Industrialization of Shoe Production in Nineteenth-Century New England

Industrialization, once labeled a revolution, is now regarded by historians as a less abrupt and more complex process: a gradual unfolding of various new ways to make things. Some industrial production in nineteenth-century America took place in factories, to which workers came each morning to operate machines run by water or steam power. Cotton textile mills in southern New England pioneered the factory system in early nineteenth-century America. Massachusetts investors copied British textile machinery and integrated all steps in cloth production into large factories. But factory production was only one model of the changing patterns of work. Older systems involving small workshops and mill villages coexisted with the new factory centers for much of the century. Some industries in major cities such as New York and Philadelphia relied on the decentralized production of limited quantities of goods handmade in artisan shops. Gradual change and uneven development marked the whole process of industrial growth.

The history of boot and shoe manufacture in New England, particularly that of Essex County in eastern Massachusetts, illustrates the diversity and gradual pace of nineteenth-century industrial change and reveals the conflicts and tensions that signified how deeply that unfolding process transformed the experiences of work, manhood and womanhood, family life, and politics. The first section of this introduction surveys the pre–Civil War period of slow evolution toward a factory system of shoe production and the responses of workers to changes that they often feared and opposed. The second section explores the reactions and behavior of factory workers who sought to build strong labor organizations to represent their collective interests. The third compares the distinctive culture and politics of New England female shoeworkers with traditional assessments of the experiences of male and female workers during industrialization in the nineteenth century.

"These *Things Ought Not So to Be!*"

Shoemaking in New England began as a household activity among seventeenth-century colonial farmers. Rough foot covers fashioned from the cured hides of livestock served until, as settlement increased, farm families could obtain the services of trained shoemakers, skilled artisans who often bartered shoes for other goods or services. Because they made shoes to individual order, their market was limited to the local population and its needs, and production remained small scale.

Beginning about 1750, however, the work of shoemakers in the Essex County town of Lynn, the innovative center of American shoe production, began to change. Groups of artisan masters, journeymen, and boy apprentices gathered together in "ten-footers"—little shops roughly ten feet square—where, instead of making shoes to order, they produced standard sizes in small lots. These goods were sold at local stores or, in some cases, carried on horseback to distant towns. Even without the aid of machinery or water power, such groups of artisans increased production and developed new standards for their work.

Local storeowners with cash assets soon began to provide tanned hides to shoemakers and pay them wages to turn the leather stock into shoes. After developing networks of information and exchange, the Essex County storeowner or merchant-capitalist also arranged to market the shoes out of town, usually to retailers in Boston or in the South. The merchant-capitalist earned the highest return from these arrangements because he owned both the raw material and the finished product. As shoemakers who could not afford to buy their own leather and sell their own shoes became wage earners, their status as independent craftsmen began to erode.

The shift in control of profits earned from shoemaking created conflicts between male artisans and merchant-capitalists during the early nineteenth century. Artisan life began with apprenticeships, rested on a group experience of training and work, and thrived on traditions of

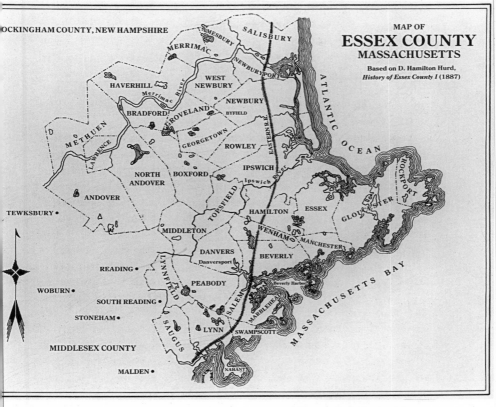

Essex County, Massachusetts, 1887. Courtesy of University of Illinois Press.

mutual obligation and loyalty among masters, journeymen, and apprentices. Artisans valued their independence as skilled workers, and they joined with other craftsmen to safeguard the welfare of their families. These values were linked with the natural rights theory of political equality learned during the struggle for American independence. Artisans believed that workers and employers possessed equal rights to work and prosperity as well as to political representation. They resisted surrendering control of the product of their labor to merchants. The merchants, however, could offer shoemakers not only the leather hides to work but access to new markets for finished footwear. They also successfully lobbied after the American Revolution for a tariff on foreign-made shoes that protected the domestic market from English competition. Slowly and reluctantly, artisan men adapted to the new ways.

Once merchants gained control of profits, shoemakers tried to earn more in wages by producing more shoes. Before 1780 the wives and daughters of artisan shoemakers did not make shoes, though like all colonial women they worked hard producing useful items both for their own households and for barter, such as butter, cheese, honey, spun yarn, or woven cloth. Thus they contributed to their family economy in ways that tied them into exchange networks in the local community. Looking around for additional hands to sew leather, artisans began to teach their wives and daughters to stitch the upper part of the shoe. In doing so, they brought women workers into the craft and created the sexual division of labor that characterized shoe manufacture throughout the nineteenth century.

Women sewed or "bound" the uppers in their kitchens, remaining outside the ten-footers and separate from the craftsmen and apprentices. The artisan system denied women the full training of an apprentice, which also involved learning how to cut leather, shape or "last" the shoe to the correct size, and put on the sole and heel. Artisan life in the ten-footers kept men and boys in a masculine world distinct from that of the women, but shoemakers had tapped a new supply of labor to increase production and provide more shoes for the merchants to sell. As a result, calculations based on both family need and market demands penetrated the homes of shoemaking families and began slowly to alter their work and their lives.

Women who sewed uppers for their fathers or husbands earned wages only indirectly through the increased earnings of their menfolk. But busy wives and daughters found it hard to meet the insistent demands from the ten-footers for sewn uppers when they had children who needed feeding or bread that needed baking. Supplying enough uppers for shoemakers required hiring additional women from the families of farmers or other tradesmen in Essex County villages. After 1810, the storekeepers of Lynn, Marblehead, Danvers, Haverhill, and other Essex County towns began to recruit women directly as "shoebinders," pay them wages (usually in store goods), and coordinate their work with that of the shoemakers. This system of domestic production, known as "outwork" or "homework," persisted throughout the nineteenth century, even after the introduction of the sewing machine and the organization of shoe factories. Working at home, by hand or later by machine, allowed wives and mothers to contribute earnings to their families, but home-work was always characterized by low wages—the very reason manufac-turers kept the system going.

Between 1810 and 1840 the economy of southern New England moved away from subsistence farming and the maritime activities of seacoast towns to the development of a series of factory centers and mill villages. Shoemaking dominated the economy of Essex County, employ-ing more men and women workers than any other industrial pursuit. Markets expanded: hand-sewn ladies' shoes and crude work brogans made for slaves were sold in the South and the West Indies. Early industrialization in shoemaking began to change the organization and location of work, introduced new divisions of labor, and reshaped family and community life. By the mid-nineteenth century, work once done in the household or nearby shop slowly shifted into new central shops and factories. Men's work, the usual measure of productive activity, moved farther away from the home and left women in charge of domestic life.

Much of women's work in the nineteenth century consisted of unpaid housework and most of the duties of child rearing. To many observers, this domestic labor appeared disconnected from the male world of in-dustry and public life and politics. Yet women dominated the first work force in the early cotton textile factories of Waltham and Lowell, Massa-chusetts. At the same time, women who remained in their homes sought ways to earn cash in order to buy the much-coveted factory-made calico and gingham. New kinds of outwork—binding shoes, braiding straw hats, or sewing garments—employed many more Massachusetts women before 1850 than did textile factory work and enabled them to earn wages as homeworkers. By 1855 nearly 20,000 women were sewing shoes for Essex County manufacturers. Throughout the nineteenth cen-tury the numbers of women involved in paid productive labor, whether at home or in the factory, continued to grow.

Because the separation of work and home during early industrializa-tion divided the worlds of male and female, however, women developed new responsibilities for the religious life and moral standards appropri-ate to the private sphere they had come to control. American society began to acknowledge and revere woman's role as the arbiter of religious values, morality, and domestic life; the homely virtues associated with womanhood contrasted with the acquisitive, competitive practices that prevailed in the male world of commerce and industry. The corruptions of the materialistic world of early industrialization incited female moral anger and impelled some women out of the home to apply domestic virtues to public life. Their moral and religious role became an active principle in engaging early nineteenth-century women in reform activities such as the antislavery and temperance movements: slavery with its interracial sexual contact threatened to disrupt white and black families alike and violated Christian morality; drunken husbands and fathers disturbed domestic order. All these new cultural forms and political activities accompanied ongoing industrial change.

Men and women shoeworkers, inspired by the artisan belief in equal rights and by the moral responsibilities of domestic womanhood, responded to the changing conditions of their employment by seeking fairer treatment from their employers. As one woman wrote in 1834: "These *things ought not so to be!*" Both shoebinders and shoemakers sought to surround their work with a proper context of economic justice and moral right. In the 1830s and 1840s separate organizations of men and women workers demanded higher wages paid in cash, not in faded and out-of-fashion store goods. Furthermore, rebellious shoebinders in the early 1830s began to recognize the importance of public action on behalf of social reform and new rights for women.

In the 1840s and 1850s, shoe manufacturers developed new ways of producing more shoes without paying higher wages by reorganizing their work forces. Essex County merchant-capitalists in Lynn, Haverhill, Marblehead, Salem, and Danvers led the way. They decided to concentrate cutting operations for leather into central shops where the sharp eye of the owner or "shoe boss" could oversee the work and protect profits. Shoe bosses issued new standards for work, baited with a guarantee of wages in cash. At the same time, using the new transportation services of teamsters and railroads, they hired additional outworkers in the rural villages and distant towns of New Hampshire and Maine. Shoemaking thus became a regional industry that bound countryside and shoe town together. Tapping new sources of rural labor created new problems of organizing the work. Nonetheless, decentralized production based on outwork—with all its inefficiencies and delays—had by the decade of the 1850s made eastern Massachusetts the center of national shoe production.

The preeminence of New England in shoemaking was clinched by the adaptation of the sewing machine to stitch leather and the rise of the early factory system just before the outbreak of the Civil War. More and more shoe bosses enlarged the operations of their central shops into factories. Steam engines ran sewing machines that produced even, regular stitches far faster than those sewn by human fingers. The spread of mechanization and centralization was slow. Most workers by 1860 were still making shoes by hand in decentralized locations—but the pace of industrial change had begun to accelerate.

Shoe bosses had persuaded some journeymen to enter the early factories in the 1850s. Inside the shops, employers divided the tasks of cutting leather into light for uppers and heavy for soles—and then assigned to different men the work of putting on soles and heels. Other bosses bought machines for various operations such as heeling, still relying on foot power to run them. Artisans who had left their ten-footers felt restive in the new central shops and grumbled about different wages for divided work. Outside the factories, employers recruited additional workers. More rural men and boys became shoemakers, hooked into the network of production by express teams and railroad lines that reached deeper into the countryside of Maine and New Hampshire. Many Irish and German immigrants to New England towns, men with little apprentice training or artisan experience, abandoned manual labor in the 1850s to become shoemakers.

Shoe bosses also began to centralize and mechanize women's work, while maintaining the sexual division of labor for stitching uppers. The appearance of stitching machines to replace hand sewing brought angry shoebinders crowding the doors of central shops in Lynn and Haverhill to voice their disapproval and fear. The majority of female workers continued to stitch uppers at home by hand or on hand-cranked or foot-powered sewing machines rented to them by their employers. Nevertheless, by 1855, hundreds of young unmarried women were running sewing machines, at first by foot treadles and later by steam power, in the early factories of Lynn, Haverhill, Marblehead, and Danvers.

Unlike the young women workers in the shoe shops, homeworkers had to "find" or "furnish": that is, provide such materials for their work as thread, wax, and cloth linings. The costs of furnishing plus the slower pace of foot-powered machines and the interruptions of domestic life created two standards in women's wages: one for factory work and a lower one for homework. The productivity of machine stitchers who worked a ten-hour day far outstripped that of homeworkers: one factory girl operating her stitching machine full time could replace eleven shoe-binders. As a result, the total number of women employed in shoe production fell sharply between 1850 and 1860.

Many of the early factory stitchers were daughters of local families living in the centers of shoe production. Mechanization, centralization, and higher wages for factory work also drew migratory female workers from small towns and rural villages to the early factories of Essex County, much as young, single New England women had once flocked to the cotton textile mills of Lowell and Lawrence in Middlesex County. Although manufacturers in shoe centers still relied on a dual system of production to get enough sewn uppers—local homework, either by hand or on rented machines, and steam-powered machine work in factories—patterns of seasonal migration to factory towns slowly undermined the outwork system in rural New England.

The economic depression of 1857 created a crisis in the shoe industry of New England and precipitated the most important antebellum incident of American labor protest. In 1860 men and women shoeworkers joined together in a great regional strike that opposed the fundamental changes taking place in the industry. The effects of mechanization and centralization of production had created widespread fear and anger among New England shoeworkers. The old ways were giving ground to powerful new forces. The family economy based on the availability of decentralized work to men and women outside the factory walls was in peril. The new factory workers—the machine girls, the heelers, and the journeymen who ventured inside the new central shops—seemed an alien group. Those in defiance in 1860 reaffirmed family, community, and artisan values. A sense of common crisis over changes being made in the system of production that bound workers in the countryside to workers in shoe centers explains the regional nature of the strike.

During the 1860 strike, shoeworkers invoked their traditional sources of artisan protest and moral outrage to fight the emerging factory system and defend decentralized work. They organized on an unprecedented geographical scale from rural areas in Maine and New Hampshire to the shoe towns of Middlesex, Worcester, and Essex Counties in Massachusetts. The center of action, however, was in Lynn, where the male leaders of the strike, in a move of far-reaching significance, rejected a potentially powerful alliance between the new work force of women in factories and the traditional work force of women at home. This female alliance represented decisions made by workingwomen at their own strike meetings whereby they sought to raise wages for all women workers. Instead, the strike leaders in Lynn chose to concentrate on higher wages for male workers in an effort to achieve the goal of a family wage that would enable a man to support his family by his own efforts. Their decision alienated the female factory workers and split workingwomen into opposing camps during the strike.

Ironically for the strikers, their activities had a buoyant effect on the depressed market for shoes: with production halted, prices began to rise. A few shoe bosses offered slightly better wages to end the strike—although they refused to sign any agreements meeting the strikers' demands. Slowly, as the weeks went by, shoeworkers throughout New England returned to work, and the great strike collapsed without any immediate effect on the relations between worker and employer. After suffering severe disruptions to the regional economy brought on by the Civil War years, the New England factory system continued to mature and to change the way shoes were produced. As factory workers, both men and women continued to fight for economic justice and moral right in the post–Civil War industrial system.

"We Will Rise in Our Might"

Between 1865 and 1873 the shoe industry of Essex County grew, changed, and prospered. The manufacturers of Lynn spearheaded the drive toward a system of production based on the centralization and mechanization of both men's and women's work, the development of new divisions of labor, and the use of steam power. In the immediate post–Civil War years, Lynn manufacturers also decided to specialize in one product: the high-cut, side-opening ladies' boot. This high-buttoned shoe became a staple of late nineteenth-century women's apparel as thousands of women moved into the work force and public activity after the Civil War. Shoe manufacturers in New England adopted new approaches to industrial production, seeking to dominate the national market in the mass production of this standard item.

Shoe bosses in Lynn led the way in developing machinery to replace hand methods. Building multistoried factories of red brick with adjacent steam-engine houses topped by tall chimneys, the large manufacturers filled them with steam-powered machines. The new technology gave the employers advantages as they sought to control production costs—

especially the costs of labor—in order to maintain their edge in the highly competitive postwar market. Threats from shoe factories in New York state and Philadelphia were met by reducing wages and increasing the speed of production. The newest machinery deepened the divisions of labor, permitted the hiring of unskilled workers, kept wages low, and undercut labor protest.

In an innovative effort to forecast demand and balance the supply of shoes manufactured to meet it, Lynn employers pioneered a new pattern of marketing. Instead of waiting for buyers to make their selections from Boston warehouses full of finished shoes, they began to send "drummers" by train to retail stores across the country. These salesmen carried special cases that held samples of the next season's shoes from which the retailers could make their choices. Only when the telegraphed orders reached Essex County did factory workers begin to make the shoes in quantity. The result of this system of making shoes only for advance orders was to reshape shoe production into alternating seasons of intensive and slack effort: the busy few months for the spring and fall trade were followed by slow periods. This pattern, created to match the supply of shoes to market demand, transformed the experience of work in shoe factories.

Each major division of work occupied a different floor in the postwar shoe factory. Large windows illuminated the work areas of cutters and stitchers; gas jets were installed next to sewing machines to augment the short daylight hours of the December-to-March busy season for the spring trade. The 1862 invention of the McKay Stitcher to sew the upper to the outer sole was followed by the development of scores of other machines that mechanized men's work during the postwar years. As each machine took its place on the shop floor, the manufacturers reduced the piece rate paid for that process. Shoeworkers had to learn how to use the new machinery as quickly and efficiently as possible to keep up their earnings.

As shoe bosses in Essex County felt additional competitive pressures from other eastern shoe factories, they continued to cut the piece rates on machine work. The results were lower wages, fewer workers required for each job, longer dull seasons in the factories, and more exhaustingly intensive work during the busy seasons. Manufacturers also experimented with changing the sexual division of labor to reduce wages, introducing women into work such as cutting and lasting, which had traditionally been controlled by men. Using these methods, Essex

County shoe manufacturers succeeded in dominating their segment of the postwar national market before the onset of the depression of the 1870s.

Shoeworkers organized to oppose the worst aspects of these changes. Men founded the Knights of St. Crispin (the patron saint of cordwainers) in 1867, and in 1868 women organized the first national union of workingwomen, the Daughters of St. Crispin (DOSC). Members of the DOSC included four distinct groups of workingwomen in postwar shoe manufacture: (1) unmarried young daughters of families resident in the growing shoe cities of eastern Massachusetts; (2) single, migratory women who boarded with local families and stayed in town only for the busy seasons: (3) single women residents who headed families usually composed of themselves and widowed mothers or dependent siblings; and (4) a small number of young wives who worked at stitching shoes until they had their first child. Between 1865 and 1905, women composed one-third of the total work force in New England shoemaking.

Because Civil War deaths and westward migration in the 1860s had depleted the number of marriageable men in New England, many of the women who joined the DOSC were unmarried and needed to support themselves; others provided for dependents. The majority of the workingwomen in Essex County shoe factories were native-born New Englanders of rural or small-town background. According to the 1870 census, 86 percent of female shoeworkers in Lynn were native-born. Yankee factory girls dominated the female work force in the post–Civil War shoe factory and remained a distinct cultural type in New England society throughout the late nineteenth century. The stitcher who, during a strike in 1871, predicted that her Yankee sisters would "rise in their might" was drawing on this New England heritage.

In the 1870s and 1880s, however, they were joined by growing numbers of American-born daughters of Irish, French-Canadian, and English-Canadian immigrant families. By 1900, 30 percent of the female workers in Lynn were native-born daughters of immigrants. The increasing ethnic diversity within the ranks of stitchers challenged the accepted meaning of womanhood based on one cultural tradition. In the 1880s Yankee females and Irish daughters struggled to develop labor tactics that might reconcile gentility with militancy.

As the streets, boardinghouses, and factories of shoe cities filled with workers who came and went with each busy season, middle-class residents and clergymen began to worry about a potential decline in public morality. Changes in the rhythms of industrial production into busy and slack seasons attracted hundreds of new people of unknown reputation into the community. Many of these were women living in female-headed families or transients who roomed in unregulated boardinghouses. Victorian moral standards stigmatized female industrial workers, who were thought incapable on their own of maintaining propriety or avoiding the sexual dangers of industrial life. Concerned middle-class women wishing to protect moral womanhood joined with manufacturers eager to defend their sources of migratory labor. Together, they fashioned the image of the "lady stitcher" as a means to confer respectability on female shoeworkers. Middle-class women of Lynn organized the Woman's Union for Christian Work to offer moral guidance and seemly amusements to lady stitchers. Shoe bosses used this image of female respectability not only to protect their labor supply but also to justify their attempts to substitute women workers for men and thereby reduce wages.

The Crispin organizations, with the support of smaller manufacturers who feared cutthroat competition with larger firms, successfully opposed the worst excesses of overwork during the busy seasons in Essex County. They defended the sexual division of labor against unwelcome changes and won higher wages for both men and women shoeworkers. In addition, the Daughters of St. Crispin, through workingwomen's associations in the Northeast, made contact with other groups of female industrial workers in garment-making and textiles. At conventions of the National Labor Union in the late 1860s and early 1870s, DOSC leaders allied with the labor reformers and trade unionists who made up its membership. DOSC delegates championed equal rights for working women and began to debate the significance of woman suffrage for female industrial workers. In doing so, they introduced labor feminism into the postwar American labor movement.

Crispinism did not survive the collapse of the economic system during the depression of the 1870s. The hard times between 1873 and the return of prosperity in 1880 exposed the sometimes desperate and divisive competition among groups of women workers which fatally weakened the DOSC. These divisions represented both ethnic rivalries and differences in marital status. Shoe bosses were still hiring female homeworkers to undercut factory wages. Low pay for men sent their wives into the overcrowded labor market on behalf of their families, while self-supporting women could barely earn a living wage, and women with dependents faced privation. New stitching machines with double needles and automatic devices undercut the skills and wages of experienced women vampers and buttonhole stitchers, whose fine work determined the quality of the finished shoe.

A decade of public debate among workingwomen revealed widespread disagreements over the proper role of women in the shoe shop, in labor protest, and in family life—even over the nature of womanhood itself. Should wives compete for jobs and wages with unmarried women who supported themselves? Should young women become lasters and thus undercut the wages of family men? Could a Yankee lady's concerns with proper behavior be reconciled with the militancy required of union girls? During hard times, serious divisions within the female work force over appropriate work for women and political disagreements over the propriety of woman suffrage made it difficult for workingwomen to organize effectively and confront their employers.

When better times returned in the early 1880s, the Knights of Labor swept through Essex County, organizing thousands of men and women shoeworkers. As an all-inclusive organization of reformers and workers critical of the economic injustice of industrial capitalism, the Knights demanded higher wages and sought political power to legislate labor reform. Women members participated in the organization at all levels. Like the Daughters of St. Crispin, they attended national conventions to advance the interests and rights of female industrial workers. They also linked up with middle-class women in the growing national movements for woman suffrage and temperance. After much activity in the early 1880s, however, internal disputes over the proper role of women in the Knights and the growing appeal of trade unions organized according to various skills and industries led both men and women shoeworkers out of the Knights and into the trade unions.

The cruel depression of the 1890s pushed shoeworkers into the new American Federation of Labor (AFL), representing all organized craftworkers. In the 1880s manufacturers had invested in additional machinery and management techniques that were transforming the remaining skilled male jobs—lasting and cutting—in shoemaking. Remorseless use of the piece-rate system by shoe bosses continued to cut wages, extort extra effort, and produce speedy work at the lowest labor cost. Ever larger factories equipped with the latest in technology (including electric motors and lights by 1900) made enormous quantities of shoes available for sale at the lowest prices. This was the typical response of

Lynn manufacturers to the intensifying competition from emerging shoe factories in the midwestern cities of Cincinnati, St. Louis, and Chicago. With heavy investments at risk in a depressed economy in the 1890s, the relations between labor and capital in the Essex County shoe industry became more and more tense and ugly.

In response to the difficult depression years that had begun in 1893, shoeworkers in Haverhill went on strike in 1895. Support for this strike in other New England shoe cities, organized in part by the activism of women stitchers, created the basis for a new federation of shoe crafts, the Boot and Shoe Workers' Union, affiliated with the AFL. Successful strike action in 1895 left women stitchers in control of their own locals within the BSWU. Their leader, Mary A. Nason, a divorced Yankee from Maine, skillfully sustained both the militancy and the loyalty of the Haverhill stitchers, who pointedly abandoned the genteel status of the lady stitcher to embrace the militant and sometimes disorderly virtues of "union women." Nason also successfully organized cross-class support from Boston women who were either socialist or reform-minded members of the middle and upper classes.

In recognition of her abilities and popularity, Nason became the only woman member of the national executive board of the BSWU. Her own commitment to socialist and feminist ideas led to her efforts to organize all women shoeworkers into autonomous locals. Her position on the national executive board later created opportunities for women shoeworkers from midwestern locals in the BSWU to form an alliance with middle-class reformers in the AFL's Women's Trade Union League, established in 1903 to organize women workers and fight for their rights.

In 1900, shoeworkers in Massachusetts still represented more than 40 percent of the work force in the national industry. Their support was crucial to the success of the new union. By 1903, however, conservatives in the BSWU led by President John F. Tobin of Rochester, New York (formerly a member of the Socialist Labor Party), had alienated most of the shoeworkers of Essex County, who bolted the union during a bitter strike in Lynn. One source of trouble was the refusal of the BSWU leaders to allow women stitchers to retain control of their union locals. Another was the shattering of gender solidarity between female loyalists in the BSWU and women workers who defended Essex County traditions of local autonomy and equal rights.

When the majority of Essex County women shoeworkers left the AFL in 1903 just as the Women's Trade Union League in Boston was getting started, they took with them the longest tradition of interest in women's rights and suffrage and the best record of effective labor protest among female industrial workers in nineteenth-century America. Throughout the century, women shoeworkers had faced multiple and sometimes contradictory realities of work and womanhood as they participated in the evolving system of shoe production. They were conscious of developing class divisions in industrializing America and condemned the unjust distribution of profits and power in the shoe industry. Those who were outworkers understood their place in the wage labor market, and beginning in the 1830s they expressed in outbursts of anger and protest their moral outrage at the negative impact of competitive market forces on the worth of their labor. They relied on their belief in Christian values, social equality, republican political rights, and the labor theory of value to justify their protests. In the important New England shoe strike of 1860, women played a crucial and controversial role.

For many women shoeworkers, a shared identity as females strengthened their common class experience. In the nineteenth century, womanhood meant a specific cultural experience. Although working-class women's lives were linked through the family with those of working-class men, womanhood also provided them significant connections with one another and with middle-class women who shared the values and experience of being female, despite class differences. This common sense of womanhood allowed women shoeworkers to build networks of support with sympathetic reform-minded women of the middle class.

Nevertheless, women shoeworkers struggled over the meanings of family loyalty, morality, and womanhood and how each might be employed as a basis of protest activity. Sisterhood, or gender consciousness, produced a nineteenth-century tradition of female-controlled organizations among women shoeworkers. Many accepted the importance of wage work for women in industrial capitalism and tried to act together to advance their interests as workers. Both the sexual division of labor in shoe production and the cultural experience of womanhood supported their sisterhood. In contrast, family loyalty as a basis for labor protest usually relegated women to a restricted public role and to an acceptance of dependence and subordination within the family.

Before the organization of the factory system, women shoeworkers expressed their womanhood in ways similar to those of middle-class women in the early nineteenth century. Although shoebinders worked hard, most homeworkers considered their domestic duties primary and their efforts at wage earning secondary. When home and children came first, shoebinding for most remained part-time and casual work. Yet their sense of the special moral capacities and religious responsibilities of females, which they shared with middle-class women, plus the added virtue for shoebinders in artisan families of being a "useful woman," justified their public action and demands for fair wages.

Although class and gender conflict as well as the contradictory appeals of sisterhood and family loyalty shaped the nineteenth-century labor protest of New England women shoeworkers, their involvement in their own organizations and in public action designed to secure their rights as workers led many to advocate new rights for all women. Traditionally regarded as appendages of their families, these workingwomen vigorously debated issues central to their womanhood and to their citizenship in American society. As a result, women shoeworkers contributed in significant ways to the development of feminism within the nineteenth-century American labor movement.

Beginning in the early 1830s, women shoeworkers united in collective action, claiming a right to public protest based on customary principles of justice, morality, and equal rights. They recognized that as workers they had to develop forms of collective power to achieve any reform of the economic system. Buoyed by their sense of self-respect and self-worth, they published resolutions and declarations, organized and conducted strikes, established labor organizations controlled by women, participated in public parades and political action, and testified to newspaper reporters, state agencies, and social reformers about their working lives. The poems, moral tales, and novels of New England writers celebrated their steadfast labor and their contributions to family well-being. Their tradition of protest reflected the view of both men and women workers in the shoe industry that their grievances could be resolved only by reshaping the terms of industrial work and altering the power relationships between labor and capital.

"We Have an Ambition Yet That Is Hard to Tame, to Dependence"

Many historians have argued that nineteenth-century industrialization did not fundamentally alter the commitment of American women to domesticity and their families. They point out that middle-class women did not commonly engage in paid work at all and contend that the (often undifferentiated) mass of young, single working-class women worked only until marriage and then expected their husbands to earn a family wage high enough to support wives and children. Wives of low-paid male workers might earn a little money working at home or venture into factories for short periods of time, but a working wife was regarded by the American labor movement in the nineteenth century as a sign of failed manhood. In this view, male hostility to women workers as competitors and women's commitment to family values limited their participation in labor organizations. Low wages and a lack of training restricted women's opportunities in the work force. Temporary and relatively unskilled work funneled most women into marriage and dependence on the family wage. Competition over industrial jobs created tensions between men and women workers and reinforced support for a rigid sexual division of labor and higher wages for working men, whether or not they actually had families to support. Consequently, working-class women supported the family wage for male workers and seemed uninterested in the politics of the women's rights movement or in woman suffrage. In short, it has been thought that the class interests of working women were embedded in family life.

But historians who ignore or overlook (whether consciously or unconsciously) the experience of working-class women thereby define working-class experience as masculine. Research that produces working-class history through studies of male-controlled work or communities or strikes, policies such as the family wage, and organizations that primarily represented the interests of working-class men imply that family values and domestic virtues (often articulated by male workers) dominated the experience of workingwomen. For examples of treatments of the New England shoe industry that ignore or undervalue women's experience, see Alan Dawley, *Class and Community: The Industrial Revolution in Lynn* (Cambridge: Harvard University Press, 1976); Paul G. Faler, *Mechanics and Manufacturers in the Early Industrial Revolution: Lynn, Massachusetts, 1780–1860* (Albany: State University of New York Press, 1981); and John Cumbler, *Working-Class Community in Industrial America: Work, Leisure, and Struggle in Two Industrial Cities, 1880–1930* (Westport, Conn.: Greenwood Press, 1979).

The documents in this collection, however, reflecting the varied experiences of the women shoeworkers of Essex County, contradict the traditional view of nineteenth-century female workers. These documents—drawn from Mary H. Blewett, *Men, Women, and Work: Class, Gender, and Protest in the New England Shoe Industry, 1780–1910* (Urbana: University of Illinois Press, 1988)—reveal an alternative experience of female class consciousness, debates over political rights and the nature of womanhood, involvement in skilled work and autonomous labor organizations, and the development of labor feminism within the American labor movement. The engagement of women in the early nineteenth-century outwork system demonstrates the invasion of family life by industrialization and the large-scale recruitment of homebound women into paid preindustrial work. Economic development transformed patterns of life and work within the family. Changing conditions of work plus disappointed expectations prompted expressions of class consciousness and feminism by female shoeworkers beginning in the 1830s and continuing into the early twentieth century. Political debates among workingwomen over the proper role of women in society and the question of woman suffrage were vehement and persistent. The defection of the women shoeworkers of Essex County from the AFL left its mark on the direction and politics of the twentieth-century labor movement.

Mechanization and the development of the factory system in the 1850s and 1860s offered many women stitchers a chance to become self-supporting wage earners. Factory work meant the possibility of developing skill, experience, and a sense of independence, self-respect, and sisterhood with other women aside from family loyalties and community ties. Geographical mobility and the sexual division of labor seemed positive experiences for many Essex County women shoeworkers. As "females in artisan families," as "lady stitchers," as "freeborn women," and as "union girls," they made the changing historic content of female gender a cultural resource for labor protest. Their involvement in the labor movement throughout the nineteenth century indicates a female tradition of activism and autonomous organization that offered an alternative to the family wage and female economic dependency. They were, as "A Union Girl" wrote in 1885, "hard to tame, to dependence." Their record as activists for labor reform and women's rights indicates that many of these female industrial workers well understood the necessity of gaining political power to represent their interests in a changing industrial society.

Nor was their experience so uniform as the conventional view suggests; on the contrary, it was complex and diverse. They struggled among themselves over the meanings of gender and class consciousness for workingwomen and over questions of family loyalty or sisterhood as a basis for their labor protest. They were drawn by moral and religious concerns to cross-class alliances with middle-class women—antislavery advocates, moral reformers, suffragists, temperance workers, and labor reformers—but often faced the submersion of their class interests within these movements. They questioned the significance of industrial employment for themselves as women and debated how best to defend themselves as workers.

If women shoeworkers clearly differed from the traditional portrait of nineteenth-century workingwomen, their experience of industrialization was also distinctly different from that of working-class men in ways shaped by gender. Preindustrial work for shoebinders had offered them no chance to learn a craft or participate as equals in the culture and politics of artisan life. Male shoeworkers sought to confine women to the family and to moral activities and often opposed representation of women's interests as workers in strikes and in male-controlled labor organizations. Yet the factory system that degraded male artisans and their independence offered many women their first chance to work together in groups away from the claims of domesticity and family. The conditions of female work in post–Civil War shoe factories meant relatively high wages during prosperous times, access for some women to skilled work, and an opportunity to dominate an important part of the process of shoe production.

But a transient woman shoeworker often faced a public suspicion about moral respectability rarely experienced by the transient man. Nor were male shoeworkers divided among themselves over issues of sexual morality or whether or not they were married. Conflicts between self-supporting single women and wives over family obligations seemed unique to working-class females and as potentially divisive to their organizations as issues of ethnicity, skill, and race.

Despite the divisions among workingwomen and the differing experience of men and women shoeworkers as industrialization unfolded, there were also dramatic moments of cooperation and unity when working-class women and men acted together and successfully defended their interests. The documentary evidence of the pre-industrial and industrial experience of the women workers of Essex County changes the traditional picture of the lives of working-class women in nineteenth-century America and highlights the human potential of overcoming divisions between the sexes.

PART I

Women Shoeworkers in the Household and Early Factory, 1780–1860

Even before women had any direct involvement in shoe work, they traded their manual labor or their household products for the services of custom shoemakers. Account books kept by Essex County shoemakers such as Deacon David Marsh and his son, of Haverhill, Massachusetts, illustrate such exchanges. The Deacon Marsh accounts (1721–39) contain notations of shoes and shoe repair bartered with families in town for products and services often representing the household work of women: butter, cheese, tallow, the spinning of shoe thread and wool, the dyeing of stockings, and the combing and weaving of wool and flax. Marsh also accepted the general labor of sons and daughters: for example, "Your Daughter with us 5 days," credited to the widow Elizabeth Page's account in April 1725. Esther Hurley's credits in 1739 listed combing wool, spinning, and two fish caught in the Merrimack River.

The better part of a century later, David Marsh, Jr., was still making custom shoes in Haverhill as his father had done, and his accounts (1791–1812) continued to list exchanges of shoes and mending for credits of labor, including husking corn and "cutting" onions. Excerpts from both account books are quoted courtesy of the Trustees of the Haverhill Public Library, Special Collections Department.

Deacon David Marsh Account
Debits:
Aug 29, 1738 then Reckoned with the widow Esther Hurley Due to
me to one pair of shoes for your Self
Nov. 9, 1738 to one pair for Betty

[21]

Feb. 12, 1739 to mending shoes
Feb. 19, 1739 to mending shoes Self
May 15, 1739 to one pair for Self
Credits:
the widow Hurley Cr Jan 1739 to Spinning 14 Skeines & half
Feb 10, 1739 to Spinning 4 Skanes [*sic*]
May 30, 1739 To 2 Shad & 2 Skanes
              Com[b]ing 5-1/2 pd wo[r]sted

David Marsh, Jr., Account
Mrs. Black Credit
1792 March 17 by one day to comb flax
     April 28 by one day to comb flax and spinning thread for stockings
     Oct   by Self & Daughter [Hannah] 1 day to husk corn by
             combing 2 pounds & 1 ounce wool

When early industrialization in Essex County introduced women into the shoe trade, at first, they labored within their households for their shoemaker fathers and husbands, brothers and uncles—one step removed from the market for wage labor. After 1800, when merchant-capitalists expanded production by recruiting additional women into the developing outwork system, these female workers became increasingly separated from combined family effort on shoes. Instead, they earned wages as isolated individuals working at home for their employers, often experiencing hardship, physical exhaustion, and low pay. Because they were outworkers, their productivity remained low, but their meager wages did add somewhat to family income. Not until the advent of machine stitching were women employed in shoe factories.

[1]

Family Labor on Shoes

When changes in the organization of production introduced women into shoemaking, they adapted traditional needle skills to binding shoes, without formal apprenticeships. Sometimes they used waxed thread attached to hog bristles to sew the heavy leather for the uppers of men's work shoes and boots. This work required tough fingers and strong hands. Shoebinders did not straddle the benches that male shoemakers used. Instead they used a shoe clamp, a tool invented for their work which accommodated long skirts and aprons. The joined end of this long, flexible wooden clamp, usually made of barrel staves, rested on the floor. The binder placed the pieces of cut leather between its ends and held the staves together tightly with her knees, freeing both hands to use the awl or needle. After making holes with a sharply pointed awl, the shoebinder sewed up the back, front, and side seams of the upper, put in a lining, bound the top edges, and—depending on the style—added eyelets or designs.

Shoebinders sewed only the shoe upper, which was then passed on to the shoe shop, where journeymen and apprentices shaped or "lasted" the shoe to size and soled, heeled, and finished it. At first, shoebinders received no direct wages. Nor did most of them learn, as did young male apprentices, to make the entire shoe; only a very few Essex County daughters and wives mastered the whole craft of shoemaking. For most women, the new work represented little immediate change; it was part of their continuing traditional involvement in pre-industrial household production for the sake of family interests.

The close connection between productive household labor and wom-

[23]

Re-creation of shoebinding at Old Sturbridge Village, Massachusetts. Photograph by Robert S. Arnold. Courtesy of Old Sturbridge Village.

anhood in the eighteenth century provided the context for the initial recruitment of women to work on shoes. Sarah Smith of Newbury, Massachusetts, born in 1787, is representative of the women drawn into shoemaking at the turn of the century on behalf of their kin. In her detailed reminiscences of her family's homestead, built in 1707, she lovingly described its interior and recalled the demanding seasonal labors whereby her mother, aunts, and grandmother contributed to family sustenance. For Sarah Smith, being a woman meant performing constant work crucial to the economic well-being of her extended family.

In her late teens, Sarah began to braid straw bonnets during the summer months for a general store in nearby Haverhill, and in the winter she sewed the uppers of boots and shoes for her bachelor uncles, who had set up a shoemaker's shop at neighboring New Rowley Corner (now Georgetown, Massachusetts). Her account of working for her uncles contains no reference to wages, and after her marriage to David Emery in 1812, she stopped sewing shoe uppers. She had bound shoes out of family loyalty, inspired by affection for kin and a desire to see her uncles prosper as shoemakers and storekeepers. Sarah Smith's *Reminiscences of a Nonagenarian* was published by her daughter, Sarah Anna Emery, in Newburyport in 1879. These extracts are taken from pages 6–9, 58, and 87–89.

. . . The back chamber—the large one under the long, sloping back roof—was set apart for manufacturing purposes. Here the chief part of the clothing and other household goods for the family were spun and woven. The apartment was conveniently fitted up with looms, woolen, linen and spooling wheels, swifts, reels, cards and warping bars. . . . My parents had married young. Their chief capital for commencing life was youth, health and mutual love. . . . Industry and economy were the watchwords of the household; still, there was no overtasking or stinting.

In those summer days, when my recollection first opens, mother and Aunt Sarah rose in the early dawn, and, taking the well-scoured wooden pails from the bench by the back door, repaired to the cow yard behind the barn. We owned six cows; my grandmother four. Having milked the ten cows, the milk was strained, the fires built, and breakfast prepared. . . . During breakfast the milk for the cheese was warming over the fire, in the large brass kettle. The milk being from ten cows, my mother made cheese four days, Aunt Sarah having the milk the remainder of the week. In this way good-sized cheeses were obtained. The curd having been broken into the basket, the dishes were washed, and, unless there was washing or other extra work, the house was righted. By this time the curd was ready for the press. Next came the preparations for dinner, which was on the table punctually at twelve o'clock. . . . If there was linen whitening on the grass, . . . that must be sprinkled. After dinner the cheeses were turned and rubbed. . . . At five o'clock the men came from the field, and tea was served. The tea things were washed, the vegetables gathered for the morrow, the linen taken in, and other chores done. At sunset the cows came in from the pasture. Milking finished and the milk strained, the day's labor was ended. . . .

Butter making commenced in September. . . . The weaving of woolen cloth was begun, in order it should be returned from the mill where it was fulled, colored and pressed in time to be made up before Thanksgiving. . . . The winter's stocking yarn was also carded and spun, and the lengthening evenings began to be enlivened by the busy click of knitting needles. As Thanksgiving approached, the hurry both in doors and out increased.

. . . Mother, a manteau-maker before her marriage, had her hands more than full, as she was not only called upon to make the gowns for our family, but to fit the dresses for her own mother and sisters and others in the vicinity.

. . . Towards Christmas the fat hogs were killed, the pork salted, the hams hung in the wide chimney to cure, and the sausages made. The women began to comb flax and spin linen thread. . . .

. . . As soon as the spring weather would permit weaving without a fire, the rooms in the back chamber were set in motion, weaving the next season's linen. Next came candle-dipping, the making of soap, and house cleaning. The calves had been sold, churning commenced, and butter was made until the warmer weather brought the summer routine.

. . . The tedium of the summer work was relieved by the cutting, curing and boating the salt hay from Plum Island marsh. . . . This brought much heavy labor to both men and women. . . .

Four miles from "Crane-Neck" was a crossing of roads called "New Rowley Corner"; near by resided Maj. Paul Nelson, a smart man, carrying on considerable business. Though a bachelor, he kept house on his estate, upon which was a large tannery. Amongst the appurtenances of the place was a small shoe-maker's shop, which Lewis Hatch hired, and commenced the shoe business on a small scale. In a short time he was joined by my uncle Joe. Little, both young men boarding in the family of Maj. Nelson. The business prospering, my uncle Ben. Little, joined the firm, which hired the whole premises with the exception of the tannery. A housekeeper was procured, and Maj. Nelson in turn boarded with the young bachelors, who now had also several youths apprenticed to them, besides employing work men outside.

As a matter of convenience and profit Uncle Joe. Little conceived the idea of setting up a small grocery and general furnishing store. One of the front rooms of the house was fitted with shelves and other accommodations, and the goods were purchased. The shop-keeping immediately prospered. The workmen were pleased at being enabled to supply their household needs so easily, and as there had been no store for miles around, custom began to flock to the place, which even then wore a bustling air of prosperity.

It would have seemed but natural, as female cooperation was so necessary, that one at least of this trio of bachelors should seek a wife, and a legend is extant, that uncle Joe did for a time entertain some such idea. Before going to New Rowley, he had formed the acquaintance of a young lady, the teacher of the summer school in our district. The new firm manufactured for merchants in Salem and Boston, and as his grocery business increased, uncle Joe. made weekly trips to those cities, driving his team, which consisted of a two wheeled spring cart drawn by one horse. . . .

The father of the young lady teacher kept a tavern on the route; thus my uncle had ample opportunity to renew his acquaintance with the daughter. . . .

It was reported that one cold afternoon on his way home from Boston, Mr. Little called on the inn keeper's daughter. Unexpectedly opening the door to the private sitting room he briskly entered, but neither the lady nor the room bore the aspect of neatness to have been expected at that hour of the day and from one who had always seemed to pride herself upon her elegance. . . .

I never heard that the visit was renewed; every matrimonial inclination disappeared; Mr. Little became wholly immersed in his business, and Miss Mary Hatch, a sister of Lewis Hatch, took her place as mistress of the bachelor establishment.

The New Rowley manufacturers were often hurried on orders. In the winter season, when the straw work was suspended, I often bound both boots and shoes for them; in an emergency I was their resource.

One afternoon at the period of which I am writing, in the early part of the week, uncle Joe. appeared bearing a hundred pairs of seal-skin boots, which he said must be corded and strapped by Saturday. At first I declared they could not be done in such a limited time, but after some demure, yielding to his ardent solicitation, I promised to do my best, and without the least delay set to work. It was a dirty disagreeable job; only love for my uncle and a desire to promote his interest could have induced its undertaking. As it was, I stitched and stitched assiduously day after day, and the task was accomplished in the given time. The last stitch was just taken as uncle Joe. entered the door. He was accompanied by David Emery. Smut from head to foot I presented no very attractive aspect. The young man snatched the completed boot from my hand, and tossing it at uncle Joe. vehemently protested against thus imposing on my good nature. The matter ended in a laugh, but thenceforward only the lighter sort of work was brought to me, and that only upon some sudden exigence.

The shoemakers in their ten-footers set the pace for the shoebinder's efforts in her kitchen. The needs of the men for sewn uppers prepared in advance for each shoe required the binders to try to keep ahead of the work in the shoe shop. David Newhall Johnson of Lynn worked as an artisan shoemaker in the early nineteenth century. Pages 336–38 of his reminiscences, *Sketches of Lynn or the Changes of Fifty Years*, published in 1880, provide a description of the prototypical shoebinder who contributed her work to the family labor system common to shoemaking before 1830. He emphasized the importance to family income of women's labor and, later, of their wages. But he overestimated the earning capacity of the majority of shoebinders by citing as typical the wages paid only for fancy gaiter boots in the 1840s. According to Essex County account books kept in the early nineteenth century, most shoebinders' wages ranged between three and six cents a pair, depending on the style.

The shoe-binder of Lynn performed a very important part in the domestic economy of the household thirty, or more, years ago. The shoemaker's wife and daughters—if he had any—were often his best bowers, enabling him to weather many a financial tempest—on a small scale—and were often the chief reliance when the head of the family, through sickness, or other causes, could no longer work to support the family. As the wife and daughters "bound" the shoes made by the workmen of the family, the "uppers," all ready to "bind," with the needful silk, cotton and thread, and sometimes beeswax, made part of the load carried home in the "little cart," or in some other way, from the boss' shop. Then there would be a little delay, perhaps, until a shoe was bound, with which to start off the new lot.

But generally, before the "jour" got his "stock" seasoned, one or two "uppers" were ready, and enough usually bound ahead to keep all hands at work. And so, now and then, the order would be heard— "Come, John, go and see if your mother has got a shoe bound; I'm all ready to last it. . . ."

Old-time shoemaker's shop. Courtesy of Lynn Historical Society.

The style of the "uppers" in vogue some forty years ago, and later, was a "foxed" boot. This foxing [overlapping vamp] was of kid, with lasting top, and the boot laced in front. A few years later the "gaiter boot" came into fashion, which usually had a lower foxing, and the "lace" on the side. These were usually made "right" and "left." The binding of these boots, when it was done well, was quite a nice job. The price of binding ranged from seventeen to twenty-five cents a pair, and a smart woman would bind four pairs a day, and sometimes even more.

It will be seen that such help was no small item in maintaining the family. Many a little home was earned by "all hands," father and mother, boys and girls, who worked for years, cheered by the hope of paying off the mortgage, so that they could have a "home of their own."

[2]

The Outwork System

As market demand for shoes increased in the early nineteenth century, the women in shoemaking families, who had many demanding household tasks and children to care for, could not work steadily enough to produce the quantities of sewn uppers needed by the men in their shops. Slowly, shoemakers and the merchant-capitalists who organized central shops where the leather stock was cut began to recruit additional women, outside of shoemaking families, to sew uppers. As a result, the work of shoemaking and shoebinding became increasingly disassociated: the two tasks were performed in separate locations, by persons not living in the same family, and for different employers or shoe bosses. Coordination of shoebinding and shoemaking became the prerogative of the shoe boss; as a result, male artisans lost control of part of the work process.

The wages earned by shoebinders who were employed outside the family labor system were often collected by their husbands, who from time to time settled up their accounts with the employer. Before the passage of the Massachusetts Married Women's Property Act in 1852, the husband was the legal owner of all his wife's property, including her wages. At first, these wages were paid in groceries and dry goods drawn on an account kept by the shoe boss at a local general store. By 1830, however, the payment in cash of at least part of shoebinding wages had become fairly common, representing for many women in rural Essex County their first opportunity to earn a little money. A document settling the account of one shoebinder was reproduced in the *Historical Collections of the Danvers Historical Society* 10 (1922), page 114.

Ipswich [Massachusetts], June 13, 1812
Mr. Z. Porter, Dr., to Sarah Scott, for binding shoes, 170 paire [*sic*]
of slippers, three cents per pair, $5.10, to 30 paire of ties at 4 cents per
pair, $1.20, to 70 paire of boy's shoes at 4 cents & half per pair, $3.15,
$9.45.

Rec'd the within in full, Nath. Scott.

As a result of the separation of binding and shoemaking, the shoemaker would often have to wait at the shoe boss's central shop for the
sewn uppers they needed. Entries in the journal of Joseph Lye, Jr., of
Lynn (1819–30), now in the archives of the Lynn Historical Society,
suggest the delay and inconvenience experienced by shoemakers who
lacked a ready supply but were reluctant to bind the uppers themselves
at the low wages paid to women. Yet like Joseph Lye, some could not
avoid doing their own "closing" (that is, binding brogans or unlined
work shoes of the sort often sold to southern plantation owners for their
slaves). The excerpts from Lye's journal are quoted courtesy of the Lynn
Historical Society.

December 9, 1819: Waited most of this day for work:—made but one
pr . . . [at] 45 [cents]. . . .

February 21, 1820: 3 pr at 25, waited 3 hours for work . . .

July 6, 1820: made 3 pr 28 waited for work. worked at haying part of
afternoon. . . .

November 2, 1820: Closed 2 pr: waited quite all day for work. . . .

March 13, 1822: 2 pr 35   closed 1 pr. . . .

June 4, 1822: 2 pr shoes 35   closed pr for myself. . . .

January 14, 1825: 1 pr 42   waited for work. . . .

June 30, 1829: Waited most of the afternoon, & made 3 pr. . . .

According to his diaries, which begin in 1828, shoemaker Isaac W. Merrill of Haverhill eagerly awaited his marriage to Lois M. Chase in part as a solution to his difficulties in obtaining bound uppers from his shoe bosses. Because Lois proved a disappointment to him in that (and in other respects), Merrill assigned the work to an apprentice. During the prosperous years before the depression of 1837, he could afford to pay his apprentice cash wages to close uppers for him—and paid him more than any shoebinder earned for the same work. The Merrill diaries are quoted courtesy of the Trustees of the Haverhill Public Library, Special Collections Department.

February 18, 1831— . . . In the evening I settled with Mrs. Brickett for binding shoes for me. . . .

June 10, 1831— . . . I expect to get married in the course of time. . . .

August 1, 1831— . . . Went down to Joe Bradley's and got a lot of unbound vamps of Hobson's. . . .

September 25, 1831—Cloudy. Published [bans] today to Lois after a short courtship of only seven years. . . .

October 17, 1831—Beautiful morning. I was married in the evening by Mr. Peckham to Miss Lois M. Chase. . . .

October 23, 1831—To meeting with my *wife!* . . .

November 5, 1831— . . . Lois spent the afternoon at Quimby's. . . . She is, at present in rather better health than usual. I have mentioned her as being unwell for a long time & I suppose you wish to know her disorder? Well, tis a delicate one and is called the falling of the womb. . . .

November 30, 1831— . . . I have been closing shoes today. . . .

December 16, 1831— . . . Made eight pair. Lois earns 25 cents per diem [binding uppers]. . . .

December 29, 1831— . . . On account of having no shoes bound I made only five pair. . . .

December 30, 1831— . . . Made five pair. Lois has a sore finger. . . .

February 15, 1832— . . . Lois is rather poorly. . . .

April 12, 1832— . . . Doct Langley came to see my wife and says— her illness is owing to hard work and taking cold which occasions a weakness in her back etc. . . .

September 16, 1833—Lucio [Joaquim De Freitas of Madeira] made a pair of shoes today. He is going to learn the trade with me because he likes the business not because he is under the neces[s]ity of *working* for he has thousands at his command. . . .

October 1, 1833—Lucio and I went to the village. Got a lot of shoes to bind of Hobson. . . .

1835 January
The past [year] has been an eventful one to me; but, however, I intend to keep up a pretty good heart. Lois went over to Andover N. Parish in the stage. In the evening, myself, Moses and Lorenzo went to North Andover and found Lucio and Lois there. Returned home before morning. . . .

January 2, 1835— . . . Put a notice in the Essex Gazette of my wifes elopement. . . . Lois returned from Andover. Packed up her cloathes [*sic*], and spent the nights at our folks. Glad I was absent. . . .

January 3, 1835— . . . I returned to Haverhill. Lois took the stage for Boston to meet Lucio there, I suppose. . . .

January 5, 1835— . . . I am alone! Well I can't help it—must be reconciled to my lot— . . . Lois returned from Boston this evening. . . . [Although Merrill does not record the event, Lois returned to him after her brief adventure with Lucio.]

February 28, 1835— . . . I carried Lois over to West Newbury to see [her relative] Sally Chase. . . .

April 16, 1835— . . . Lois has a very bad cold in her head. . . .

September 4, 1835—David Clough says he intends to come here and learn the shoemakers trade. He is 16-1/2 years old and nearly six feet in height. . . .

December 26, 1835— . . . Made 9 pairs again today. I give David 12 cents a pair for sewing. I do the rest. . . .

January 16, 1836—David and I have made 60 pairs of shoes this week . . . at 40 cts. a pair. He sewed them for 12-1/2 cents a pair. I done all the rest so that I have earned $16.50 cts. this week. . . .

March 26, 1836—Shoemaking is real prime. . . .

Shoe bosses and shoemakers had trouble getting enough uppers sewn promptly in an outwork system that stretched for miles throughout rural Essex County and into southern New Hampshire and Maine. Further, most shoebinders regarded their work as a part-time effort that represented only a small supplement to their families' incomes. Young, unmarried women were often the most productive shoebinders; wives and mothers who sewed uppers worked intermittently unless they faced economic hardship and desperately needed store goods. Hence, delays were common, and productivity and wages for shoebinding remained low. The correspondence of his outworkers to shoe boss William Richardson of Stoneham, Massachusetts (housed at the Baker Library, Harvard Business School), illustrates the problems and complaints of shoemakers about the difficulty of getting enough bound uppers to keep them on schedule.

Bedford [Massachusetts], July 17, 1835
Capt. Richardson,
  Sir, I send you 48 pr Leather Boots & 30 pr A [ankle] ties and they are part made. I am very much troubled to get them bound. Mr. Webber's wife have bound all he has made as yet except those that came bound. If you can bring up some that are bound you help me

verry much. You will please bring some more upper stock when you come. Mr. Webber would like some Morocco. . . .

Enough till I see you.

Yours with respect

William K. Cooke

New Ipswich [New Hampshire], November 21, 1838

Sir I shall have 2 Lots of your shoes done next week & shall send them in Saturday if it comes right for the teamers to be there that day. I wish you to have some ready for them to take back. . . . I am very much in want of a little *money* say *ten dollars* for this is a cold country. I should like you to send one Lot of the shoes bound on part of a lot for I have but one binder Bacon's. . . . Have but hard work to get them bound. . . . Tell Sam to write & tell the news & roll the money up in it so I can get it before next week a Thursday or I shall have to go without a *Pudding* no mistake, the rest is hurry & Blunder. We are all well.

From yours,

Jesse Reed

[3]

Outbreaks of Early Labor Protest

In the 1830s both men and women shoeworkers protested against changing conditions of work. Early episodes of collective action reflect the interplay of class and gender experience and illustrate how the early phases of industrialization were changing the meanings of work, manhood, womanhood, and family relations for shoeworkers.

For example, when the work of early nineteenth-century shoebinders moved outside the family labor system, women still remained inside a family social system that decreed for females an important but separate and subordinate place. Yet though they accepted the sexual division of labor, which consigned them to work in their kitchens at low wages, shoebinders in the early 1830s developed their own organizations and leadership, acting together as women to protect their interests and to achieve better treatment from the owners of central shops. The decentralized nature of outwork denied them an experience of group work but not a collective sense of womanhood.

It was hard for isolated and vulnerable outworkers to organize, but they managed to create an extensive network among women living in the scattered shoe towns of Essex and Middlesex Counties. Their protest drew on their experiences both as workers and as women and signaled the beginnings of a female alternative to both the craft allegiance of male workers and the family wage as an organizational principle of labor protest.

Although shoebinders were not directly involved in the group work and male culture of artisan life, beginning in 1831 they borrowed ideas from artisans to justify their positions in public disputes with their employers. The bedrock of their argument was the labor theory of value being used by artisan shoemakers themselves to defend resistance to mistreatment: if shoeworkers created the essential worth of the shoes that their employers sold, then they deserved wages representing a fairer share of the value they created. Shoebinders reworked ideas from artisan culture to reflect their own experience as female members of artisan families. Yet recognizing that they now worked outside the protection of a family labor system, activist shoebinders also drew upon other social networks, such as those of female churchgoers. The Reading, Massachusetts, binders' society in 1831 published its protests in the *New England Christian Herald*, a Methodist newspaper. Their meetings were often held in churches, especially those in which women participated freely in religious activities on equal terms with men. The Lynn Female Society in 1833 met in the Friends' (Quaker) meetinghouse, for example, and the Saugus binders in the Methodist church. The activities of women in evangelical religion and in labor protest reinforced each other.

Rebellious shoebinders claimed that the morality of their cause justified a move by workingwomen into public political activity. Their statements also reflect a developing awareness of the privilege and wealth of shoe bosses and the exploitation of shoeworkers. Their words convey their class-conscious anger at the growing power of capital and demand redress of their grievances in the interests of justice and morality.

The first public protest occurred in 1831 among the shoebinders of Reading and in the surrounding towns of Essex County. The *Lynn Mirror*, August 6, 1831, quoted part of their public statement.

Shoe Binders. The Shoe Binders of Reading and vicinity have promulgated the following advertisement, which was signed by two or three hundred persons. They say the *bosses* are unwilling to allow them a fair price for their work, and threaten to get their shoes done elsewhere, when it may be done cheaper. It is contended that their price is very low. The object is to "have a general understanding["] throughout the country, of what prices are paid, and beneath which the labor is not compensated so that inexperienced persons may not "work for nothing and find [furnish] themselves." The prices named, we are informed, do not materially differ from those now given in this town.

Reading, July 26, 1831

We, whose names are undersigned, and whose employment is generally that of binding shoes, wishing that a greater degree of regularity might take place among us, as it respects the prices of different times, that no one may do good work for a less price than another, and that fair prices may be obtained, so, in order to carry the foregoing into effect, form ourselves into a Society, to be called the "Reading, South Reading, Stoneham, Malden, Lynn and Woburn Society of Shoe Binders." . . .

The initial response of shoemakers to developing labor protest by women was encouraging, but journeymen expressed their support in terms of family economic interests, for which men held major responsibility. The Society of Journeymen Cordwainers in Lynn, organized in 1830, included the low wages paid to shoebinders among their own grievances in a statement to the *Lynn Mirror*, August 14, 1830.

Address to the Craft. . . .
    And are you willing to be crowded to the depth of misery and distress, which is your future destiny, if something is not done to prevent it? Then arise, shake off the lethargy from your minds—come forward and act like men. . . . It is by the establishment of a General Trade Society and by union and a determined spirit, that we hope to achieve our purpose. . . . Cash is the living principle; the only article you ought to receive in return for your labor. . . . Look, and see how they have depressed the price of female labor, and reduced it down to almost nothing! This has an effect on us as husbands, as fathers, and as brothers. This, gentlemen, ought to be looked to—there is a remedy and it is within our control. . . .

The second public protest from shoebinders occurred in Lynn and Saugus in late 1833, when they claimed for women, as artisan shoemakers did for men, the inalienable right to public protest, based on the political heritage of the American Revolution. They accused their employers of "manifest *error*." Their declarations were published in the *Lynn Record*, January 1, 1834.

Preamble to the Constitution of the Female Society of Lynn and Vicinity for the protection and promotion of Female Industry, 1834.
    Whereas numerous in this and neighboring towns have, for a long time past, devoted themselves to the employment of binding shoes, with a reasonable expectation, that by close application of personal

industry, they might be able thereby to obtain a comfortable support; instead of which, they have found their means of living gradually diminishing, while necessity has driven them to inquire into the causes, and to seek relief. They believe that no class of females have tasked themselves more severely, have been effected [*sic*] more by their personal exertions, or have proved themselves more worthy of encouragement, protection and support; and yet few have been so inadequately compensated.

They would reluctantly impute to their employers of the other sex, any unworthy motives, or any willingness to oppress them; but there appears to be somewhere a manifest *error*, a want of justice, and reasonable compensation to the females; which calls imperiously for redress. While the prices of *their* labour have been reduced, the business of their *employers* has appeared to be improving and prosperous, enabling them to increase in wealth. These *things ought not so to be!* Equal rights should be extended to all—to the weaker sex as well as to the stronger. The disadvantages which nature and custom have entailed upon females, as to the common transactions and business of life; are sufficiently great of necessity, without the addition of others, which are unnecessary and unjust—Under these circumstances, driven by necessity, to seek relief, a large number of females from this, and the neighboring towns, many of whom have families, as well as themselves, dependent on their industry for support; and impressed with the belief, that women as well as men, have certain inalienable rights, among which is the right at all times, of "peaceably assembling to consult upon the common good," have assembled accordingly, at the Friends Meeting house, in Lynn, this thirtieth day of December, A.D. 1833—. . . .

Another, and in our opinion, a very philosophical, as well as reasonable consideration, is the propriety that all individuals in the community should receive something like a corresponding remuneration for their exertions. It is highly reasonable, that those who perform a considerable portion of the labor, should receive a considerable portion of the recompense. Neither those who bind the shoes nor those who make them, and who of course perform the greater part of the labor, receive so much as those who cause them to be made, is evident from the fact that manufacturers frequently become wealthy, while the more laboring portion of the community, are obliged to struggle hard for a competence, and are frequently distressed.

But we do not ask, nor expect, to make as much money as the manufacturer, who employs many hands. We do however, think it reasonable, that while his income far exceeds his expenses, ours may, at least to be equal to them: and that while he is making thousands of dollars, we may have some reasonable chance of making hundreds. . . .

It has been said that we are forming a combination against the manufacturers, and one that will be detrimental to the prosperity of the town. To the latter part of this objection, we can only say, that we regard the welfare of the town as highly as any one can do; and that we consider it to consist, not in the aggrandizement of a few individuals, but in the general prosperity and welfare of the industrious and laboring classes. . . .

> Mary Russell, Chairman
> Elizabeth K. Keene, Secretary
> Female Society of Lynn and
> Vicinity, for the protection and
> promotion of Female Industry

Many shoebinders, as reported in the *Lynn Record*, January 1, 1834, saw themselves as homebound women workers reaching out from within their families to make common cause with other females.

> Address of the Shoe-Binders of Lynn at a Public Meeting, December 30, 1833. Considerations of an important nature have induced the Ladies of Lynn, who endeavor to obtain an honorable subsistence by the needle, in aiding the principal branch of our domestic manufacture to demand a reasonable increase of their wages.
>
> The idea that their wages ought to be increased is not merely the opinion of a few avaricious individuals, desirous of becoming rich in haste; but it is the deliberate and settled conviction of a very large number of steady and intelligent females, who are willing to render an equivalent for all that they receive.

Instead of basing their wage demands on the value of their productive labor, however, shoebinders in 1834 measured the worth of women's work by a domestic yardstick: the preindustrial view that the contribution of "a comfortable support" to their families was the rightful measure of a just wage for women workers. Comfortable support represented a female version of the male artisans' demand for a "competency," a wage high enough for a man to support his family and to yield some savings for old age—in effect, a family wage. For themselves, women workers demanded a wage high enough to make an important but essentially supplemental contribution to family income. In calculating such wages, shoebinders estimated the cost of their duties and responsibilities as domestics rather than the worth of their labor as shoeworkers. For example, in her address to the first meeting of the Female Society in 1834 as reported in the *Lynn Record*, January 8, 1834, Mary Russell figured the price of household services and personal expenses of shoebinders and demanded a wage high enough to cover these household costs, though she did acknowledge the necessity of "widows and orphans" to support themselves.

. . . The poor man who employs help, must pay as much as the rich man. For the servant girl he must pay one dollar, or one dollar and a quarter per day besides her board. For the seamstress [*sic*] he must pay fifty cents per day. For the wash woman, he must pay seventy-five cents, and in some cases, one dollar per day. For the nurse he must pay two or three dollars per week besides her board. And these expenses are all that the rich man is required to pay for the same services. It is therefore evidently reasonable, that the wife of the mechanic, should receive a sufficient remuneration for her services, in order that she may assist her husband to defray their expenses, and to provide for their children.

. . . Again, the mechanic may have daughters grown up, and in that case they should pay him at least, one dollar and twenty-five cents a week for their board. . . . But the mechanic is induced to board his daughters for one dollar per week because he knows that they cannot earn enough to pay more and at the same time provide themselves with suitable clothing. He is therefore at a continual loss on their account. . . . All this inconvenience might however be easily remedied, by such a reasonable increase in wages, as would enable young ladies to pay a suitable price for their board, and to support themselves respectably and independently. . . . Yet more, it is well known that in factories young ladies receive a high price for their services; and unless our females received nearly an equal amount, they may be induced to seek employment in the factory, the printing office, or some other place. . . .

. . . Many families in this town consist of widows and orphans, who depend entirely on their own exertions for their support. If their means of subsistence are stinted, they are under a constant liability of calling upon the town, or upon their friends, for relief; and this is a source of unhappiness, in addition to the continual grief and affliction, which must rise in their hearts and surround them at every step, from a sense of destitution. . . . To allow such a just compensation, for their industry is an [act] of right and benevolence, which affords the means of supporting themselves respectably, and without a sense of dependence.

In 1834, however, the rebellious shoebinders of the Lynn Female Society were also criticizing the subordinated position of females and extending the equal rights doctrine of artisan life to include women. They claimed for women workers "inalienable" and "natural" rights, specifically the right to public assembly and the right to a reasonable wage for their labor. This feminism based on natural rights arguments appeared in their protest statements in the *Lynn Record*, January 1 and 8, 1834.

Preamble to the Constitution of the Female Society of Lynn and Vicinity for the protection and promotion of Female Industry
. . . Equal rights should be extended to all—to the weaker sex as well as to the stronger. The disadvantages which nature and custom have entailed upon females, as to the common transactions and business of life; are sufficiently great of necessity, with out the addition of others, which are unnecessary and unjust—Under these circumstances, driven by necessity, to seek relief, a large number of females from this, and neighboring towns, many of whom have families, as well as themselves, dependent on their industry for support; and impressed with the belief, that women as well as men, have certain inalienable rights, among which is the right at all times, of "peaceably assembling to consult upon the common good," have assembled accordingly at the Friends, Meeting house, in Lynn, this thirtieth day of December, A.D. 1833—. . . .

All that we have ever demanded or expected, is such a reasonable compensation for our labor, as shall enable us to defray our expenses, and ensure us that freedom from want, which is the natural right of the honest and industrious.

After several months of partial success, including the development of a standard list of prices for binding and plans to share work and start a shoebinding cooperative, the Lynn Female Society lost its momentum.

Chairman Mary Russell, in an effort to revive the organization, used the *Lynn Record* of June 18, 1834, to exhort the members to act together as "a band of sisters" and prove their loyalty to each other as women and to their cause. Her sense of sisterhood as an organizing principle extended also to the textile mill operatives of Lowell, Massachusetts, and their simultaneous labor protest in early 1834.

Ladies!—The present state of this Society calls for our serious and candid attention; it seems that but little regard is paid to the rules and regulations; that they have been disregarded and broken by many of its members who have taken work under price. . . . We cannot see the propriety of denying the shoebinders that liberty which other females have [a reference to the first walkouts by Lowell mill operatives in February 1834], that of setting their own prices upon their own work; and we have but little doubt in saying, that if all the members of this society were to be firm and determined that it would be but a short time ere they might be equally free from oppression. But if we are indifferent to our own interests, as the irregular and confused manner of the affairs of this society indicates, we shall soon make prophetic, the language of our oppressors, that women are too fickle minded and vain to accomplish any thing of importance. . . . Ladies, let us be alive to our own interests and honor. . . . Let us become a band of sisters; each considering the welfare of the society as her own peculiar interest. . . . Let us be willing to make some sacrifice if necessity require it. . . . If our dress is not quite as fashionable as it was last year, let us be willing to be a little out of date in these trifles, rather than be fashionable slaves. . . .

And in conclusion; Ladies, I beg leave to say, be not discouraged— our prospect daily brightens—we have not made these exertions for nothing—those who have stood foremost in defending and espousing the rights of females, will have the reward of well done! . . .

Serious divisions among shoebinders in Lynn over proper conduct and tactics had already emerged in public. Signing herself "A Shoebinder," Russell defended her personal attacks on a shoe boss she called, "Philadelphius" against criticism by "Another Shoebinder," whose vulnerability as an isolated, wage-dependent worker seemed to motivate her defense of the employers. Their exchange appeared in the *Lynn Record*, March 26 and April 2, 1834.

Mr. Editor, . . . I have felt deeply interested in the shoebinders' cause being myself one, and in a great measure dependent upon this employment for a living. When Philadelphius appeared to advocate our cause, I felt grateful to him for the disinterested spirit he *appeared* to manifest, and the good feelings which I *supposed* dictated what he wrote. I must confess I had not sufficient discernment, to discover, that he was "in reality our worst enemy"—"a snake in the grass," nor am I yet convinced that this is the case, the strong and unqualified assertion of "A Shoe Binder" [Mary Russell] to the contrary notwithstanding. . . .

As we are bound to believe every man honest till he is proven to be the contrary, I have found myself quite at a loss to account for the unsparing invective, and wholesale declamation [*sic*], which, without measure, has been poured upon the head of our professed friend Philadelphius. My first impression on reading the first piece, was, that it could not be the production of a female hand, but that of some enemy, wishing to injure our cause. . . . If it be indeed a female, I should think that the very good advice of Philadelphius gives us, . . . came too near home to that individual, and feeling herself piqued, she determined to consider him an enemy, and perhaps induced others to the same belief. I am prepared to say, that she has not expressed the opinion of all the shoebinders, nor of any I have conversed with on the subject. . . .

Another Shoebinder

Mr. Editor—A correspondent in your last paper, who signs herself "Another Shoebinder," has made a long story, which seems to amount to but very little. But as there now and then seems to appear the glimmering of an idea, I shall endeavor to pick out all the meaning I can find, and reply to it. In the first place she says she is a "shoebinder, and feels deeply interested in the cause." If so she has a very strange way of showing her interest, by opposing another Shoebinder, and by endeavoring to build up one part of the cause of he who has proved himself a recreant, and she has come out against one who is doing all in her power for the shoebinders' cause. . . . She says, that we are bound to believe every man honest, till he is proved to be the contrary. Well, I have proved that Philadelphius is dishonest, by which I mean, that he is not sincere in espousing our cause; else he would come up to the work, and give us our prices. . . .

Some of our society proposed that we should establish a manufactory by a fund, raised among ourselves, and as he [Philadelphius] had promised such great things, with his "fortune and sacred honor," we applied to him, not to give us money, but simply to aid us, by engaging to *buy our shoes.* . . .

After some conversation, he replied, "I sha'nt do it!" And now he calls it a "Quixotic scheme." Thus all his pledge of "fortune and sacred honor" has vanished into empty air. Instead of giving us any assistance he utterly refused either to help us by giving our prices, or buying our shoes, and insults us with what he calls our "Quixotic scheme." . . .

A Shoebinder

This public disagreement in 1834 reflected the many divisions among women which undermined the sense of sisterhood for Lynn shoe-binders. The material conditions under which they labored—isolated from each other in private households, outside any group setting, and combining wage work with many other tasks—discouraged collective activity. When they used artisan values to justify their demands, the contradictions between wage work for women and the role of women in artisan family life began to surface. The patriarchal logic of artisan ideology and family loyalty undercut female arguments for higher wages. Artisan values that defined women's work as domestic and supplemental and regarded womanliness as nonaggressive ran counter to the aspirations of female labor protest. Mary Russell's appeals to sisterhood could not change this, and the activities of the Lynn Female Society ceased within a year.

After the shoebinders' societies of the 1830s disappeared, at least two of their leaders in Lynn and Saugus, Miriam B. Johnson and Martha C. Hawkes, joined middle-class women active in the local antislavery move-ment as "moral warriors." At the second annual meeting of the Lynn Female Anti-Slavery Society in 1837, women openly advocated equal rights and the extension of female moral activity into the political realm in spite of the opposition of "corrupt" public opinion. Antislavery lec-turers Angelina and Sarah Grimké attended this meeting in Lynn. That evening they lectured to an audience of both men and women, thereby violating the early nineteenth-century taboo against women speaking in public and precipitating the historic controversy over women's rights within the antislavery movement. Excerpts from the minutes of the Lynn Female Anti-Slavery Society for 1836–38 are quoted courtesy of the Lynn Historical Society.

The Female Anti Slavery Society of Lynn held their second Annual Meeting, June 21st 1837.

The meeting was called to order, and opened by reading a selection from scripture by the President [Deborah Henshaw], prayer was then offered by A. G. [Angelina Grimké].

The annual report was read by Abby Kelly[,] Corresponding Secretary.

Second Annual Report of the Lynn Female Anti-Slavery Society

. . . There was a decrease in our members during the first of the year, but through the influence of anti-slavery publications[,] individual exertion, but more than from any other cause through the influence of lectures we have received a considerable accession of members within the last few months. . . .

We consider this mode of operation [gathering names on antislavery petitions] one of the most efficient that we can employ as the very first step we take in it brings us in direct contrast [*sic*] with classes of the community—with the pro-slavery, with the indifferent, with those who are as much as ourselves opposed to slavery, *but,-but,-but*—and in fine with all, whatever may be their sentiments so that many who would not otherwise think at all about it are induced to give it a little place in their minds, and we hope some are by this means led to examine thoroughly, with a desire to find the truth and consequently are brought to embrace Abolition principles. . . .

We would as moral warriors adopt this motto—"We consider nothing done while anything remains undone."

We do not wish to think ourselves divested of any individual responsibility by becoming members of a society—each has a duty of her own to perform; and in the parlor, in the kitchen, in the shop, in the school, in the walk, in the ride, and in every other situation, whenever opportunity presents, she may be performing that duty by instilling correct principles, and awakening Christian feeling for the crushed and withering slave.

We trust that what woman is doing in the present struggle, will accelerate the approach of that time, when instead of the contumely and scorn which are now heaped upon her who enlists in a moral conflict against wrong with a determination to do her whole duty, even should that duty require her to overstep the bounds "prescribed by a corrupt public sentiment" she shall be hailed as a minister of Heaven, sent on an errand of mercy to the erring and wandering of earth—

When it shall be practically acknowledged, that man and woman are both one in Christ.

In the early 1840s the moral activism among women that had fired the shoebinders' societies shifted to temperance as well as antislavery senti- ment. The middle-class temperance movement in Essex County attract- ed the support of many Lynn women, especially among those who lived in Wood-End, the section with the greatest concentration of shoemak- ers. Their activities suggest that male drinking added an intolerable burden to the low wages paid to shoeworkers. A letter and a report published in the *Essex County Washingtonian* on December 29, 1842, and January 26, 1843, reflect a zealous commitment to temperance.

Mr. Editor: Feeling a deep interest in Temperance, I wish to enquire through your valuable paper how the Cause flourishes in the Western part of the town, and what its friends are doing for its promotion. I would ask, have they followed the example of our Wood-End friends, by forming Ward Associations, and establishing Reading Rooms where they can meet and converse on the great and important subject of Temperance and devise ways and means for its promotion? . . . I have attended the meetings of the Wood-End Association from their com- mencement and find them very interesting. . . . The meetings are well attended, the Hall is literally packed. . . . Much credit is due to the Ladies of Wood-End, for their punctual attendance on those occa- sions. They feel a deep interest in the cause, and they manifest it by their presence. It is hoped that the Ladies in the West part of the town will partake of their spirit.

Yours, S.H.M.

Second Annual Report of the Washington Total Abstinence Society of Lynn

. . . One year ago, after a mutual consultation, the Female Society in this town was disbanded, and its members attached themselves to this Society. We have since labored indiscriminately in the promotion of the great cause for which we are associated. The obvious increase of zeal and energy and effectiveness which has been the result, has abundantly proved the advantage of the union. . . . "It is not good for man to be alone." Peculiarly appropriate does it seem that woman should be admitted to an equal participancy in an enterprise, whose object is the removal of an evil from which she has, if possible, suffered more than men.

> "When woman's heart is bleeding,
> Shall woman's voice be hushed[?] . . . "

On behalf of the Directors,
Wm Bassett, Secretary

Lynn, January 11, 1843

[4]

Women Workers and Artisan Protest

In the 1840s, shoe bosses such as Christopher Robinson of Lynn attempted to raise the standards of shoe production by issuing directions to shoebinders and shoemakers, specifying exactly how the work should be done and offering the incentive of paying all wages entirely in cash rather than partly in dry goods and groceries. Robinson's instructions, owned by the Lynn Historical Society, were reprinted on page 22 of the *Lynn Business Magazine* 1 (June 1907).

Directions to Binders

1. All the seams in shoes or boots—both outside and lining—must be closed tight and with a short stitch; and be smoothly rubbed down or pressed.

2. A double thread must always be used when the stock is stout enough to bear it.

3. The stock must be handled carefully, and kept perfectly clean, both outside and lining.

4. Every part of the work must be done in the neatest and most tasteful manner—and brought in well trimmed and bunch tied up in good order.

5. The book must always be brought in with the work, and when money is wanted.

I expect every person who works for me to comply with the above directions, in every particular.

C. Robinson

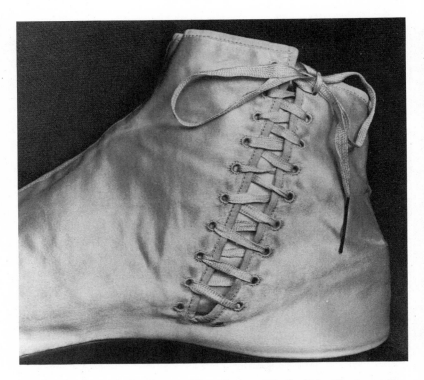

Shoebinding on satin bootine, wedding slipper of Emily Alden Davis, c. 1840. Courtesy of Lynn Historical Society.

Robinson and others were heartily disliked by both shoemakers and shoebinders for interfering with their autonomy as workers and the customs of their trade, and labor protest against new work standards and low wages broke out again in Essex County. Protest societies of journeymen shoemakers sought to utilize the morality and usefulness of women on behalf of their activities in 1844–45 (and later, during the New England shoe strike of 1860). Women's involvement in this labor protest proved similar to that of middle-class women in the antislavery movement: male reformers welcomed women's special moral influence to advance the cause but did not permit them to influence policy or undertake independent political action.

Although shoebinders in the early 1830s had clothed their own protests with moral imperatives—especially when they declared in 1834:

"These *things ought not so to be!*"—the image of the moral female took on exaggerated shape in the 1840s through editorials and articles in *The Awl*, the newspaper of the Lynn Society of Journeymen Cordwainers. The editors were eager to associate the moral power of local females with their activities. An editorial of December 21, 1844, defined moral agency as central to womanhood but pointedly excluded women from political action. Working-class men thus defined the meaning of womanhood in ways that served their own interests.

Woman

Thank heaven, our movement is not a political one. If it were, it would not be warmed into life by the bright sunshine of woman's smiles, nor enriched by the priceless dower of her pure affections. But as it is strictly a moral enterprise, it opens to her willing heart a wide field of usefulness, and is sure to be gilded by the light of her countenance. . . . She will hallow and enoble [*sic*] it. It is a cause on which she can lavish all the wealth of her soul and feel that her treasures are well placed. It is the cause of the poor and down-trodden. . . . What wonder, then, that the mind of woman is inclining toward our movement, . . . She finds in it "ample scope and verge enough" for the exercise of all her sympathies. All about her she sees her lovely sisters toiling from morn to noon, from noon to dewy eve, "yes far into the still watches of the night,["]—to gain a scanty subsistence,—ruining their health with close confinement to labor, and compelled for want of time to forego all the enjoyments and refinements of life—and her heart beats quickly at the thought that now is the time to better their conditions and enlarge their sphere. . . .

We rejoice that this is to some extent true of Lynn. We hope it will be more and more so with every returning Sun. Every woman in town, especially every laboring woman, ought to be actively at work in our high vocation. . . . Let her then enliven our meetings with her presence. Her "still small voice" will sound in the ears of the griping manufacturers like the noise of many thunders. They cannot face her indignant look—they cannot answer her proof-laden charges. The story of her wrongs is full of bitterness, and the guilty wretch who has caused them, trembles in his shoes lest she will expose them. . . . Let her be present at all our counsels, and shed new glory on that sex which in all time has been first at the cross and last at the grave of crucified humanity.

The editors of *The Awl* who saw women as moral beings and as useful family members encouraged them to attend their meetings and participate in the temperance tea parties that served as major social gatherings for the society. Some women, among them "Girtrude," whose letter appeared in *The Awl* on September 11, 1844, accepted this role without question. In the paper's September 18 issue, "Centre Street" detailed further the ways in which women might contribute to the work of the journeymen's society.

Messrs. Editors—Reading your worthy paper, and observing the true spirit of equal rights, so clearly exhibited in its columns, prompts a friend of humanity to speak a word to those who have not enlisted their energies in an object truly worthy of the co-operation of every philanthropist, of whatever class or grade. Will any refuse their aid to paralize [*sic*] the hand of oppression . . . ?

. . . Will not the ladies engage in this work, on which so much depends? Yes, I hear you say. Come, then, one and all. . . . Mothers, daughters, all, suffer no longer the cruel oppressor to take that which is your due. Need I ask, why is education so limited among the laboring class? Why is that promising youth obliged to quit his or her school, at an age when knowledge is the most attainable? The question needs no reply. . . . Ladies, one and all, arouse to action in this toil of mercy. Then shall your sons and daughters no longer wear the oppressor's yoke; peace, comfort, education, and all that is desirable, shall be theirs. Then shall we behold, unitedly, the darkening cloud of oppression dispersing, and the noon-day of equality shedding its peaceful rays, around our hallowed associations and quiet homes.

Girtrude

Messrs. Editors—I was much gratified on last Saturday evening, to see so large an attendance of *ladies* at the Town Hall. This is right; for certainly the females are as much interested in any undertaking, which has for its object the bettering of the condition of the males, as the males are themselves. . . . Then, ladies, continue to give us your presence. You have influence, and can do much. Your attendance, of course, will cause a larger attendance of the young men, who, when they visit your houses, and find by your mothers that "you are out," and at the Town Hall, where they ought to be, and that you are attending to your immediate interest, this will nerve them to action, and they eventually will act; they will come; and if they attend, they will soon discover the necessity and importance of their influence, and that in union there is strength. Then I say, give us your presence; learn our songs, and help us to sing them; make speeches, if the men wont, and tell to us and the world whether there are any bosses in the town of Lynn that will cheat a *woman* or not; or whether there are not some that will pay you in calico at twice its value; or whether there are not some that will make cash contracts with widows who have families to support, and pay them off in orders, or shave the cash debt at the rate of ten per cent. If these stories are true, let the sufferers make them known; tell the men's names, if they can be called men, and where they live; let them be published to the world; and by persevering in this course, you can exert an influence that shall prevent the reputation [*sic*] of these things. . . .

Centre Street

Despite the appeal of "Centre Street" and others, no shoebinders came forward with grievances. The editors of *The Awl*, regarding the work of shoebinding as inherently virtuous and useful, advised shoebinders to use the moral power of female indignation as a collective weapon against mistreatment by the shoe bosses. They seemed oblivious to the isolated vulnerability of the individual shoebinder who worked alone in her kitchen, dependent on the good will of her employer. Moral indignation, however satisfying, might prove dangerous: shoe bosses could identify the discontented and give them no work.

In early 1845, E. C. Darlin, an *Awl* editor, announced that he had found a shoebinder who had been cheated by Lynn shoe bosses and encouraged her to speak out. The case of Mrs. Jane Atherton, who herself played no direct role in the controversy as reflected in subsequent letters to *The Awl*, illustrated the reluctance of shoebinders to make their grievances public and risk focusing the anger of employers on them as individuals.

[January 4, 1845]

The *Awl* and the *Needle* ought to go together. . . . To come to the *point*, we mean by this little figure that the Binder ought to unite with the Journeyman in carrying on the great work of reform. . . .

The interests of the Awl and the Needle are one. They both point to the same thing, they are brother and sister, and should work together in perfect harmony. The bright eye of the Needle ought to see this? The Needle that don't see it must be very dull.—It aint worth threading. . . . But the Needle that does see this and is willing to be used for the purpose of "binding" us together and "finishing our work" is of the true Hemmings brand, and not one of those miserable counterfeits which "snap" at the very idea of "joining us." . . .

We assure you, sister Needle, that the oppressor dreads your point more than the point of the bayonet. . . . He knows that you can "bind" him hand and foot, and plead his own "orders" as your excuse. He'll threaten to break the thread of your existence if you look favorably on the Awl—and will try to make you sew (sue) for mercy. . . .

He [the shoe boss] may tell you, sister Needle, that your grievances are "all in your eye." Tell him there is more truth than poetry in that, as many a sleepless hour . . . can testify. He will call his brother bosses to prove that his tyranny is all imaginary. If so, appeal to the *Bench!* Nay appeal to the *Awl—* —and that will end the matter. . . .

Speaking of "figures," . . . we examined a poor Binder's book [wage account] the other day, and became satisfied that even figures by a little timely alteration can be made to lie most effectively. . . . The low price which is paid for binding shoes is intolerable. . . . [Shoebinders] are working, many of them, from twelve to fourteen hours a day for from two to four cents an hour for their labor. . . . It is known that in some instances the Manufacturer is cruelly hard and exact upon his Binders—taking most ungenerous advantage of their position. . . .

[January 25, 1845]

Messrs. Editors—If the writer of those uncharitable allusions and insinuations in a few of the back numbers of the Awl . . . where it says a wealthy shoe manufacturer has defrauded a poor shoe binder etc., will be so good as to publish the whole matter as he has threatened over his own proper name, giving names and dates, . . . a shoe manufacturer would like a fair chance to reply. . . .

I respect the person of the "Shoe Binder" and would not do or say, anything to give her trouble or anxiety, any further than I am compelled to vindicate my own character. She has told me that she did not wish any trouble made about it, that if other folks would mind their own business and let mine alone it would be better for them—that she had never *thought* nor *said* that I had ever *defrauded* her. . . .

I expect to be able before I get through to prove a reckless, if not malicious design to injure the character of a

Shoe Manufacturer

[February 15, 1845]

Messrs. Editors— . . . I hereby testify that in a conversation with Mrs. Atherton, she told me that she never *said* that Mr. [Nathan D.] Chase ["Shoe Manufacturer"] had defrauded her—that the transaction in regard to his paying four cents *cash*, instead of *five* in *orders* [for store goods] was agreed to by her at the time. That she never had a wish that anything be published about it—that the most she ever did say, was that she thought it rather a hard case, to make so much difference for the money.—Still, if she now wanted a favor, Mr. Chase would be one of the first men she would go to.

Asa L. Breed [sexton at
the Friends' Society]

[February 22, 1845]

Messrs. Editors— . . . Mr. Chase thinks that she [Mrs. Atherton] is "perfectly satisfied," as she has expressed a kind disposition towards him. She may have expressed a kind disposition towards him, but does that prove that she don't feel herself injured? And furthermore, Mr. Chase says, that she told him that she never thought he defrauded her, and he should try to prove it. That is right, give us a testimony from her that she never thought herself wronged, and that she was perfectly satisfied with the transaction, and that it was agreed to at the time that she commenced work, that she should have 5 cts. orders, or 4 cts. cash. . . . *But suppose she did agree to it, does that make it right in a moral point of view?* . . .

E. C. Darlin

Womanhood meant usefulness as well as moral virtue to the journeymen's society in the 1840s. David Johnson's portrait of the Lynn shoebinder's role in the family labor system (see Chapter 1) emphasized the importance of her contribution to the work process and to family income. Johnson's attitudes reflected those of other journeymen shoemakers who had been trained in the artisan tradition. John Greenleaf Whittier celebrated the strengths and joys of the preindustrial family labor system in an 1845 poem, "The Shoemakers" (published on pages 291–

93 of *Anti-Slavery Poems, Songs of Labor and Reform,* vol. 3, of *The Poetical Works of John Greenleaf Whittier* [Boston, 1892]).

> . . . Rap, rap! Upon the well-worn stone
> How falls the polished hammer!
> Rap, rap! the measured sound has grown
> A quick and merry clamour.
> Now shape the sole! now deftly curl
> The glossy vamp around it,
> And bless the while the bright-eyed girl
> Whose gentle fingers bound it! . . .

The Awl printed several stories and articles that illustrate the artisan view of the "useful" woman as the ideal "mechanic's wife." In "Old Fudge of an Uncle," published in the issue of September 11, 1844, a young wife triumphs over the "demon" of gentility by abandoning the leisured life of a lady to contribute as a shoebinder to her family's economic well-being. In the story "Charles Do-well," published on February 22, 1845, Eliza D—, the daughter of a merchant, is attracted to a handsome young shoemaker but feels that she should marry within her own class. At the end of the story, however, she happily awakens to her true destiny as a useful woman.

> " . . . Yes Mother, . . . I am determined henceforth, to be a woman, and see if I can't do something for a living. I will go immediately and join the 'shoe binders society of mutual improvement,' and what is more, I mean to bind shoes myself, for I have come to the conclusion that if we would be good members of society, we must be useful. . . ."
>
> A few days after the above conversation took place Charles Do-well, who long had had an attachment for Eliza—for he perceived, in spite of the foolish notions which had been instilled into her by her acquaintances, an undercurrent of strong good sense, and he doubted not the time would come when the film would drop from her eyes, and she would dare to be herself, a sensible, intelligent, *useful* woman. . . .
>
> Judge then how delighted he must have been to behold her whom he so highly prized, engaged so honorably.
>
> "You seem to be surprised," she said, "in seeing me for once in my life, usefully employed."
>
> "Not more surprised than pleased, I'll assure you," he quickly re-

plied. "Oh, Eliza, if you but knew the rapture of this moment, you would cease to wonder at my altered looks. Can it be possible, Eliza, that anything that I may have said has led thee to renounce thy former notions, tell me, Eliza, *dearest* Eliza, *dare* I hope that I am connected with this improvement[?] . . . Say Eliza, say, am I too presumptuous, or may I indeed prepare for joy?"

Eliza's countenance . . . confirmed the soft impeachment, and Charles Do-well *felt* that he was *truely* loved. . . .

Women supporters of cordwainer protest in the 1840s arranged temperance tea parties to raise funds for the journeymen's society, but they did not participate in shoemaker protest on the same terms of equality that they achieved in the temperance movement. The irritation of one woman supporter over the subordinated position of women surfaced in the last two lines of her poem, published in *The Awl* on February 22, 1845.

> On the Art of Shoemaking
> . . . And now the Awl and Needle are combined,
> Ladies your talents show with intellect refined;
> Though men still take the lead in politics and shoes,
> Yet, when they ask our aid, oh! let us not refuse!
>
> But help them in this work, with willing heart and hand,
> And let not man be left alone, within this happy land;
> Yet when we own this claim, (let not despotic sway,)
> Arouse the woman's wrath, (with that *old* term, Obey.)
> Lynn, 1845   Constance

The reality of shoebinding in the 1840s meant hard work under such taskmasters as Christopher Robinson of Lynn, but little money—at best a dollar a week. The 1849 diary of Sarah Trask of Beverly, Massachusetts, now at the Beverly Historical Society, reveals the experiences of a shoebinder who often worked for Lynn shoe bosses and chose to do so rather than make garments or do domestic work because she believed that she could earn a little more money. This occupation, which she learned from other shoebinders in Beverly, was to be temporary while she and her friends waited for their young men, who were sailors, to return and marry them. On one occasion she helped her friend Lydia finish up her work and then turned wearily to her own.

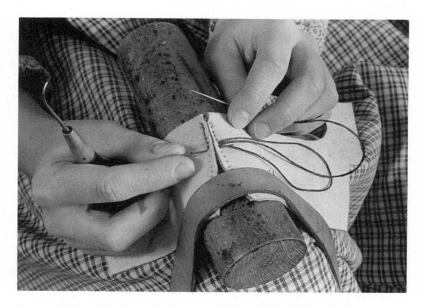

Close-up of shoebinding techniques at Old Sturbridge Village, Massachusetts. Photograph by Robert S. Arnold. Courtesy of Old Sturbridge Village.

For a full account of the work and life of Sarah Trask, see Mary H. Blewett, "'I Am Doom to Disapointment': The Diaries of a Beverly, Massachusetts, Shoebinder, Sarah E. Trask, 1849–51," *Essex Institute Historical Collections* 157 (March 1981): 192–212. Diary excerpts are reprinted by permission of the Essex Institute, Salem, Massachusetts, and the Beverly Historical Society. The original spelling and punctuation are unchanged.

Jan 25 [1849] Stay down to C. [Sarah's friend Catherine], all night for her to show me about my shoes, but did not do much, but I will try and see what I can do, for I cannot afford to make a coat for 33, Cts for, L. O. Hale if I can get anny thing else to do.

Jan 26 Stitched on three pairs of shoes, have I not done bravely. . . .

Jan 31 winter seem so dull. At home all day and in the evening. Oh my shoes they do go of[f] so slow only four pairs and a half today, I wish they were all done, but what is the use of that it will not get them done anny sooner; so I must not despair. . . .

Feb 20 Just for fun I counted the stiches in a shoe, the size was fives, 719 in the whole, 250 on the top, 173 in the filling, 120, on the side seams or 65 in one side, 69 in the closeing or 23 on a seam, 58 in the lineing, or 29, on a side, 99 on the surgeing. . . .

April 17 . . . today I have had another lot of shoes come, although I have not got my others done, but I hope I shall soon. . . .

April 21 This day I have been trying to finish my shoes, and have got them done and I am so glad. . . .

April 23 This day I have begun my gaiter boots, I have not finish anny tonight but hope I shall tomorrow. . . .

April 26 This day have finished four pairs of boots, just fifty cents this week, I hope I shall do four pair more before Saterday.

April 28 At home today, finishing my week work eight pairs of boots one dollar: how smart, beside my housework, and last tuesday I work for Lizzy [her married sister], so there the duty of the week. I almost think I shall make my fortune soon. . . .

July 12 At home today finishing my shoes, or boots. . . . [Her friend Lydia has gone to Salem] I almost went with her, but thought that I should not get my boots done to send up to Lynn tomorrow.

July 27 Well I have got L.A.B. [Lydia] shoes done, and I am glad of it, for her and me to[o], today I go to work on mine, and I must make haste and get them done. . . .

Sarah Trask longed for the return from a dangerous sea voyage of the man she hoped to marry, yet she was ambivalent about marriage and feared the consequences of dependence as a wife. Like many women in Lynn, she devoted what time she could to the local chapter of the Daughters of Temperance and worried about the fate of her friends in marriages with unsteady partners. With a strong belief in her own rectitude, she joined other women to try to redirect male behavior toward moral ends. Although her activism did not lead her into labor protest, Sarah's piety and self-scrutiny suggest the religious basis of her moral politics. However, her diary also reflects a deep pessimism about her own lack of effectual power and the uselessness of complaint.

Feb. 5 [1849] . . . three brothers and two sisters I have and after Lizzy [her sister] is Married, there will be a bachelor [Joshua, her brother] and old maid left. Never mind, the happy life that ever was had is always to court and never to wed. . . .

Feb 19 . . . M.A.R [Martha Rogers] and E.A.F. [Eliza Foster] called in the evening to see Lizzy once more before she leaves us for good on wensday night at seven, or half past, she will be a bride, then she must go just where her husband says . . . untill he can get a house, then a home of their own . . . and may it be a happy one. . . . Marriage to me seem a great responsibility for then you must act for yourselve, and almost all the care come upon the wife. . . .

March 14 Another wedding last night one of our shop girls, all getting married. Mr. Shale [the shoe boss] will not have anny to work for him, if they go so fast as they have done, this two or three years. It is three years last November since I went [to work], there as been 20 Married. . . . Married on the 13th of March, Thomas Cook and Hannah J. Herrick. May their life be a happy one, But rather a poor prospect I should think.

April 3 M. told me that T. Cook, was not very steady, now he was married, last saterday he was so drunk, he could not walk strait, I pity her, Yet I dont know as she needs my pity, for she knew what he was before she married him, why did she not have a mind of her own, but she alone must suffer. . . .

April 12 Uncle Foster and I have been looking the maps over to see where L.W. [Luther Woodberry, Sarah's beloved] had gone, to see what course they had taken, he says that he expects that when L.W. gets home there will be a wedding, but I guess he will be mistaken, a laugh at me. . . . They spoke of tobacto chewing, M.E.R. [Mary Rogers] and L.A.B. and I are going to tell L.W. that he must leave [off] chewing tobacto, or I guess, but it won't do to say what I shall do, if he does not.

May 22 . . . No news from L.W. yet, and I am almost discourage, it seem as though I have look for news a year; I think some times I will not think of it, but I cannot help it, it will come up in my mind, But this will never do for me, and so I will not write my wicked thoughts, always complaining, if things are not just so, oh what a wicked girl I am. . . .

May 24 . . . And now Mother foretells a dark future for me, But what [makes] her I cannot tell, none other of the family but me are destine to so dull a life. . . . But I shall hope for the best, and trust in god and in the end, doubt not all will yet be well, But this would not cheer anny one up, if they should read it. . . .

May 30 . . . I believe that [God] has guided L. so far; and I hope he will ever; o that I were good, I often wish I were, for then I should be happy, but I am not now, I am wicked and everything thats bad. . . .

July 22 . . . M.E. Rogers and H.P. Gates called in the evening, as I did not go anny wheres, A convention on California [opposed to their prospective husbands joining the Gold Rush of 1849], All four against it so we can pull together very well. . . .

Writer Lucy Larcom, a former Lowell textile operative originally from Beverly, knew well the situation of shoebinders like Sarah Trask, and her 1854 poem "Hannah Binding Shoes" provided a pathetic image of womanly faithfulness and became a popular nineteenth-century song lyric. Unable like Hannah to earn enough to support themselves, most shoebinders remained isolated at their work and dependent on others. The poem is included in *The Poetical Works of Lucy Larcom* (Boston, 1884).

> Poor lone Hannah,
> Sitting at the window, binding shoes:
> Faded, wrinkled,
> Sitting, stitching in a mournful muse.
> Bright-eyed beauty once was she,
> When the bloom was on the tree:
> Spring and winter,
> Hannah's at the window, binding shoes.
>
> Not a neighbor,
> Passing nod or answer will refuse,
> To her whisper,

"Is there from the fishers any news?"
  Oh, her heart's adrift, with one
  On an endless voyage gone!
Hannah's at the window, binding shoes

    Fair young Hannah,
Ben, the sunburnt fisher, gayly wooes:
    Hale and clever,
For a willing heart and hand he sues.
    May-day skies are all aglow,
    And the waves are laughing so!
    For her wedding
Hannah leaves her window and her shoes.

    May is passing:
Mid the apple boughs a pigeon coos.
    Hannah shudders,
For the mild southwester mischief brews,
    Round the rocks of Marblehead,
    Outward bound, a schooner sped:
    Silent, lonesome,
    Hannah's at the window, binding shoes.

    'Tis November,
Now no tear her wasted cheek bedews.
    From Newfoundland
Not a sail returning will she lose,
    Whispering hoarsely, "Fishermen,
    Have you, have you heard of Ben?"
    Old with watching,
Hannah's at the window, binding shoes.

    Twenty winters
Bleach and tear the ragged shore she views.
    Twenty seasons:—
Never has brought her any news.
    Still her dim eyes silently
    Chase the white sails o'er the sea:

> Hopeless, faithful,
> Hannah's at the window, binding shoes.

Some shoebinders eagerly sought better-paying work in textile mills away from home, where they might relish the personal freedom and economic independence that factory jobs could bring. In 1847 Ann Swett, who had lived unhappily with relatives in Haverhill, Massachusetts, where she bound shoes for low wages, moved to the home of an aunt and uncle in Manchester, New Hampshire. The letters she wrote to her sister Sarah between 1847 and 1850, now located in the collection of the Manchester Historic Association, are full of her delight at being a textile worker.

February 1847

My dear sister,

. . . And now about work. I like it very much, it is just the prettiest work you ever did see. . . . Yesterday forenoon Mr. Sage says Ann you may step out here and get your pay. He paid me four dollars for two weeks work. What do you think of that! Do you see anything green? By and by when I get to knit [loom harnesses] real fast then I shall pay my board and after all that shall have twice as much as though I were binding shoes. I guess you [won't] catch me to do that little thing [shoebinding] again, not I! You cannot think how funny it seems to have some money. . . . I tell you it is a first rate thing to have the time when I get my work done. Just the neatest you ever did see. Some of the old knitters make $3.00 besides their board, guess I will one of these days. . . .

Your dear sister Ann Swett

April 4, 1847

My dear sister,

. . . I will say to you that as to my work I get along very well indeed. Since I have wrote to you another payday has come around, I earned 14 dollars and a half, 9 and a half dollars besides my board. The folks think I get along just first rate, they say. I like it well as ever and Sarah don't I feel independent of every one! The thought that I am living on no one is a happy one indeed to me. . . . I tell you Sarah, it is grand to be a boarder. I leave my work at seven o'clock then I come home and I do what I please. . . . I [now] board with a Mr. Morse. . . . There is in all 17 boarders. . . . I don't have even my bed to make. Quite a lady to be sure. . . . Aunt M. now thinks I better begin and put my money at interest. . . . I get up early, eat my breakfast, go to the shop, do my days work, come out any . . . hour I please, come home, then do anything I wish to. Grand thing, I tell you, so different from what I have been used to. . . .

Wives and other homebound women who could not leave for textile factories, however, endured tedious labor binding shoes to earn a little money for their families. In some instances even this pittance proved crucial to the family's well-being. Harriet Beecher Stowe captured just such a situation in describing Sam and Hepsey Lawson, characters in her 1869 novel *Oldtown Folks* (Cambridge: Harvard University Press, 1966, page 77). The setting is her husband's hometown of Natick, Massachusetts, a center of preindustrial shoe production.

"An eternal torment," said Aunt Lois, with a snap. "I'm sure, if there's a mortal creature on this earth that I pity, it's Hepsey Lawson. Folks talk about her scolding—that Sam Lawson is enough to make the saints in Heaven fall from grace. And you can't *do* anything with him: it's like charging bayonet into a woolsack."

Now, the Hepsey thus spoken of was the luckless woman whom Sam's easy temper, and a certain youthful reputation for being a capable fellow, had led years before into the snares of matrimony with him, in consequence of which she was encumbered with the bringing up of six children on very short rations. She was a gnarly, compact, efficient little pepper-box of a woman, with snapping black eyes, pale cheeks, and a mouth always at half-cock, ready to go off with some sharp crack of reproof at the shoreless, bottomless, and tideless inefficiency of her husband. It seemed to be one of those facts of existence that she could not get used to, nor find anywhere in her brisk, fiery little body a grain of cool resignation for. Day after day she fought it with as bitter and intense a vigor, and with as much freshness of objurgation, as if it had come upon her for the first time,—just as a sharp, wiry little terrier will bark and bark from day to day, with never-ceasing pertinacity, into an empty squirrel hole. She seemed to have no power within her to receive and assimilate the great truth that her husband was essentially, and was to be and always would be, only a do-nothing.

Poor Hepsey was herself quite as essentially a do-something,—an

early-rising, bustling, driving, neat, efficient, capable little body,—
who contrived by going out to day's works,—washing, scrubbing,
cleaning—by making vests for the tailor, or closing and binding shoes
for the shoemaker, by hoeing corn and potatoes in the garden at most
unseasonable hours, actually to find bread to put into the mouths of the
six young ravens aforesaid, and to clothe them decently.

[5]

Mechanization and the
Early Factory System

The successful 1852 adaptation of the Singer sewing machine to stitch light leather undermined the status of shoebinders. As machine stitching began to replace hand work, homebound women quickly identified and fought the threat that mechanization and centralization of their work into small factories posed to their ability to earn wages. For other women, however, the shift of shoe production into steam-powered factories offered the chance of full-time work in groups outside their homes. Factory work also paid higher wages. Many women responded positively to the new terms of shoe work, but, like operatives in the early New England textile mills, many also demanded reform of the factory system, asserting their social and political equality with their employers.

Essex County shoebinders became outraged at shoe bosses who placed stitching machines in their central shops and thereby threatened to deprive women with home responsibilities of their customary paid work. Employers in Lynn, Salem, and Marblehead responded by renting and leasing machines to women homeworkers. But young, unmarried factory girls who worked under the constant discipline of centralized production earned better wages and were not required to "furnish"— that is, pay for some materials and tools out of their own pockets. As a result, mechanization and decisions by shoe bosses to centralize production began to divide women shoeworkers. Some worked a ten-hour day on steam-powered machines in factories, while others worked at home at their own pace on foot-powered machines or by hand.

Although mechanization did not centralize all shoebinding, it did solve some of the shoe bosses' problems of delays, low productivity, and uneven standards of stitching. Women's work was the first to be mechanized by shoe manufacturers; most of the work of shoemakers continued to be performed by journeymen and apprentices in artisan shops. As a result, the sexual division of labor introduced in the 1780s survived both mechanization and the early factory system. Women's control of the stitching process in shoe factories persisted until the early twentieth century.

Shoe cutter John Bliss Nichols figured out how to convert the Singer sewing machine to stitch leather and, in the early 1850s, helped organize small stitching shops that hired young women workers. Other shoe bosses integrated stitching operations into their central shops and intensified their control of the work process. Nichols recalled his experiences in an interview reported in the *Lynn Item*, November 10, 1903.

He had for a long time watched the development of the sewing machine by Elias Howe, Jr. and Isaac M. Singer, and one morning while perusing one of Singer's advertisements in the Boston Times he decided to invest in one of the new machines. Accordingly he went to the place where they were being manufactured in Harvard square, nearly opposite the Old South, and purchased either a No. 5 or No. 7 machine, which was one of the first 15 manufactured. For this he paid $125. . . . He experimented for a considerable length of time, but without success, and finally struck upon the novel idea of sewing pantaloons which had hitherto been done by hand. . . . This business subsequently proved to be a very profitable investment for Mr. Nichols, and he opened a stitching room on Sudbury Street, Boston, where he employed eight girls and a pressman.

During his spare time he continued to experiment on the stitching of leather by machinery, and after six months' time succeeded in perfecting a machine so that it would stitch leather in good shape. . . . Mr. Singer provided him with bench room in his factory, and before long the Singer leather sewing machine was placed on the market. . . . When George W. Keene, John Woolbridge and Scudder Moore, three prominent shoe manufacturers of this city, purchased the exclusive control of the Singer leather sewing machine for Essex County, he [Nichols] accepted an offer from them to instruct their employees how to operate the machine. . . . Then he established a small stitching plant and did a lucrative business in the stitching of shoes for various manufacturers.

Philip C. Swett, nineteenth-century resident of Haverhill, Massachusetts, recalled stories of the angry reactions of shoeworkers to the shoe boss who brought the first machines to town. Excerpts from Swett's unpublished reminiscences, "History of Shoemaking in Massachusetts," are quoted courtesy of the Trustees of the Haverhill Public Library, Special Collections Department.

. . . In [1853] . . . the first stitching machine was brought into [Haverhill] . . . by Isaac R. Harding, who manufactured on the north side of Merrimack Street near White's Corner.

The late Daniel Goodrich was in business with Mr. Harding at the time, and in later years gave an interesting account of the great excitement and bitter feeling of the shoe fitters [binders], who thought they were about to lose their occupation. A Mr. Pike was the first operator and so many people came from far and near to see how the great curiosity worked, that the firm was obliged to keep the factory doors locked. The women were fully excited as the men, and some of them shook their fists in Mr. Goodrich's face telling him that he was destroying their means of livelihood.

. . . Other manufacturers ordered machines but for a time it was difficult to run them satisfactorily owing to the inexperience of the operators. Mr. Alfred Ordway who was a boy at the time, was working in those days for Sawyer & Wheeler, and the firm was among the first to purchase stitching machines. Some of the best shoe fitters were selected to operate them but they could not do so satisfactorily and gave up in despair. Mr. Ordway, who is an ingenious man, worked over one of the machines until he thoroughly understood it, and one day closed the seams of three sets of uppers without difficulty. One of his employers, when he saw what had been accomplished, was so delighted that he rushed down stairs into the cutting room and danced on the floor, shouting, "The boy's done it, the boy's done it." . . .

In those days all ladies' shoes were made with straight side seams and the machines were used to close the seams and stitch flat binding on the uppers which were afterwards lined by hand. Some seven or eight years later, a folder attachment for the binding was invented which enabled an operator to fit the uppers complete on a machine, but a great many shoes were lined in by hand as late as 1862.

Shoe bosses who did not immediately purchase Singer sewing machines faced ruinous competition from those who did. One who recognized the implications of mechanization for faster and more standardized production expressed his fears in a letter published on March 19, 1859, by the *New England Mechanic*, a publication of the Lynn Mechanics' (journeymen shoemakers') Association. A few copies are on file in the Essex Institute, Salem, Massachusetts.

The sewing machine has effected a great change in the modes of manufacturing. Ten years ago, the small manufacturers, known then as bag bosses who did their own cutting, and sold directly to the retailer, enjoyed almost a monopoly of the best quality of stitchers and binders, which gave them a great advantage over manufacturers of great capital and credit, which went to compensate for the lack of those essentials in trade. In a word, skill as a general rule, resided with the small manufacturer. The sewing-machine has changed all this; it knows no difference between cheap cotton backed with silk warp lasting, and the best satin Francaise; the lines of stitches are laid with a mathematical regularity and beauty that but few handworkers can rival. Capital can buy the machine, and hire the operator, and skill is confined to the small manufacturer. But the most astonishing change worked by the sewing machine, is that enabling the manufacturer to get up a thousand pair of shoes in less time than it would have taken to get up two or three dozen, seven years ago. When women did the stitching and binding, uppers were in the hands of binders from a week to six months, and it would take four or five weeks for the manufacturer to get up a hundred pairs of shoes, to fill an order. Within a year, I have known a manufacturer to receive an order for seven hundred dollars worth of goods in the morning, have them all cut out, and a large part of them stitched and bound and a small part of them made, before night. In three days the order was filled, and the cash paid.

E.

During the New England shoe strike of 1860, Robert Hassall, pastor of the Unitarian Church in Haverhill and an active supporter of the striking shoeworkers, denounced the impact of mechanization on shoebinders. The result, he argued, was a double standard: low wages and hard work for homeworkers who sewed shoe linings by hand, and higher wages and better conditions of work for the female shop workers who worked on machines. His letter to the *Tri-Weekly Publisher* appeared on March 3, 1860, and condemned the influence of the market forces of supply and demand on wages as sinful, unjust, and antirepublican.

This is a large class of workers. Many of them, I know, have husbands whose earnings can support them. They line shoes when they can do nothing better, and they can work for less compensation than those who are dependent altogether upon their own industry. But woman's time and labor are not lessened in value by the fact that she can call some man her husband. Married or unmarried, her work is of the same value. But who knows not that the prices of lining shoes are miserable low? Two days of close work in stitching from morning till night will earn but about sixty cents. . . .

But look at the difference in the earnings of [some] females who labor on shoes. The wages of twenty girls in one shop in this town average from six to seven dollars a week. . . . The following statements I obtained from John Gardner and Sons. One young lady whose name I need not mention earned for sixty weeks $7.31 a week; another $6.70 per week; another $5.30 a week. All must admit these are good wages. . . .

Let some addition we say be made to the prices of [wages for] linings and make the shoe buyers pay for it. If the manufacturers will avoid the sin against God and still more the sin against man of reducing their goods to the very last cent of profit and placing themselves in such circumstances that they feel compelled to lower the price of labor; if they could be united amongst themselves to sustain better prices [for shoes], and could be made to feel that the interests of the laboring classes were to some extent in their hands, a better state of things would exist. But as it is, what a strife we witness to sell! The stock *must* be disposed of. Money *must* be had. Above or below value the shoes *must* be sold. To gain custom, goods *must* be reduced to a very low figure and men, women, boys and girls *must* work for less and down go the wages, lower and lower still, and heaven knows where they will go if this competition continues. . . .

R.H.

Even though they were paid better than homeworkers, the lot of the first factory girls was hard. They worked at hand-cranked or foot-powered sewing machines for ten exhausting hours a day. Attracted by the good wages for machine stitching in the 1850s, some women, among them Martha Osbourne Barrett of Salem, forced themselves to accept the long hours and physical burdens of foot-treadled machine work before the introduction of steam power. In her diary of 1855 she record-

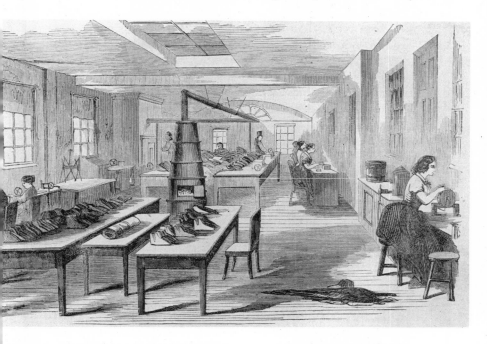

Interior of stitching room. From *Frank Leslie's Illustrated Magazine,* March 17, 1860. Courtesy of Lynn Historical Society.

ed her reaction to factory work. Within a year, however, forced by circumstance to board away from her mother, Barrett abandoned the relatively high wages for stitching shoes to accept a milliner's position. Excerpts from the Martha Osbourn Barrett diary, 1854–59, are reprinted by permission of the Essex Institute, Salem, Massachusetts.

July 2, 1855

The 22d of April—Went to work at Danvers-Port in David Mead's 'Machine Shop' Have continued to work there and board at home—and at night after my days work am to[o] weary for much thought. . . .

July 6

A day of toil, hard physical labor. . . .

July 16

. . . Have been to the shop and am weary. . . .

July 29

Work, hard and almost unremitting has made me necessarily very negligent of my pen. . . .

. . . Some pursuit than what I am at present engaged in would be more congenial to my taste—but mere *taste* cannot be always consulted. It is absolutely necessary for me to do something to earn *money* and this work seems to be the most available just now. So I am steadily at work.

Eliza A. Bartlett, with her widowed mother arrived in Lynn from New Hampshire in the 1850s, and like many others, after learning machine work in a shop, found a way to avoid the discipline of the long ten-hour day by working at home on a rented machine. Bartlett's recollections were reported in the *Lynn Item*, October 26, 1895.

She came to Lynn in her youth from her birthplace, Portsmouth, New Hampshire, with her mother and sisters. Her father had died, and at an early age she found employment, like hundreds of lassies then, from the shoe shops, beginning in the old George W. Keene factory, on Willow street, stitching in congress uppers for $3 per week, and when she had become skilled turning out from three to four 60-pair lots a day. She afterwards worked in the old Tozier shop, using an old-fashioned three-wheeled Singer machine, and at the time of the strike [in 1860] was taking uppers from the L. B. Frazier factory to stitch at the home of her sister . . . on one of the old Grover & Baker machines.

Editor Alonzo B. Draper, in the February 26, 1859, issue of his *New England Mechanic*, criticized the factory system in the February 26, 1859 issue as injurious to the health of female machine operators and bemoaned the low wages earned by shop stitchers. Draper became one of the leaders of the 1860 strike in Lynn.

Machine Girls, and Their Compensation

Throughout the whole range of Female labor there is no branch which makes such cruel inroads on the physical energies as the present wretched system, which the numerous and indispensable class of our city are daily submitting to. The first point of objection is the incalculable injury which originates from want to exercise. Sitting hour after hour nearly motionless, nothing to relieve this dull monotony for hours, but the short time outside in going from house to shop and shop to house. To imagine for a moment that any person can follow up unremit[t]ingly these habits without incurring the penalty which is sure to follow these palpable infractions of the physical laws, is sheer folly. Look at the rugged girl of to-day, glowing with health, strength & vigor, before entering one of these machine-shops and, meet the same person one year hence, and in many instances you would hardly believe the change possible,—weak, pale, and emaciated, hardly able to do half the labor which she could have performed before she commenced this health destroying calling.

Thus the health and happiness of females are sacrificed (for without the former there is not much of the latter,) and where is the motive for surrendering all these blessing[s], for they are paid the poorest and work the hardest of any class in the County of Essex. The following is from a book furnished by one of these unfortunate girls: Prices in 1854, stitching tipped Congress boots, no heel price, heel seam not stitched 17 cts. 1858, the same kind of boot with two rows of stitching and find trimmings, 8 cts. 1855, Congress foxed heel seam, not stitched, 20 cts. Same kind in 1858, 10 cents. Pages might be furnished showing the similar reductions, but we turn from the task with loathing and disgust that human beings professing to be meek and lowly followers of Jesus Christ would commit such outrages upon any of the human family. Can such people lay claim to Christianity? We pause for a reply.

In a letter published in the *New England Mechanic* on March 19, 1859, one shop stitcher, replying to Draper's editorial, agreed that the work was physically debilitating but refused to criticize the wage rates paid for factory work and accepted centralized machine production. She wanted to work eight hours a day rather than ten and advocated more prompt payment of wages, but she called on the employers rather than on her fellow workers to reform the factory system.

Machine Operators

The introduction of sewing machines, for the purpose of stitching and binding boots & shoes, has wrought a revolution in this branch of industry, which for so many years has so largely engaged the female labor of our city and its vicinity. This revolution, like all others, whether political or social, has worked out unlooked for results—some good, some evil. Some of the evils are inseparable from the benefits which accompany them—others admit of a mitigation, if not of a radical cure. The prudent statesman will not seek the destruction of existing forms of government, until he sees a reasonable prospect that they may be supplanted by those which will better subserve the interests of the people; for he knows that in a greater or lesser degree, imperfection must inhere in all human institutions. Neither will the social reformer labor for the demolition of prevailing systems, until he is convinced that others more just in their operation will take their place, and thus work out a grander result for humanity. This has been the true philosophy of reform, in all ages. Old abuses have gradually yielded to the force of public opinion, whose silent, and often unnoticed power has changed the forms of government, and moulded anew the social and political institutions of mankind. But, to follow out the thoughts thus suggested, would carry me too far from my special purpose at this time, which is to call the attention of those whom it may concern to two points which seem worthy of consideration. First, a reduction in the hours of labor performed by machine operators; and second, the more frequent payment of wages.

1. The ten hours of labor, required whenever the length of days will admit, are too many for the physical strength of the operator. If this point can be established, no consideration of a pecuniary nature ought for a moment to be admitted as valid.

That the labor of running a machine is very exhaustive, few acquainted with the subject will deny. From some causes, not now perhaps well understood, the effects of unremitted labor, on the part of machine operators, are often disastrous to health.

Few persons except those blessed with unusual vigor of constitution can pursue this employment steadily ten hours a day, for any considerable period, without finding themselves injuriously affected. The only remedy for this is a reduction in the hours of labor. This can be accomplished without materially diminishing the profits of the employer, while the beneficial results to the employed, on the score of health, will be incalculable.

It may safely be assumed that eight hours of labor, performed with the vigor of complete strength, will be as productive as ten, part of which is performed while the system is exhausted by too long continued exertion. Under the present system, in the short days of winter, the operator is obliged to get her breakfast before daylight, and hurry off to the shop with the morning meal simply swallowed, not eaten, thus laying the foundation of dyspepsia, and a long line of evils that follow in its train; and, at the close of day, must resort to gaslight to finish her work.

These are but a few of the points that would be gained by adopting the eight hour day.

The operator would have more time for moral and intellectual culture[,] an object, the importance of which no intelligent person will undervalue, but which is almost entirely out of the question when the bodily and mental energies are prostrated by severe toil.

Who among our employers will inaugurate this reform?

Secondly. In the mind of the employer, it may seem a small matter whether the operator receives her pay once a week, or once in four weeks; but with *her* it is a matter of great importance, making all the difference oftentimes, which lies between the ability to meet her regular expenses, and inability to do so—a vast chasm.

A few years ago, when sewing machines were first introduced, it was the uniform practice for employers to pay their hands every week, or, at the longest every fortnight; but more recently some employers have adopted the plan of paying only once in four weeks. The practical workings of this system are somewhat as follows: The operators [*sic*] receiving her pay but once in four weeks, as a matter of course, most generally, she cannot pay her board oftener than she receives her wages. This subjects the boarding housekeepers to serious inconvenience, inasmuch as many of them are persons in moderate circumstances dependent upon their weekly incomes for their support. There is now no alternative but to resort to credit; and credit, every businessman knows, must be paid for. The final result of all this is an increase in the cost of living, the burden coming, ultimately, where it always comes—upon the laborer.

Why this retrograde movement, after once established a better system? Why should the machine operator be compelled to wait four weeks for her pay, while the shoemaker receives his whenever his lot is returned? Can the plea of the necessary be urged in the one case more than in the other?

Employers, pay your operatives every Saturday, and you will confer a benefit, the extent of which it will not be easy to estimate.

D.

[6]

The New England
Shoe Strike of 1860

The participation of women in the New England shoe strike of 1860, particularly in Lynn, reflected the new possibilities in factory work for them as well as the influence of traditional artisan ideology and family loyalties. The strike, involving shoe towns throughout the region, represented the most powerful demonstration of American labor protest prior to the Civil War. The choice for women between collective action as working sisters and labor protest as members of families became central to the 1860 strike in Lynn.

Strategies based on sisterhood promised to overcome the divisions created by the new factory system between homeworkers and shop girls. Women workers could join together to support the interests of all females in the industry, married or single, resident or boarder, working at home or in a factory. Sisters could pursue female-defined organizational tactics. In contrast, women who supported family loyalty during the strike reflected the gender relations within artisan family life, values that defined women workers as secondary earners in a family wage system within which they were socially and economically subordinate.

During the strike of 1860, journeymen shoemakers appealed again for the support of women for the same reasons as in the 1840s: the moral power of females would ennoble and elevate the cause of labor protest. Strike leaders recruited sympathetic women following outbreaks of widely criticized physical violence on the streets of Lynn between male strikers and the drivers of wagons that carried machine-sewn uppers and leather stock into the countryside to nonstriking shoemakers—violence that threatened support for the strike in other New England

shoe towns. The view of womanhood expressed by the striking journeymen in 1860, and accepted by many Lynn women, emphasized self-
sacrifice, family loyalty, and female moral power. Female support for the
strike would erase those scenes of male violence and replace them with
family and community values consistent with artisan harmony and solidarity.

The foremost advocate of female involvement was Alonzo B. Draper,
editor of the *New England Mechanic* and president of the Lynn Mechanics' Association. But he and the other male leaders initially confined
women's activities in the strike to a labor boycott of shoe bosses who
refused to pay higher wages to journeymen. No one on the men's strike
committee considered increased women's wages as part of the strike's
objectives until the women themselves made these demands. Alonzo
Draper expressed the views of the men's strike committee at two meetings held on the evening of February 23, 1860. He declared to the men
strikers that the women, who were meeting that same night at another
public hall in Lynn, were "as devoted to your cause as were the Mothers
of the Revolution in the cause of American liberty." A reporter captured
Draper's later remarks to the assembled women—and some signs of
their divided response—for the *Boston Herald*, February 24, 1860.

. . . he proceeded to urge the ladies present to unite with the men in
their strike, and go in with them in their endeavor to get better prices.
He stated what the men had done in their strike, and said that if both
men and women would lay their heads together, and neither work until
each was paid their bill of wages, the thing would be done. Now ladies,
will you do this? Loud cries of "we will! Yes sir—we will!" A voice—
"Binding shoes at two cents a pair I think is abominable!" (Great
laughter.)

Another voice—"Yes, and find [furnish] your own silk!"

Mr. Draper continued—He appealed to all his hearers—to see that
their husbands, their brothers, their sweethearts—

A voice dolefully—"We ain't got any!"

Mr. Draper—Now ladies, you all remember Molly Stark, how she
behaved in the [American] revolution.

A voice—I'll bet we do.

Mr. Draper—Shall I tell the men at the other hall that you are with
them, heart and hand, and will strike with them[?]

A hundred voices—"We will strike and stick to it—it's the men who always give out first!" (Great applause.)

Draper—Remember ladies—especially you young and blooming ones—(great attention paid on all hands) that if you want husbands (great sensation) wages must go up, for no one can get married at present prices. Renewed sensation and cries of Shame! Shame!

Lewis Josselyn, editor of the *Bay State* and an adviser to the strike committee, was among those who feared that street violence had deprived the strike of its moral justification. His poem "To the Strikers," published in the *Bay State* on March 22, 1860, portrayed the moral females whose association with the journeymen's strike would elevate its objectives.

> . . . Then up, fair daughters of the free!
>   Assert your rights anew;
> Let those who seek to wrong us see
>   Our hearts are firm and true!
>
> That though our arms may be less strong,
>   Our hearts are full of might;
> And they will find that human wrong
>   Must yield to moral right!"

As Josselyn hoped, the moral and religious convictions of the protesting shoebinders of the early 1830s were echoed in the angry speech of one elderly shoebinder of Lynn at the second public meeting of the women strikers, recorded in the *Boston Journal*, February 29, 1860. The shoe bosses' violation of customary justice and morality again provoked female outrage.

A lady, advanced in years, here rose and stated that she gloried in this honored cause. It was the same cause that brought the Israelites out of Egypt. . . . The time was when they [the shoebinders] were furnished even with beeswax; but now the workingwomen had to find everything, and do the work cheaply. She wished she could stand upon Lynn Rock and talk so that every boss could hear her. There was to be an awful shaking of things, and the bosses would feel it. . . . the bosses took their last farthing to *grandize* their houses with. It was heartrending to her to see her Lynn friends out of work, when work was being sent out of town.

As they had in the 1840s, protesting shoemakers in 1860 attempted to define womanhood in ways useful to their cause. Many women in Lynn, especially those with husbands, fathers, and brothers who were shoemakers, agreed with the men's definition; other women had their own ideas. Clara Brown, a twenty-one-year-old unmarried factory stitcher from Medford, Massachusetts, who boarded in Lynn with a shoemaker's family, expressed a different view of womanhood during the 1860 strike. Like Mary Russell in 1834, she emphasized the power of sisterhood as the basis of female labor protest. Representing the young women engaged in machine-stitching shoe uppers in early Lynn factories, she recognized the strategic position of female factory workers to halt shoemaking in rural areas by refusing to stitch any uppers by machine. With this power to paralyze production, they could also aid their sisters who worked at home as well as men and women in other towns. For Brown, womanhood meant the power to unite women as workers.

Some of the voices in the audience of women at their first meeting on February 23 had indicated that they had no husbands or sweethearts and that family loyalty was not workingwomen's only interest in the strike. After Draper left the women's meeting, a large and vocal contingent of factory girls who worked a ten-hour day at steam-powered machines took charge. Many were not members of resident Lynn families but, like Clara Brown, represented migrant women from the New England region who boarded in the city and worked in the shoe shops during the busy season. Factory girls would strike on behalf of raising women's wages as well as men's wages. They wished to be led by women who represented their interests as workers.

The appropriate role of women in the 1860 strike was fought out at four meetings in which Clara Brown and the shop girls battled the male and female supporters of the men's strike, who wanted the workingwomen to put aside their own wage grievances. At the second meeting, on February 28, the women voted for "the high wage list" that would raise the pay of both factory girls and homeworkers. Determined to prevent the women's demands from complicating the strike, Alonzo Draper and Willard Oliver, who chaired the second meeting, called the women together the following night, February 29, for a third meeting to reconsider their vote. In these and a fourth meeting on March 2, the

Women's strike meeting, February 28, 1860. From *Frank Leslie's Illustrated Magazine*, March 17, 1860. Courtesy of Lynn Historical Society.

debates over the proper relationship of Lynn women to the 1860 strike featured Clara Brown and other factory girls, Alonzo Draper, James Dillon, and Willard Oliver of the men's strike committee, and homeworkers Mrs. William Graham and Mary Damon, who supported the men's strike. The dispute was detailed in both Boston and New York newspapers.

[*Boston Herald*, February 28, 1860] Shall binding and eyeleting be done for 8 1/2 and 9 cents? that was the question.

Mrs. [William] Graham [a homeworker] thought that for the very poorest quality 7 cents was enough.

Cries of "oh dear! that is *too* cheap!"

. . . Miss Clara H. Brown . . . opposed the motion of Mrs. Graham to have a third price on binding and eyeleting.

The seven cents idea met with no favor and was scouted with derision.

Mrs. Graham said that it would be of no use to vote these prices; they could not get them.

Miss Brown replied with spirit—"yes we can!" said she, "only the Lynn girls can bind shoes as they should be bound and the competition of the girls out of town would be of no account. . . ."

[*Boston Journal*, February 28, 1860] A lady said she had been through the Salem [Massachusetts] machine shops and the girls there would strike if the prices are not set too high here.

A voice—Don't be bluffed. We shall get our prices if we are not faint-hearted. . . .

Another thought if they had the spirit of our Revolutionary ancestors they would put the bill of prices through as first reported. . . .

[*Boston Journal*, February 29, 1860] He [Draper] was well aware that if the ladies refused to bind and stitch, the bosses must either accede to their demands or go out of town. . . . It appeared to him that the ladies of Lynn had struck for a pretty high bill of wages. But it appeared to him that it was more important that their husbands should get their prices, than the ladies. A voice—We haven't any husbands. . . .

After reading the two bills, the President [Oliver] asked which they would accept.

Many voices—The first one.

A few voices—The second one.

One lady wanted to know what kind of a strike it was if they adopted the last [low] bill of prices?

One lady said the bosses thought the first bill of prices too stiff.

Another was having better prices than the second bill provided. She didn't want [her wages] to be cut down when she was on a strike.

[*New York Times*, February 29, 1860] The leading spirit of the meeting, Miss Clara Brown, a very bright, pretty girl, said she called at a shop that day and found a friend of hers hard at work on a lot of linings. She asked what she was getting for them, and was told *eight cents for sixty*. "Girls of Lynn," said Clara, "Girls of Lynn, do you hear that and will you stand it? Never, Never, NEVER. Strike then—strike at once; DEMAND 8-1/2 cents for your work when the binding isn't closed, and you will get it. Don't let them make niggers of you; (Shame, there are colored persons here.) I meant Southern niggers:—keep still; don't work your machines; let 'em lie still till we get all we ask, and then go at it, as did our Mothers in the Revolution."

The speech was a good one; it seemed to suit all parties. . . .

Brown apparently used the word "niggers" to insist that unjustly compensated or "slave" labor could never replace the free, skilled labor of Lynn binders and stitchers. Angry Lynn women who had held anti-slavery views since the 1830s rebuked her for using a racial insult (*Boston Journal*, February 28, 1860). Nevertheless, ignoring the pressure from the men's strike committee, a large majority of women at the third meeting voted a second time for the high wage list and ordered it circulated to all women strikers in Lynn. Still the male leaders did not give up. Their sympathizers on the women's canvassing committee conspired with Willard Oliver to substitute a second, lower wage list, which they had printed and circulated for signatures among the women workers of Lynn.

Some homeworkers who opposed the high wage bill regarded the factory workers like Clara Brown as "smart girls," irresponsible and selfish young women without family obligations or connections in Lynn. Higher wages for smart girls, they believed, would be foolishly spent on extravagant dress. To homeworkers, the interests of shop girls seemed to endanger family economic security. They feared that higher wages for women would push all stitching operations into the more productive, steam-powered factories and destroy homework for homebound wives and daughters. To prevent this, they called a fourth meeting, as noted in the *New York Times* for March 6, 1860.

We [the reporters covering the strike for out-of-town newspapers] . . . were met by one of the Lady Committee women, who said she hoped "we could be at the [March 2] meeting tonight, for they were going to have high old times, and if Clara B— dared to open her head, she was to be kicked down stairs." We gently asked the cause of all the inveighing against Miss Clara, whose straight-forward manner and blunt way of coming to the point had rather excited our admiration, and were told that Clara was one of a few smart girls who could get higher wages than the majority of girls, and that regardless of the general welfare, she was stirring up the working-women to strike for higher pay than the bosses would be willing to pay, other than to such as she.

Outraged over changes in the wage list, the shop girls, led by Clara Brown, confronted their opponents' deceit at the tumultuous fourth meeting on March 2. Brown tried to heal the divisions among the women strikers with renewed appeals to the power of sisterhood and to the strategic leverage that women factory workers wielded in shoe production. She also made it clear that the shop girls would not support the strike at all if their wage demands were ignored. Both the *Boston Herald*, March 3, 1860, and the *New York Times*, March 6, 1860, recounted her energetic efforts.

At this juncture—critical for the high price advocates—up rose Miss Clara Brown to the rescue. "Where?" said she, in silvery pealing tones, "is the use of striking, if you gain nothing by it? It has come to a pretty pass if the machine bosses of Lynn were to govern the girls as they chose. If Mr. Fred Ingalls—the meanest man in Lynn—can rule us as he pleases, then where is the use of the strike? His machines are worth nothing if he can't get girls to work them; and if they only hold out, the list would have to be met by the bosses." (Applause and much hissing—ladies will hiss now and then.)

Mrs. Damon made a most earnest appeal for unity. We must have the machine men with us, said she; we can't get along without them, can we ladies?

A voice—We must have them!

Another voice, derisively—Get them, then!

"Clara Brown wasn't going to strike for less than she got now, that was certain. She could get $5.50 and $6, why should she strike for $5. "For God's sake, don't act like a pack of fools. We've got the bosses where we can do as we please with 'em. If we won't work our machines, and the out-of-town girls won't take the work, what can the bosses do?"(Cheers, hisses, "Shame," "Hoe her out," "Pest," etc.) . . .

Clara Brown—"Mr. Oliver, I say if we are going to strike for anything, let's strike for something worth having."

James Dillon, vice-president of the Lynn Mechanics' Association, made a final appeal to the women strikers on behalf of the men's strike committee. The *New York Times*, March 6, 1860, printed his speech.

> . . . we rest on you; you, who suckle us in our infancy, who court us in our prime, who succor, support, and comfort us in our old age and declining powers, we rest on *you* to help us *here*, now, at *this* time; give us, journeymen shoemakers, your encouragement and cooperation, and we'll go on, on, on e'en to Death's grim door. Tremendous applause, great clapping, immense sensation, followed by a hum of approbative remarks from the fair crowd in the pit. . . . Remember the noble stand we men took [to strike] on the glorious twenty-second [of February], and if you love us, if you love your little ones, and your God, stand still, and when the day of trial comes, still stand.

Swayed by the rhetoric of family loyalty, the majority of the women strikers reversed themselves and voted for the low wage list. Sisterhood was rejected, and the shop girls abandoned the strike. Most of the other striking women decided to march in a gigantic procession on March 7 through Lynn, where their presence attested to the morality and justice of the journeymen's battle. Their banners and actions indicated that the marching women refused to work like slaves and that they agreed with the definition of their womanhood made by the supporters of the men's strike. The *New York Herald*, March 9, 1860, quoted the words of the banner carried by the female delegation from Ward 4, while the *Lynn Reporter*, March 10, 1860, described its ceremonial conveyance to the striking journeymen of Ward 4 by Miss Ellen Darlin, daughter of E. C. Darlin, former editor of the *Awl*.

> Weak in physical strength but strong in moral courage, we dare to battle for the right, shoulder to shoulder with our fathers, husbands and brothers.

> " . . . It is the wish of the ladies of Ward 4 that you maintain your stand like men in a peaceable and orderly manner, committing no violence on person or property, and conducting yourselves in such a manner as to secure that sympathy from the people which is now yours." [Striker] Davis N. Johnson responded: " . . . without woman's sympathy and cooperation, no noble work was ever consummated."

The women's procession on March 7, 1860. Detail from *Frank Leslie's Illustrated Magazine,* March 17, 1860. Courtesy of Lynn Historical Society.

The strikers held out throughout March, but by early April the protest had collapsed in New England.

The strike of 1860 represented the last stand of pre-industrial artisan protest against the emerging factory system, the end of a tradition that had equated the interests of women workers with family economic interests and female morality. Despite the divisions among women shoe-workers and the rejection by many of Clara Brown and the strategy of sisterhood, the increasing numbers of women employed as full-time factory operatives in Essex County shoe shops after 1860 meant that their interests and their demands would shape labor protest after the Civil War.

P A R T   I I

Work and Protest in the Post–Civil War Factory, 1865–1910

In the years immediately following the Civil War, the factory system throughout Essex County, especially in Lynn, matured rapidly. After the McKay stitcher mechanized men's work in 1862, journeymen began to join women workers in new steam-powered, centralized operations.

Inside these factories the operations of the stitching room, which produced the uppers for ladies' high-cut, buttoned shoes in the 1870s and 1880s, involved complicated divisions of labor. Women workers who dominated the stitching process gained dexterity and experience. The structure of factory work offered opportunities for some to develop the skills that determined the fine appearance of the finished boot or shoe. The most skilled stitchers—the stayers, closers-on, vampers, and over-lap vampers or foxers—exhibited a feminine pride in their craft and often became leaders in strikes and labor protest. Howard Mudge Newhall described the process of stitching uppers in shoe factories in *Harpers' New Monthly Magazine* for January 1885.

The first clatter of machinery is heard in a room which is "all windows," where "girls," who are always girls, no matter the age, sit with eyes and hands busy at sewing machines. No longer the "stitch, stitch, stitch" of the weary binder, but machines speeded at the rate of six hundred stitches in a minute! Their introduction came early in the "golden age" of invention, and with the advent of sole-cutting and sewing machines, foot-power began to assert its rising importance. Now even the foot is relieved, and the machines are run almost altogether from steam shafting. In this "stitching-room" the small quarter

[87]

A stitching room, 1885. From "A Pair of Shoes," *Harpers' Magazine*, January 1885.

[of the upper] and button piece are "closed" on the quarter, the seams are "rubbed down" on the inside, and a "stay" is sewed over the inside of the seam with a row of stitching on each side. The different parts of the lining are stitched together in a similar manner, when outside and lining are passed along to be "closed on." A small cut on the front of the lining is the only guide by which an experienced "closer-on" knows where to begin her work, yet as with accurate eye and practiced hand the needle and the "trimming knife" follow the winding outline, it seemed as if she must be following a traced pattern. Lining and outside are stitched together on the wrong side, and to get them right side out, a "corder" forms the top and button scallops over a round pointed piece of steel securely fastened to a table. The seam thus left on the inside forms a cord or "bead" on the whole outline of the boot, which is held in place by "stitching round" one row of stitching to follow the outline. One machine cuts and works a button-hole in each button scallop, doing the work so regularly that an exacting seamstress would not hesitate to commend it. After the "vamp" has been joined to the quarters by two or three rows of stitching, there is no use to look for more pieces because they have all been sewed together. They have become an "upper."

[7]

The Factory Girl as Moral Lady

The increasing demand for female labor in the post–Civil War shoe shops attracted not only women residents in Lynn but additional migrants from surrounding Massachusetts towns, the New England countryside, and Canada. The scarcity of marriageable men resulting from Civil War deaths and westward migration seemed to guarantee a ready supply of stitchers among those women who needed to support themselves.

Lynn manufacturers, eager to assure themselves ample numbers of young female machine operators during the busy seasons of production, promoted the image of shoe stitchers as ladies. Manufacturing interests joined middle-class residents, who worried about public morality in their rapidly changing city, to define the young women shoeworkers as morally respectable ladies. On December 23, 1865, the *Lynn Reporter*, a pro-manufacturer newspaper, launched this effort to elevate the status of female factory workers, and particularly of those "young ladies" who came from distant country towns in New England and from the Maritime Provinces of Canada.

Twelve hundred thousand dollars has been made in Lynn during one year. . . . Where is concealed this machinery, these hands, this industry, which so prospers her? Much good judgment, great business faculties, thought, knowledge, all are taxed; but I see also in the train of workmen, of business men and manufacturers, another that attracts me, that calls forth my tenderest interest. That train is composed of the working women of Lynn, who help you to this wealth. I have not only looked upon them, but with spiritual ear heard the sound of many a sigh—sighs from motherly hearts. Far away they are uttered . . . as they cross the New Hampshire hill—fainter as they sweep up the sea coast, from villages and country homes—fainter from distant Canada and Nova Scotia. . . .

The prosperous city of Lynn! Two thousand, and sometimes four thousand girls congregate here. To whose flock do they belong? Who loves these strangers? Who invites them? Who urges them to think of home and God? . . . And today she who earns . . . [her daily bread] has won a title better than in common parlance called "lady." Yes, lady! with thy silks and satins, rolling in the luxury of wealth, the simplest sewing girl is far better, filling her place in God's world, than those in thy indolence and ease. . . .

Clergymen, it is not enough that your churches stand ready for a congregation. Not only "invite to the feast," but gently "compel" the guests to come. There should be in every church free seats for strangers and those who cannot afford to pay pew rent. Mothers and daughters, extend your invitations to those "sociables," reading societies, and pleasant gatherings of yours, to those who would be pleased to come. Young ladies, strangers in Lynn, accept the advances made you: form societies among yourselves; attend church, Sabbath schools, for the sake of your mothers at home. Intelligent, and numbering so many, doing your work nobly in the world, you are of vast importance in the community of Lynn. Already you have formed societies of your own—already, many have attended churches and Sabbath schools, and may heaven prosper you, as it always has all true women, at all times, and under all circumstances.

In promoting the gentility of the factory stitcher, the shoe manufacturers of Lynn created a public image of a well-paid and highly respectable class of female operatives whose labors at their sewing machines were light and easy and who moved with social grace among the better families of the community. Their social status, according to the *Lynn Reporter*, November 2, 1870, equaled that of female clerks, teachers, and stitching-room supervisors. For the lady stitcher, there was no contradiction between respectable womanhood and working in a shoe factory.

"What in the name of wonder do all these girls do?" asked a gentleman the other day, while passing through our streets at the hour when from all the places of business came troops of laughing, smartly-dressed girls. . . .

. . . here we are in the third story of one of the most flourishing shoe manufactories in the city. Here, in a large, well-lighted room sit some thirty, forty or fifty young women, not languidly bending over a piece of work for which they will receive perhaps a pittance, such as remunerates the operatives of the manufacturing districts of England, but before a magic little sewing-machine, driven by steam power. . . . With skillful fingers they guide the different parts of the boot beneath the glittering needle, and these are in turn taken by others to be stitched together ready for the maker. . . .

And so they work and sing and smile from day to day, some of them earning ten or twelve dollars per week, few less than one dollar per day, which enables them to "pay their way" and move in the best walks of society. The labor hours being over our working girl is the lady, and you will find her on the fashionable promenade, at the popular lecture, mingling with the musical associations of the day, attired in the most stylish costumes and forming an attractive feature of the social assembly. . . . But we have not quite finished our investigations in the stitching-room. There must be some governing spirit here, and if we look about we shall see one of these Lynn girls of whom our friend asks, flitting here and there, carefully inspecting the work as it passes through the several stages, scolding a little to this one, commending that one, and all in such a way that even the delinquents cannot but admit is just. This is the overseer, and everything is under her immediate supervision. . . . Some of these overseers, wishing to venture still farther out on the ocean of independence, have set up for themselves, and more than one can point to a nice little residence which they have erected as the result of their enterprise.

But let us descend to the counting room. . . . Here again, we see a young woman in charge of the journal and ledger, to whom "double entry" is no mystery whatever, and who can give the head of the establishment a trial balance with all the readiness of a veteran knight of the quill. These fair accountants can be found in many of the counting-rooms, not only of the shoe manufactories, but the banks, insurance offices and other places of business in the city. . . .

We will now pay a flying visit to the public schools, where we find eighty-one teachers. . . . Of this number, seventy-five are females, nearly all of whom are Lynn girls. . . . We shall see this same class of workers in our private institutions of education, some of which are entirely under the control of female principals. . . .

This is the way in which "all these girls" gain a livelihood. Whether as operators, overseers, proprietors of stitching-rooms, clerks or teachers, their work is accomplished steadily and satisfactorily. . . . So to our inquiring friend we would say, this tide of humanity, which you see whenever you visit our city, is not drifting to and fro without purpose. . . . In the merry groups which you meet in our streets you will find all we have described, and we take a peculiar pride in telling "What they do."

Despite this carefully crafted image of the lady stitcher, many middle-class people in Lynn worried about the fast pace of social change created by rapid industrialization and about the moral behavior of the numerous women without family ties who lived and worked in their community. Most migrant stitchers boarded with private families in the city, but the specter of young women living outside the moral influence of home life concerned many observers. Dangers to respectable womanhood seemed to lurk most ominously in the streets of Lynn. "The Stitching Girls," a poem published in the *Lynn Transcript*, June 26, 1869, transformed the image of the lady stitcher into that of a tempting and heartless flirt.

> When walking on the crowded street,
>   A lovely lass attracts your eye,
> and while you gaze your glances meet,
>   You smile—alas! you soon will sigh
> For Cupid from her beaming eyes,
>   His shining arrows thickly hurls;
> And hard indeed must be the heart—
>   That can withstand the stitching girls.
>
>   The stitching girls, the witching girls.
>   The jaunty, dainty, stitching girls
>   With Cupid's dart they pierce the heart—
>   The pleasing, teasing stitching girls.
>
> . . . Again you meet her and she plys
>   And sings and smiles for you alone,

Charmed by her gentle, loving ways,
    You hope to call her all your own,
But should you kneel and tell your love,
    With cruel scorn her lip will curl:
And you'll be left alone to sigh:
    I'm jilted by a stitching girl.

    The stitching girls, the witching girls—
    The singing, clinging stitching girls
    They break your heart and then depart
    The naughty, haughty stitching girls.

The promenade of working girls on Saturday nights in Lynn became a symbol of the moral dangers and pitfalls of a city crowded with migrant working men and women. A novel titled *The Queen City!: or Life in the Shoe Factories of Lynn*, serialized in the *Lynn Record* in 1872, captured the scene that troubled so many. In an episode appearing in the April 20 issue, Eben Poole, a new recruit or "green hand" in the shoe shops, ventured out one evening after work.

On Saturday night, Eben, dressed in his "best," promenaded the streets of Lynn, in the height of his pride. He saw other young men with ladies, and thought that a lady would be a pleasant companion in promenading.

The evening was partially cloudy. Notwithstanding the state of the weather, multitudes flocked the streets. Girls paraded up and down, having no visible avocation. On the corners and under the lamplights "rings" of young men gathered for the purpose of saluting passers-by.

The flirting that was carried on surprised Eben; he tried to imitate the same, but he found himself "green" at that, as everything else.

The outer door-way of a building on Market street is a position noted for being the place where the first step is taken by a young man who desires to flirt with a girl. It is generally dark in that place. There is room for but one. Solitary, friendless fellows occupy it.

Eben, as soon as the door-way became vacant, mounted the step. A continuous rush passed the building. A young woman, apparently two years older than Eben, glanced at him interestedly.

He returned the look.

She passed by.

Eben fancied the girl; and wished she might return. It was not five minutes later when the same person passed by again, *going in the same direction.*

"Whew! that's queer," muttered Eben. "I wonder how that happened!"

Five minutes later she came along as before, still keeping one direction.

When this unaccountable manoeuvre occurred for the fourth time the young man's curiosity reached its highest pitch. . . .

Accordingly he started after her. She perceived his movement and said nothing. It was a long tramp, lasting for quite half an hour, leading Eben through street after street, and . . . stopping at his new lodging house, where she entered the front door, disappearing up the stairs.

He *was* puzzled! . . .

She had entered and left no trace behind her. . . . There were eight rooms on the second floor, but by whom these were occupied, Eben Poole yet never learned. He had heard words spoken at night in other rooms, and seen, in the main halls, persons whom he supposed were the occupants of the several rooms.

Possibly this girl . . . lived in the *same* lodging house that he did.

Her appearance was quite mysterious, her ways too deep for the young man. Whatever may have been her character—good or bad—there could be no doubt but that the maneouvre on Market Street was prepared for the occasion, to entrap the young man.

Eben knew nothing of the "dark ways" that abounded in Lynn. His eyes were shut; his sense of perception inert. But what he had seen thus far had aroused his curiosity; he wished and was determined to know more. . . .

Middle-class women organized the Woman's Union for Christian Work (WUCW) to address the threat of immorality among the female members of the "floating population." Encouraged by local clergymen and newspaper editors, this organization, beginning in November 1869, offered lady stitchers proper recreation by opening a reading room on the popular thoroughfare of Market Street. Workingwomen could spend their free time there and keep away from the dangers of promenading the streets. The WUCW also kept a list of private boardinghouses where stitchers could find homelike surroundings that might preserve moral virtue. Unlike the textile corporations in other New

England cities, the shoe manufacturers had built no corporation-owned boardinghouses for their factory operatives. The Woman's Union believed that ties of friendly support and benevolent interest between middle-class and workingwomen would guarantee the preservation of respectable womanhood to the benefit of the community and of women in general. The *Lynn Reporter*, March 19, 1870, avidly supported its activities.

There are in Lynn several thousand female operatives, single women, who come here from places more or less distant, attracted by the profitable remuneration afforded by labor in the various shoe manufactories. These young women find it extremely difficult to obtain comfortable boarding places, . . . In the cotton and woolen manufacturing places the corporations supply this want . . . procuring suitable people as keepers of what are known as the corporation boarding houses. Nothing of this kind has been done in Lynn. . . . The result has been very bad, and many a young woman, lately the occupant of a pleasant and comfortable home, has suffered mentally, morally, and physically from this serious neglect. In order to correct in some measure . . . this grievous error, some benevolent ladies of this city, formed, a few months ago, a society called the "Woman's Union for Christian Work." . . .

The duties of the members are fully described in the following sections [of the constitution]. . . .

The members shall interest themselves to assist ladies taking up a residence in Lynn, by striving to bring them under moral and religious influences, helping them to obtain suitable employment, and inviting them to some place of worship on the Sabbath. . . .

The great need of the association now is the cooperation of the manufacturers and business men, that they may secure some place where they can establish a good boarding-house for young women. . . . Something must be done for these helpless women, if we would save them from the evil influences that will surely surround them.

This association ha[s] a pleasant room at No. 54 Market street, where free lessons are given in music, writing, drawing, sewing and wax work, and where books and periodicals are free of access to all the young women of Lynn. . . . The room is open every week day until ten o'clock in the evening, and afternoons and evenings on Sundays. . . .

The annual report for 1872 by P. M. Merrill, superintendent of the reading room, was published in the *Lynn Reporter*, October 23, 1872. In it Miss Merrill reviewed the services and kinds of sympathy which as a concerned sister she believed the Woman's Union should offer to workingwomen.

. . . Many touching incidents cannot be made public without violating the confidence and needs not only of the young and trusting, but of those in maturer years, whose li[v]es have been darkened by such trials as a deserted wife can know, with helpless infancy dependent upon her, with no means of support, and in some instances with poor health, and wholly unable to bear with courage the contest. . . .

. . . What good has the reading room done? or is it appreciated?

It is enough to say that each day brings within the precincts of our room, not only those who seek enjoyment in reading and other recreation, as a recess from toil, weariness, and the close atmosphere of the shop or store, but often there come those on whom press heavily the cares and trials of the *working women*, and who look us in the face with the eager, questioning glance of suffering and anxiety:—seeking sympathy and counsel—and often with the thought plainly expressed in the countenance, "Can I find a friend here to help me?" "Is this a place for protection and rest?" Many who are obliged to earn their living in poor health are sometimes forced to leave their work for hours and seek the room for rest, instead of the confusion of a large boarding house. Such, thankfully, and often with tears, accept the proffered pillow, or a cup of tea, and other attempts to relieve their suffering.

With thankfulness, and the consciousness of a great lack of wisdom on her part, and sense of dependence on God for direction, it has often been the sacred duty and sad privilege of the Superintendent to minister comfort and the needed word of counsel and sympathy, or to quiet the excited imagination of the homesick girl, who finds herself in a strange city, far from home and friends, without employment or funds to take her home, or to obtain a meal or night's lodging, and told, as she goes from shop to shop, that *only Crispins* can have work. Under such circumstances, the offer of food and a night's lodging at the reading room, with assistance in finding employment and a home, are very gratefully accepted. A few words of kindly interest and inquiry have helped them to look calmly in the face obstacles in the way of success, which have in solitude, without the judgment of friends, seemed almost insurmountable. The exclamation is often heard, "What should I do without this room?" and "This is the most homelike place in Lynn to me." And sometimes with joy we hear the remark, "This room has saved me from going astray."

. . . The knowledge of our work is not confined to our own city, for young girls in other States have seen advertisements of the room in the Lynn papers, and have decided to come to Lynn to earn their living, feeling that they should find *friends* here. Even from the West, young women have come to enjoy the privileges offered. Mothers at home have blessed the "Woman's Union" for remembering their daughters. . . .

The interest of many members flagged during the depression years of the 1870s, however, and P. M. Merrill resigned her position as superintendent of the reading room, expressing regrets in the *Lynn Reporter*, April 11, 1874, for the failure of the Woman's Union to fulfill the promise of sisterly support. For Merrill, the personal involvement of middle-class women "meeting on the common ground of womanhood" was the only way to elevate and sustain the moral condition of working-women.

In preparing my last report my mind turns back with a mingling of grateful pleasure and regret upon the past four years. . . . A feeling of pleasure in remembering the hundreds of young women over whom I have been permitted, even imperfectly to exert a good influence . . . to keep some young feet in the right path. . . . It is often a question with me whether I have done all in my power to win those who seem inclined to choose the downward road. And have we, as an association, carried out as we intended the principles embraced in our preamble and constitution . . . ? This query has been forced upon me more of late, as some have said, "I do not consider the reading room a success, as it does not bring in all classes of girls, and the number of those who seek recreation on the street is not diminished." . . .

In order to do so, we, as members, must come in personal contact with those whom we wish to elevate, and thus assure them that we are willing, at least, to meet them on the common ground of womanhood, giving thereby the best endorsement we can give to our preamble, that we wish to aid in their highest development. Are we trying to solve the vast social problem—as to how to bridge the gulf that divides the favored and cultured women of our land from those less fortunate, whose only dower is the ability to earn their own bread, or perhaps the privilege of supporting a helpless parent, child, or other friend? Our

American industrial young women are largely from country homes, and, to a great extent, educated and refined (usually) beyond the same class of city girls. . . . But let her like many who come to our city from country homes—as I know some of these girls have—come to the cheerless shelter of such boardinghouses as our city affords, only to realize as did Christie in her "experiment," [in Louisa May Alcott's 1873 novel, *Work*] that she is only a working woman with a working woman's accommodations, in society inferior even to that in which she had been chafing at home. . . . As the members of the association never meet these girls at the rooms, they fail to be of service to them. . . . they are obliged to settle down to the commonplace, tedious life of most working women—disappointed, discouraged, and sometimes even glad to accept the companionship of such as only drag them down. . . . Life has little of light and sweetness to our young working women . . . and attention bestowed upon them from those in the more favored walks in life has a great influence towards elevating them. . . . if these young women are to become mothers, to rear the sons and daughters of the next generation, are we excusable for withholding from them in any degree just that influence the most powerful, (our personal influence) thus encouraging them to feel less the distance between the lady of means and the working woman? . . . The working woman can be made a great power in the moral elevation, at least, of their own class, and, on locating myself in business here, I feel that my work with them will not cease; for never before have I seen so clearly that real sympathy with and for them in their daily life can attach them to those who labor for their good.

In early 1871 the moral behavior of the workingwomen of Lynn had become the focus of a sensational series of public talks by the Reverend Joseph Cook of the First Congregational Church. Cook shared the worries of the Woman's Union about the respectability of the floating population, but he located the dangers of moral contagion in the uncertain character of the migrant female worker herself and in the fact of women working together with men in the city's factories. The controversy he aroused (see John T. Cumbler, *A Moral Response to Industrialism: The Lectures of Reverend Cook in Lynn, Massachusetts* [Albany: State University of New York Press], 1982) threatened to eclipse the lady stitcher image and to interfere with manufacturers' decisions about work assignments.

On January 22, Cook addressed a large gathering in a public hall on the subject of labor reform. His speech, "The Moral Perils of the Present Factory System of Lynn," reviewed in the *Lynn Reporter* on January 25, 1871, criticized the practice of employing male and female operatives in the same rooms as highly detrimental to moral welfare. Manufacturers were just beginning to integrate women into work procedures such as lasting, traditionally performed by men; in some factories, female stitchers and male cutters as well as men and women lasters shared the same work areas. Cook cited the seasonal fluctuations in the work force as the root cause of the danger and strongly advocated the adoption of the more regulated conditions of boardinghouse and factory life common in the textile cities of Massachusetts.

He commenced by saying that he should doubtless be criticized in what he said, but that the subject was one which he had regarded seriously and with much thought, and should treat it independently, not with a desire to find fault but with a view of calling the attention of the thinking portion of the community to what he considered an evil. By this, he meant the practice which was adopted at the present day, of male and female operatives being employed in one room, whereas in the speaker's judgment, a separation of the sexes was demanded. He would not be understood as saying that Lynn was the seat of all of the evil in the State; . . . but the transition state of the shoe business from the old to the present factory system, had called in a floating population, which had changed the general character of the place. The present method of doing business, necessitated the employment of large numbers in one building, men and women being often times found at work in the same room, which he regarded detrimental to their moral welfare. The main point urged was a separation of the sexes, or else the most stringent regulation in regard to the characters of those employed. . . .

During a subsequent lecture, Cook referred explicitly to one shop he had visited where he was told the moral atmosphere was bad. Once the identity of the shop became known, the operatives—eight women and seven men—responded angrily in the *Lynn Transcript*, February 4, 1871.

To The Public—
Rev. Joseph Cook, of Lynn, made a statement in Music Hall, during his last lecture to this effect—That he visited a room in Lynn, from sixty

to seventy feet in length, and some twenty feet in width, at one end were six or eight girls employed as stitchers—at the other end were as many men. They were coarse, low, vulgar, bad-featured girls. A man who showed him the room informed him that no young man could come to that room a virtuous man and remain so any length of time, because the girls were so bad.

We, the undersigned, believing we are the persons alluded to, feel that his charges are very unjust and unchristian, and we feel justified in appealing to an honest public to investigate our characters, and see whether the investigation will warrant any person in making such charges as these against those whom we believe have nothing to condemn them but that they are compelled to labor for their own maintenance.

Lydia D. Bates, Ella G. Hoyt, Phebe C. Stone, Mrs. Maggie Miliken, Miss Julia A. Merrow, Miss Katie A. Farrell, Miss Emma A. Collins, Mary Conway.

George F. Stevens, Wm. P. Flint, T. T. Crane, S. R. Pedrick, Cas. F. Lewis, B. Johnson.

Six of these eight women appear to have been migrants; they were not listed as residents of Lynn in the 1870 census. Of the two who were, Lydia D. Bates was the sole support of her widowed mother, and sixteen-year-old Katie A. Farrell contributed her earnings to a large family headed by her Irish-born father.

That the Leaders of Central Lodge No. 1 of the Daughters of St. Crispin in Lynn issued no public statement during the Cook controversy reflected the discomfort that wage-earning women felt when their sexual morality was questioned. Even the suggestion of impropriety prompted fear and silence. Six months later, the women stitchers of Lynn took on their employers over the issue of their morality, but while the war of words over Cook's allegations raged, women workers let manufacturers and other clergymen speak for them.

The Reverend George W. Perry of the Second Universalist Church, himself a former shoeworker, defended the moral influence of women workers in the shoe shops in the *Lynn Reporter*, February 1, 1871.

. . . The young people who work in our factories are nobler than we are apt to think. There are hundreds of shop-girls in our midst who would die rather than lose their virtue. They are among the best workers in our churches, and sacrifice more than almost any others for the cause of religion. . . . There is no shop so bad that a man or woman of any principle need be contaminated therein.

. . . It is far better that bad people be scattered among the good than that they should congregate together. . . . Neither will it help the matter any to separate the sexes.

[He] had worked in shops where they were separated and where they were not, and with the same class of workmen, everything was ten, if not a hundred times better, where they worked together. . . . In those schools and colleges where both sexes are admitted, the moral and social habits of the students are a hundred per cent better than where either sex is by itself. . . .

. . . It matters far more who are the associates of the young people where they live, and in the streets, than in the shop. . . .

Patrick Strain, pastor of St. Mary's Church for over twenty years, objected to Cook's attack on the character of Katie Farrell, who was one of his young parishioners. His letter appeared in the *Lynn Reporter*, February 11, 1871.

. . . Now so far as the Rev. Mr. Cook . . . advocates appropriate rooms or halls for girls and men to work apart, and that no communication should be held between each other during the hours of labor, and that competent women superintend the girls department, and competent men the men's department, so far as practicable, I heartily agree with him; not because I condemn the present system, but that this separation would be more fitting, more conducive to good order, more beneficial for the public good, and more in harmony with Christian civilization. . . . But so far as the Rev. Mr. Cook used language to convey the impression of the immorality of the girls and men working in shops and halls, I am opposed to him. . . . Indeed, hardened must be the heart—I had almost said soulless must be the man—that would attack poor, honest, industrious and defenseless girls, who wend their way on foot, by the dawn of morning, amid the cold blasts of winter, to these shops and halls, and when the labors of the day are over, tired and weary, at the shades of evening they return to perhaps comfortless homes. Thus they toil to earn an honest livelihood for their parents, for their little brothers and for themselves. . . .

George W. Keene, shoe manufacturer and vice-president of the Lynn

Board of Trade, publicly rebuked Cook in the *Lynn Reporter*, March 4, 1871. Keene, like many other manufacturers, feared that allegations of female immortality, raised by a clergyman, would interfere with the seasonal movement of female stitchers from surrounding towns to Lynn. Furthermore, employers knew that their experiments with the introduction of women workers into labor processes traditionally performed exclusively by men were strongly opposed by male Crispins. The support of Keene and other shoe bosses for the moral influence of womanhood in the shoe shops represented class-interested efforts not only to defend their regional sources of female labor but to reduce labor costs.

The consideration of the various statements recently made concerning the system adopted by the manufacturers of Lynn, and the liability of the present system tending to the moral degradation of the operators, has led me to examine somewhat into the facts, and review the situation of affairs in relation thereto. . . .

I have been intimately connected with the shoemaking business in Lynn, since 1826. I have watched carefully and interestedly the course of events though all the changes since that time, and have lived in Lynn over a half century. . . .

It would not be surprising if some defects should appear in a system of manufacture suddenly introduced as the present mode of manufacturing shoes among us, for within the memory of most of us there were no females employed in our manufactories or in the shops of the workmen. . . . *Now* there are from three to five thousand women employed in the various factories in this city, in almost every department of industry connected with the business. They are found not only useful and efficient, but generally faithful and trustworthy. . . . In those places where woman is held by man in the lowest esteem it is most destructive and degrading, and in those places where woman is elevated to the true dignity and majesty of her womanhood, there we find the purest morality and the highest virtue.

. . . The girls employed in our factories are largely composed of Americans, and mostly from good, honest, Christian homes. Is it fair or honorable, in any true sense, to hurl the imputation broadcast, that these shop women are immoral, and it would be dangerous to the morals of the young men to be in their company? . . .

Without calling in question the motives of anyone, I must give it as my solemn conviction that the personal allusions that have been made and which have found expression in our public journals . . . have caused a large increase of public scandal, greatly to the detriment of public morals. Moreover, the high position from whence it emanates has fixed in the minds of the people in our neighboring towns and cities a most foul aspersion against the moral character of our young and prosperous city, which it will take years of our best efforts to undo. . . .

The first attempt to introduce women's labor, to any extent, into our factories, was on the introduction of the sewing machine. . . . Then the question of moral propriety was fully considered and freely discussed by the manufacturers. Then our conveniences were unfavorable; there were no factories of sufficient size to properly accommodate them. Yet the attempt proved a success, and I think the universal experience of every manufacturer who this early introduced the sewing machines is that the girls created a favorable influence in the factory. They earned better pay, and were more independent in their labors. And the moral result is practically this, that these girls, thus early called together, have become in most cases worthy members of society, and are now honored as wives and mothers among us. . . . Every day their shops are visited by strangers coming in at different times, and they are always found busily engaged, decorous, respectful and orderly; and whoever visited the fair of the Grand Army, held at Music Hall last week, must have been profoundly impressed, on seeing that great crowd of both men and women . . . intermixed and intermingling throughout the entire building, consisting of thousands of our fellow citizens of both sexes, and not a word, a look or action observable by anyone that could detract from the lady or the gentleman; and the ladies in these gatherings were largely composed of our Lynn shop girls.

. . . With the favorable experience had in the employment of female help thus far, the manufacturer believed that many parts could be as well performed by women as by men; and wherever the circumstances are favorable, they invariably improve the condition of things around them. . . . Women are employed wherever their labor can be available, and in a large majority of factories, where they are at work with men, better order and decorum is manifest. . . .

The Cook controversy created a great sensation in Lynn and widespread interest throughout the region in the spring of 1871. Its effect, however, was not to introduce moral reform into the factory system but to confirm both the moral respectability of women shoeworkers and the traditional sexual division of labor in the shoe shops. Opposition by shoeworkers prevented manufacturers from transferring young women in significant numbers to jobs normally occupied by men. Women workers continued to control stitching operations and avoid competition with men over work. The traditional job structure in the shoe shops encouraged stitchers to use their virtual monopoly over stitching operations as a basis of labor organization and protest.

[8]

The Daughters of St. Crispin

The efforts of middle-class members of the Woman's Union and reform-minded moralists to control the behavior of workingwomen were rejected by the Daughters of St. Crispin, the women's shoeworkers' union organized in 1868. The DOSC developed separately from the men involved in the Knights of St. Crispin (1867) and produced a group of leaders primarily from among the unmarried and self-supporting New England women who worked in the shoe industry in New York and New England. The DOSC tried to represent the diverse elements within the work force of stitchers: those who were skilled, well paid, experienced, and committed to their work, as well as young women with their eyes set on early marriage and domesticity.

Massachusetts labor reformer and textile operative Jennie Collins, who as an observer attended the organizational convention of the national DOSC in July 1869, commented in the *Lynn Transcript* of August 14, 1869, that the character, bearing, and accomplishments of the women shoeworkers there appeared to fit the image of the lady stitcher.

A Reminiscence of the Lynn Convention

I passed three days never to be forgotten, and was delighted to witness the combination of skill of the working-girls, and the dignity, grace and refinement of the most fashionable ladies of the land. Mrs. Franc[e]s Jones, of Stoneham, presided over their deliberations with modesty and ability. I wish some of the crusty old fellows who have so much to say about women's tongues could have been present and witnessed the true genius which manifests itself by admiration for others. Each one preferred to listen to somebody else rather than speak herself, but when one did speak it was to the purpose. What was the most remarkable feature of the convention was the manner in which they would suggest measures and amendments to by-laws: it was with the gravity of profound statesmen; and while they were waiting for a committee to report, one of them would seat herself at the piano-forte and play an accompaniment whilest a sister sang a beautiful piece, and nearly all possessed both accomplishments. . . . The business was transacted with wisdom and ability that was marvelous in girls so young and of so little pretensions. Not a harsh word was spoken against their employers nor anybody else.

Thursday, the day of their entertainment, is one long to be remembered in Lynn and out of it by those who had the good fortune to share the courtesy and hospitality so freely accorded them. . . . Miss Carrie A. Wilson, the First Directeress [*sic*] of Lodge No. 1, took charge of the evening admirably. She looked charmingly, being dressed in green silk. Mrs. Emma Lane worked very hard throughout the convention, and especially behind the scenes. . . . She is a most estimable little lady, and her sisters testified their appreciation of her merits by making her First Grand Directeress of the National Lodge. . . . Miss Bancroft is very prepossessing in her appearance, and played her parts well. . . . Miss Wilson sang very prettily, and others whose names I cannot remember.

The Crispin farce was well gotten up, well acted and decidedly funny. Mrs. Blaisdell added much by her performance on the piano and her sweetness of manner. Miss Lawrence looked exquisitely as the "Goddess of Liberty." . . . Miss Lily Dole seemed like a doll to me. Miss Martha Wallbridge, of Stoneham, understood her business well. Miss Ora P. Bates, of Auburn, Maine, is imperial—she would sit on a throne as gracefully as she would sit at her machine stitching shoes. They all seemed very lovable to me, and although I cannot remember their names, their faces and forms will pass through my memory in grand review for many a day. . . . The charming little city of Lynn is an honor to the Commonwealth, and St. Crispin has reason to be proud of his fair daughters.

Jennie Collins

In an address to the convention about the labor reform movement in Massachusetts, Collins described the DOSC members as leaders of an independent womankind. As a participant in recent textile strikes, she was well aware of female hesitancy to join unions and attempted to allay that fear. Her speech was reported in the July 31, 1869, *Lynn Transcript.*

> The State House has been made a central countinghouse for the Capital of the Commonwealth, but next fall the people will take possession of it and attend to the legitimate business of the State. . . . If we had just and equal laws every man and woman could be well-dressed, and society would move as regularly as the machinery in a shoe factory. Now a few favored ones have more than they need—wasting thousands of dollars in luxury—while we see God's children picking cinders from the gutters to keep themselves warm. . . . Who are these D.O.S.C.? Many of them were the pride and joy of their homes, but one or the other of their parents, perhaps, were taken away, and they must go out into the world to labor. And they do not complain of their lot, not envy the lady who rides in her carriage. They only ask the respect due them from their employers, and fair pay for the work of their hands. . . . Some working girls are afraid to join the Daughters, because they may be called "strong-minded women." It is better to be independent—acting and thinking for yourself—than to be the little echo of somebody else. Who was ever ashamed of the girl who stood at the head of her class in school? . . . We will consecrate our lives to the cause of the laboring men and women, and work for it while life remains.

The Daughters of St. Crispin was the first national labor organization for female industrial workers. Its lodges stretched from Maine south to Baltimore and west to California, but most members were workingwomen in New York and New England. Because many shoeworkers moved from one town to the next during the busy season in search of better pay, the organization functioned as a chain of lodges serving the interests of both local members and transients. The most active were in Lynn and Stoneham, Massachusetts, but no membership lists have survived. Many shoe stitchers did not join the DOSC lodges, but wage levels in Essex County benefited from their activities.

During the prosperous years before the depression of 1873, the DOSC held national conventions, participated with men in the conventions of the National Labor Union, supported labor reform in Massachusetts, and joined with other women workers in the Northeast to advance their rights. Its membership was small—a total of only 2,000—and no doubt unstable, fluctuating in response to economic conditions and strikes, but the national DOSC leadership was continuous and devoted to labor reform.

In the early years DOSC members found sisterhood a useful organizing principle. In 1870 Mrs. Emma (Emmie) A. Lane of Lynn and Miss Martha Wallbridge of Stoneham, the two national "directeresses," testified before the Massachusetts legislative committee on labor in applying for a corporate charter. Their arguments, reported in the *Middlesex Journal*, March 5, 1870, emphasized the gender solidarity of the members.

> Mrs. Lane said that the first and second grand directeresses and the treasurer reside in Massachusetts. . . . Of the 2000 [national] members 1200 live in Massachusetts. The subordinate lodges [23 in total] assist largely in educating and bettering the condition of their members. The central body was intended partially as a bond of union and to secure uniformity. The lodge rooms had been centers of good influence, and afford places for many girls to pass their evenings in a satisfactory and profitable way.
>
> Miss Wallbridge gave a sketch of the order in her town. Music and discussions at the evening meetings had proved attractive to the members, and the charitable element was one to be considered. . . . It was a benefit to girls going from one place to another. Her lodge had never yet refused permission to its members to teach others their trade. . . .
>
> Mrs. Lane . . . explained the condition of the female workers on boots and shoes, spoke of the amount of their wages, etc. The subordinate lodges did not have a scale of prices, but the members never took the place of a sister discharged on account of wages, except with her consent. . . .

In the late summer of 1871, a group of subcontractors in Lynn who provided machine-stitched uppers to shoe factories decided to cut the wages of stitchers. Further, in an effort to control the high turnover rates among women workers who moved about the shoe shops seeking better wages and conditions, the bosses adopted a system of "honorable" and "dishonorable" discharges. In the aftermath of the Cook controversy and with their sensitivities heightened to any charge reflecting on their morality, honor, or character, the stitchers—"feeling insulted"—

rebelled and went on strike. Especially for migratory women workers, the moral stigma of a "dishonorable" discharge was too much.

In addition to these "degrading" and "obnoxious rules," the shoe bosses' attempts to "equalize" wages undercut the skill and experience of many older women workers. The strikers based their demands for justice and fair treatment on the value of their labor as skilled workers and on their political heritage and social standing as "free-born women." The Knights of St. Crispin assisted the successful stitchers' strike, affirming that Crispin men believed in "good and wholesome moral regulations" in the shoe shops but denied "the assumed right of any individual to hold the interpretation of any employee's moral character after leaving his employment." Their newspaper, the *Little Giant*, printed the stitchers' resolutions on September 2, 1871, as did the *Lynn Transcript* for September 9.

Preamble and Resolutions

Whereas, We, the Workingwomen in convention assembled, do accept the following resolutions as an earnest expression of our sentiments.

Whereas, We have long felt the need of protecting our rights and privileges as free-born women, and we are determined to defend them and our working interest to the fullest of our ability. Therefore, be it—

Resolved, That we, the Workingwomen of Lynn, known as Uppers Fitters and Finishers of Boots and Shoes, do enter a most solemn protest against any reduction of wages, on any pretext whatever; neither will we submit to any rules binding upon us that will not likewise affect our employers.

Resolved, That we feel grateful to the shoemakers of Lynn for their interest and determination to stand by us in our time of need.

Resolved, That we, the free women of Lynn, will submit to no rule or set of rules that go toward enslaving or degrading us.

Resolved, That we will accept no terms whatever, either with regard to a reduction of prices, notices to quit, or forfeiture of wages. That while we utterly ignore the spirit of littleness and illiberality which prompted the late action of our would-be oppressors, we will not forget to resent, in a proper manner, the unjust encroachments upon our rights.

Resolved, that a copy of these resolutions be given to each one of the Committee, by them to be presented to each girl in the shop, and her signature there on obtained, that will adhere to the terms of the resolutions, and should any one of the members of the shop be reduced in her wages or ill-treated, we will drop our work until she is righted. . . .

Her sense of maturity and skill as a "good workwoman" persuaded one Lynn striker in 1871 to reject with anger the various attempts of the subcontractors to cut wages. She expressed a sense of craft consciousness that distinguished her from most women industrial workers, who regarded wage earning as a short prelude to marriage. Her letter, originally sent to the *Lynn Reporter*, was reprinted as "Voice from the Stitchers" in the *Stoneham Amateur*, September 9, 1871.

Mr. Editor:

What an immense amount of encouragement and philanthropy was contained in that soul-stir[r]ing "Answer to Stitcher" in your last Saturday's *Reporter*! Ought not the girls at once to surrender their flag, throw down their arms, and at once disband, at such a call for peace from him [an employer] who signs "Leslie"? By the way, if we mistake not, we know the gentleman in question, and we rather surmise that he has not been as many months in the business he is endeavoring so heroically to s[t]raighten as the most of us have been years, and we think him hardly old enough yet to govern the stitchers or operatives of Lynn. Let him work a little longer, look a little more thoroughly into the "whys" and "wherefores" of the case, before he lays down rules so complacently to govern those better posted than himself, and quite as capable of understanding what they want and need. Enough of him for the present. . . .

With regard to the three objects of the [shoe manufacturers'] organization. First "equalization of prices [wages]." That sounds well, but look at the absurdity of the thing. To take from one and give to another, robbing Peter to pay Paul. For instance, I am a fancy stitcher: I have worked a number of years at this part of the business, trying to perfect myself as a good workwoman. Are my services of no more value to my employer than Sarah B.'s—a young miss of fourteen who has just commenced her labors, or of Nellie C. who may have worked a year or two for pay, with no interest in her work to perfect herself, or no interest for her employer, only carelessly indifferent as to whether she can do a fine job or not? Are the services of the master workman on yonder stately pile of no more value than those of the humble hod-carrier equally needed to aid in its completion? If so then of what use will it be for mechanics to attempt to excel in their craft? Of what use is a collegiate education to our physicians, our ministers or our lawyers, if their services are to receive no higher remuneration than those of the man who mends our streets or digs in our gardens? Valuable services, and of course to be appreciated; but are the same talents and education needed? Just so with our labor. Should not the first-class operator, in any branch of his business, receive better pay than the workman who turns off a job hardly fit to be seen? If that is to be the case, then the one comes down to the level of the other; and then farewell to excellence, for who cares to excel where all are alike rewarded?

Then again, to my certain knowledge for I have it from the young lady's own lips—there are two stitchers from the same shop, I think side by side, at the same work, on the same machine, and at the same prices, both equally steady and industrious—the one older at the business, understanding just how to turn off her work. She earns regularly her twenty dollars per week; the other barely reaches, by straining every nerve, her ten dollars. Now sirs, we ask you what can be done to equalize wages in this case? And this is only one in a hundred cases. If you endeavor to cut the one down, where will be the other? So I say to this part of the matter—*let well enough alone.*

Now as to giving a week's notice or forfeiting wages. Absurd! that will never go as I rather guess one of that body is beginning to find out. The plea that Monday morning often finds absent the girls who were there on Saturday night is a feeble one to the last degree. Let the foreman of the shop do what is right by his girls, and I will wager they will do what is right by him. Sitting in a neighboring shop, with an immense cigar in his mouth, while his girls wait for work, will never retain good help. And, Mr. Editor, here let me say, and contradict it who dare that the best stitchers, or the best operatives anywhere, will always be found where they are best appreciated; and if a boss stitcher has in his employ good hands, who are doing his work well, and laboring for his interest—let him look to it that he keeps them. They are the girls, and that is the stitching room that finds no help lacking on Monday morning.

As to a uniform code of prices [wages], we say that too cannot be attained at present, for there are no two shops that do exactly the same kind of work. Some are particular, their work is of a higher grade, and they require far more accuracy in line and stitch. To that I say that if I were the proprietor of a stitching room, I should know exactly what to give, and would be governed by no cabal nor ordered by any organization.

I would in closing advise the members of this [employers'] club to look well at what they are doing. They have roused the lion, and they little imagine the strength they will find opposed to them in their attempt to prove themselves masters of the situation. We will not submit to being crowded; we will not be enslaved. We are freeborn American women; and when they attempt to tell us what they will do, we will rise in our might, and three thousand voices will tell them what we will do.

Stitcher

After the strike had been won, the DOSC used Old Testament language to ridicule the shoe bosses' dishonorable discharge threat and insisted that they would not accept any certificate beneath their dignity or degrading in any respect. In its report on their November lodge meeting, the *Little Giant*, November 18, 1871, applauded their spirit and printed their satire of a boss's "honorable" discharge.

Annie Blank—a good girl. When you get her, keep her. She hath been in our employ so long a time. All kinds of abuses and deceit have been heaped upon her; thrice has she been discharged; in perils of steam, in dull times often; in perils of Breed's Pond Water [drought], in weariness often; in hunger, in thirst, and debts hath she stuck by me. I therefore recommend her to you. Greet her in our name, and make her as profitable to you as she has been to me; and great will be your recompense.

Not all stitchers in Lynn joined the Daughters of St. Crispin or shared their anger at the shoe bosses. Hannah Richardson (1844–80) emigrated to Lynn in 1871 from rural Yarmouth County, Nova Scotia, to work in the shoe factories. Twenty-seven years old and engaged to be married, she spent only about two years as a stitcher. According to the accounts she kept of her earnings and expenditures, she spent almost all her wages, which averaged $12.71 a week, on items of personal apparel, gifts, music lessons, and instruments. Hannah's diary reveals no awareness of the Crispin women or their activities. Her interests included the letters that she wrote and received from Canada, her religious and temperance activities, her love of music, and her social life with her shopmates and her brother, who was part of a small circle of Nova Scotian friends in Lynn.

Hannah Richardson's diary is located in the archives of Acadia University, Wolfville, Nova Scotia. These excerpts are from entries transcribed by Margaret Conrad, Acadia University (to whom I am grateful for drawing my attention to Hannah Richardson) and are quoted by permission of her granddaughter, Ruth J. Morton.

Monday, January 1, 1872
Mild and warm, but cloudy all day. Went out in the morning with Abbie Moody [a shopmate from Rumford, Maine], we each bought a Diary gave 42 cents. In the evening Jenny & Susy Smith and I went and spent the evening with Than [her brother Nathaniel]. . . .

Tuesday 2
Clear and cold. Went to the shop [P. P. Sherry] in the morning did not have any work till most noon. When I went home to dinner stopped on my way, bought me a hat gave 50 cents. Went to the shop after dinner had work till night. Went to singing school in the evening with Than and Joe [Bain, the brother of her fiancé Sam Bain of Yarmouth].

Wednesday 3
Cloudy and cold. To the shop at work all day. . . .

Thursday 4
Wet and rainy all day. To the shop hard at work. . . .

Friday 5
Cloudy all day. To the shop all day. got a letter from Sam at night. In the evening Than and Joe came in. Than and I went to Mrs. Williams to see the Smith girls [Jenny and Susy]. . . .

Saturday 6
Beautiful in the morning but cloudy in the afternoon. To the shop all day. . . . In the evening Than, Joe, Susan & Jenny and I went to Miss Mercy Smiths, spent a very pleasant evening.

Sunday 7
Fine but very cold. Went to meeting in the morning with Joe. . . . got

dinner . . . then went to meeting. I home in the evening, wrote to Sam and Sister Tabby. . . .

Thursday 11
Fine in the morning clouded up just before night, to the shop all day. One caller Jenny S. In the evening Joe and I went down to Nehemiah McCormack [a Yarmouth County man], found his wife very sick. She wanted us to sing we did. Wrote a part of a letter to Sam after I got home.

Friday 12
Fine all day. To the shop. . . . The evening, Joe, Than, May and I went down to Mrs. Hamiltons had a nice sing and a real good time. . . .

Saturday 13
Fine and warm, more like Spring than winter. To the shop all day. In the evening Joe and I went down to Nehemiah McCormacks. His wife just alive, she wanted us to sing we did so. . . .

Tuesday [January] 23
. . . To the shop. Went to the young ladies reading room to get a boarding place. Got the ladies [*sic*] name went after tea to see her think I shall go there. Went to church and singing school in the evening. . . .

Sunday [March] 10
A rainy day. Home all day and evening. wrote letters to sisters Susie and Tabbie & Sam B. played on the flutina a little read a little and retired at eight. lonesome. . . .

Monday 18
. . . To the shop all day. steam came on this morning but we did not work by it [instead they used foot power]. . . . No letters yet.

Tuesday 19
. . . To the shop. worked by steam it seems good to have steam again I tell you. got a letter from Sam. . . .

Wednesday 20
. . . I to the shop but had no work in the forenoon. Mr. Sherry fixing the shafting [for the steam power]. work in the afternoon. . . .

Saturday 23

. . . May & I left Mrs. Pearls and came to Miss Patch's to board. seems like going from a prison to a Palace.

Sunday 24

. . . like my new boarding place since so far had roast turkey for supper tonight. Went to meeting afternoon and evening. . . .

Friday [April] 19

. . . To the shop. Went to meeting in the evening. A year ago to night I was to Mrs. Bains sitting on the lounge beside Sam. I did not feel very well in my mind.

Saturday 20

. . . To the shop. . . . A year ago tonight I left Yarmouth for Lynn. . . .

Sunday 21

A lovely day warm as summer. to meeting all day & evening. . . . In the evening Joe, Susie Walsh and I went to a lecture in the Methodist church. It was very good. he was very much against the Catholicks. . . .

Sunday 28

. . . To meeting all day and evening. went to the Methodist in the evening with Joe heard a nice lecture on the evils of intemperance. Wrote to Sam. . . .

Saturday [June]1

Fine and warm. I went to Boston in the afternoon Hattie [her future sister-in-law] & Kiss Patterson went with me we had a nice time but we got awful tired. I got myself a set of hair curl[ers] a set of jewelry and a sunshade [parasol]. . . .

Monday 24

. . . not much work in the shop. . . . [When the spring production season began to slacken in late June, Hannah began to think about going home for a while.]

Tuesday 25
. . . to the shop but not doing much. came home at three o'clock and sewed on my dress. . . .

Wednesday 26
. . . Worked a little in the forenoon. to the shop but did not do any work on shoes in the afternoon. . . .

Thursday 27
. . . To the shop worked till three oclock. . . .

Friday 28
. . . Went to the shop in the morning finished my work came home after dinner. . . .

Saturday 29
. . . went to the shop with May and helped her finish her work. . . . In the afternoon went to the shop for my pay. . . .

Monday July 1
. . . I went to the bank in the forenoon and drew my money. . . .

Tuesday 2
. . . left Lynn at eight oclock for Yarmouth. . . . [Hannah stayed with her family for two months and saw a lot of Sam. On August 3 she returned to Lynn, where the fall busy season was just beginning.]

Tuesday [August] 27
. . . To the shop, plenty of work. . . .

Tuesday [September] 3
. . . to the shop lots of work. . . .

Wednesday 4
. . . To the shop earned [$]3.20 for the first time. . . .

Friday 13
. . . To the shop hard at work earned [$]15.55 this week. home in the evening. went to bed quite early, for I was sleepy. . . .

Friday [November] 1
. . . To the shop business commences to grow dull. . . . got a letter
from Sam. He seems pleased because I bought a Melodean [a small
foot-pumped organ]. Joe Bains birthday. I made him a present an
Autograph Album.

Saturday 23
. . . To the shop in the forenoon. Stopped work at noon for a week.
went to the shop in the afternoon for my money. . . .

Monday [December] 2
. . . went to the shop this morning but no steam yet. came home,
practiced [music] two hours, pasted some pieces in my scrap book in
the afternoon. . . .

Wednesday 4
. . . went to the shop this morning. steam on but not working. . . .

Thursday 5
. . . went to work this morning. . . .

Tuesday 31 [The last entry for 1872]
. . . Snowy. To the shop. Home in the evening. took my [music]
lesson. . . .

During the active years of the Knights and Daughters of St. Crispin, a
stitcher who used the pen name "Americus" corresponded regularly
with the pro-labor press in Lynn: the *Record* and the *Vindicator*. Americus had migrated to Lynn from a country town in New Hampshire after
the Civil War; she married, bore seven children, and worked on and off
as a homeworker and in the shoe shops as a vamper. She was a member
of the Daughters of St. Crispin and a strong supporter of the cause of
labor reform in Massachusetts. Although opposed to the woman suffrage movement, she worked to organize women to resist wage cuts, or
"cut-downs," and to improve conditions. Her experience and skill as a
vamper, in addition to the common sense and skeptical rationalism
reflected in her nearly fifty surviving letters on religion and politics, led
her to depict in two of her letters the craft knowledge of the skilled
female worker who often led labor protest. These letters appeared in the

Lynn Record for December 28, 1876, and the *Vindicator* for November 3, 1877.

I am writing this article for the edification of any person who chooses to be edified thereby, but I am writing it most especially for shop girls; they will understand what wages they would be likely to make vamping sixty pairs of boots for thirty-three cents. Sixty pairs of boots in shoe shop vocabulary is called a set, and two sets and a half is a good day's work for an ordinary vamper. What wages for a girl who works perhaps seven months in the year, and is obliged to live the other five! I mention the price this man [the meanest man in Lynn, according to Americus] pays for vamping, not because it is the meanest price he pays, but because vamping is usually considered the best paying part of shoe stitching, and the prices paid for other parts of the work depends [*sic*] greatly upon the prices paid for this. . . .

. . . A man invents an attachment for a sewing machine, by means of which the stitcher is enabled to stitch with two threads of silk instead of one, thus stitching with double silk. This attachment is to be used, we will suppose, in vamping boots. The man for whose interest it would be to see the attachment in general use, stands by, while the stitcher vamps a few boots after the improved (?) method; he then inquires:—"Well, what do you think of it?" The girl replies frankly—"I fail, Sir, to see its merits." "Why!" exclaims the man in astonishment,—"what fault can you find with it?—is it not stronger?" "No, Sir," replies the girl, "it is not as strong." "My dear lady," says the man, "you must be crazy! Are not two threads of silk stronger than one?" The operator then gives the reasons for her opinion—she tells him that the needle she is using is the largest she is allowed to use upon that kind of work, and that the groove in this needle is not large enough to carry two threads of coarse silk, therefore she must use a finer silk, two threads of which does not in reality equal in strength one thread of coarse silk which she has formerly used. Then, again, she tells him one of these threads is very likely to break, through the friction consequent upon stitching, and the girl is quite likely to stitch an inch or two before she perceives that her silk has broken; the average girl [is] not sufficiently conscientious to take out the row of single stitching and set her needle back to commence with the double thread; she knows that the little blunder would never be noticed, so she threads her needle and goes on her way

TWO HANDSOME SHOES, MADE BY THE GEO. E. BARNARD CO., LYNN.

The two standard products of Lynn: serge and all-leather high-buttoned boots. *Boots and Shoe Recorder,* August 10, 1982. Courtesy of Lynn Public Library.

rejoicing, leaving a space stitched with a single thread of fine silk, scarcely more than sufficient to hold the boot together while being made. The man listens to the arguments, and answers:—"Ah! yes, I see, *but don't you perceive that a boot vamped with double silk is stronger than a boot vamped with a single thread?*" . . .

So, also, in the case of a man who invents a machine for stitching with cotton instead of silk. His machine does not stitch well with silk, and it does stitch well with cotton, consequently cotton must be better for stitching boots than silk. You may tell him that silk as a material has a long fibre, while cotton has a short fibre, and, for this reason, silk must be stronger than cotton, and more durable: and the man answers:—"Pooh! nonsense! Just look at my machine and see how much better it will stitch with cotton than it will with silk." The lady tells him she does not like her boots stitched with cotton, because, after they have been exposed to the light and air for a short time, the cotton fades and looks badly, and the man replies: "My dear Madam! A boot stitched with cotton is much more elegant than one stitched with silk; why, my machine will not stitch with silk at all!"

In bidding a poetic goodbye to her shopmate Miss Mattie M. Byrne, a stitcher who had worked in Lynn for six years at the stitching shop of Morgan and Dore, Americus revealed her class sentiments openly in the *Lynn Transcript*, June 9, 1877.

> Farewell Mattie—Heaven's Blessing
> Rest upon you evermore;
> Boots and cut-downs be forgotten,
> In the shop of Brother Dore.
> And when once you leave the shoe shop
> May the mem'ry pass away
> That you ever rendered mortal
> *Over-work* for *under-pay*.

[9]

Workingwomen and the Women's Rights Movement

After the Civil War, middle-class advocates of women's rights made significant efforts to build a coalition with the labor movement, especially with organized groups of women factory workers such as the Daughters of St. Crispin. Issues of woman suffrage and equal opportunity for job training became part of labor politics. These feminist issues provoked great controversy within the labor movement and within the DOSC. Working-class women debated among themselves and with middle-class women the significance of political rights for women and the proper relationship of women workers to labor protest. Many DOSC leaders supported labor feminism in the 1870s and provided a link between the women's rights movement and the labor movement in the late nineteenth century.

In April 1869 labor reformers Mrs. E. L. Daniels, Aurora Phelps, and Jennie Collins organized a Workingwomen's Convention in Boston, and Daniels (as reported in the *American Workman* for May 1869) called on shoe stitchers and other skilled women workers to organize their unskilled sisters in the garment trades.

> Such of the working-women as are now employed on mere parts of products and who have been taught to put the parts together, are, with a few exceptions, deficient in that industrial training which is equivalent to an education. Their moral energies have, moreover, been repressed by seclusion, monotonous labor at long hours upon tasks stultifying to their mental as well as to their physical natures, and also by the privations naturally consequent on extreme poverty. These women are, therefore, (of course with exceptions), timid, incapable of self-

assertion, and not provided with such clothing as would justify them, to their own eyes, in presenting themselves at places where they would have an opportunity to defend their own cause. The skilled working-women, who have constant work at good wages, are, on the contrary, in the enjoyment of a high degree of independence, and of the moral and physical qualities which are its fruits; these skilled working-women are, moreover, in continual contact with the unskilled or half-skilled laborers, and are perfectly cognizant of the wants, privations, and helplessness of their less favored sisters. It is thought, therefore, in view of these considerations, that the skilled workwomen are the natural counsellors of their less skillful sisters, to the almost utter exclusion of men, and to the absolute exclusion of ladies of refined leisure.

That convention produced the Boston Working Women's League. Three months later, both Daniels and Collins attended the national DOSC organizing convention held in Lynn and later drew its leaders into their activities in Workingwomen's Association of Massachusetts on behalf of labor reform and woman suffrage. Organizers of the Boston league looked to the DOSC as a sisterhood of skilled workers who could provide effective leadership for other workingwomen.

Both Susan B. Anthony and Elizabeth Cady Stanton of the National Woman Suffrage Association had attended the 1868 convention of the National Labor Union (NLU), looking for allies for women's rights. Seated as delegates, despite the opposition of antisuffrage men from trade unions in New York City, they succeeded in organizing a Committee on Female Labor and in gaining the support of the NLU for equal rights for workingwomen, though the convention did not endorse woman suffrage. By the following year, NLU opposition to the suffragists had grown, and Anthony, representing a New York City workingwomen's association, was expelled from the 1869 convention. Because she had been a delegate to the 1868 convention, the chair did grant her the privilege of the floor to answer the charges of M. R. Walsh, of Typographical Union No. 6 in New York City, that she had encouraged women to become strikebreakers against the men's union. Walsh's charges were based on information received from Augusta Lewis, president of the New York City women's typographers' local. The exchange was reported in the *Workingman's Advocate*, September 4, 1869.

[Walsh insisted that] . . . "she [Anthony] did not represent a bone fide [*sic*] labor organization, also because during the recent struggle of that Society [Typographers' Union No. 6], she had striven to procure situations for girls from which men had been discharged, at lower wage than they had received. . . .

"If Miss Anthony was a workingwoman I would be willing to take her hand as soon as any man. We have one here from the St. Crispin Society [Martha Wallbridge]. Who objected to her admission? Nobody. . . . She is a bone fide working woman, and we want her with us. . . . The lady [Anthony] goes in for taking women away from the wash tub; and in the name of heaven who is going there if they don't? I believe in a woman doing her work, and men marrying them and supporting them."

[Anthony answered:] "The objection [raised by my admission] was that Susan B. Anthony had been a renegade to the principles and interests of the workingmen of New York, and I suppose that they want me to answer these specific charges, that exist according to Miss Lewis' letter. . . ."

She [Anthony] agreed that it was proper for men and women to be married and that the former should support the latter; but she worked for a class of women that had no husbands and who were on the streets penniless, homeless and without shelter. "Now I ask you what we are to do with these girls? Shall we tell them to starve in the garrets because the printers, by their own necessities, open their doors and give a slight training to a few girls for a few weeks? Shall I say to the girls, 'Do not go in, but starve'? or shall I say, 'go in and get a little skill into your hands, and fit yourself to work side by side with men'? . . .

"The question is whether every single labor organization that knows nothing of trades union, but is formed for the purpose of establishing the principle of equalizing the rights of laboring women with those of men is to be represented or not. Now I think men have great wrongs in this world between the existence of labor and capital, but these wrongs as compared to the wrongs of women, are not as a grain of sand on the sea shore, and if some of us who advocate the wrongs of down-trodden women do take a position which you do not like you must remember that our clients are in a very suffering condition, and we must act and speak for them. . . .

"I grant you married men, that it is very important that you should earn money enough to support your wives and little ones; but then it is also important for us single individuals to earn money enough to support ourselves honestly.

"All women in this country are in the power of men. We ask for a change, and we demand a change. There is no solution to the problem of prostitution but to give them a chance to earn an honest living with men; not merely a pittance, enough to keep body and soul together, but sufficient to enable them to invest in building societies, and to have houses and homes of their own, and make them just as independent as anybody in this country. . . . "

Martha Wallbridge of the DOSC, who later became an advocate of equal rights for women in the labor movement and an ally of Massachusetts suffragists, defended Anthony's presence at the NLU convention in 1869. The *New York World*, August 18, 1869, cited her argument.

Martha M. Wallbridge of the St. Crispin Association of Massachusetts said as one of the working women of the State from which she came, she considered Miss Anthony to be a representative woman, and one whom she would indorse. If her claims were not sufficiently valued—and upon that ground they were to be rejected—then let there be an investigation into the equally invalid claims of male delegates [claiming to represent workingmen] who were present, some of whom she knew were not fully qualified.

Although she failed in her effort to get Anthony seated as a delegate, Wallbridge became the chair of the Committee on Female Labor. The committee's resolutions supporting equal rights for workingwomen were adopted by the NLU in 1869 and in 1870 and vindicated the arguments of the banished Susan B. Anthony for equal opportunity in the skilled trades.

[*Workingman's Advocate*, September 4, 1869]
Resolved—the National Labor Congress immediately make an effort of all trades unions to organize Female Labor and demand equal pay for work equally well done by women as that done by men.

Resolved—every avenue of labor for which woman is physically capacitated should be freely opened to her on the same terms and conditions as allowed to any class of laborers.

[*Workingman's Advocate*, August 27, 1870]
Resolved by the National Labor Congress, that we demand for our

toiling sisters the same rate of wages for equal work that we received for ours.

2. We also ask all who are represented [by delegate] in this convention, and also all working-men of our country, to do all in their power to open many of the closed avenues of industry to women, and welcome her entering into just competition with men in the industrial race of life.

The resolutions were unanimously adopted.

In October 1869 the Daughters of St. Crispin joined women labor reformers in Massachusetts to support equal rights for workingwomen, including equal wages for equal work, reduced hours of labor, and woman suffrage. Leaders of the DOSC also attended state conventions of Massachusetts and New York workingwomen, including a convention of the Working-woman's State Labor Union of New York held at the Cooper Union in New York City and reported in the *New York World*, March 11, 1870. But ambivalence among DOSC leaders and members on the question of suffrage was beginning to surface.

. . . Mrs. [Emma] Lane of Massachusetts [First Grand Directeress of the Daughters of St. Crispin] . . . said it would have been more acceptable for me to have heard a working-woman of New York first come forward to address the meeting. ["]I have even heard it said that this is a Massachusetts affair. I hope you will not think so; although you must admit that in the Eastern States we have organized well. I am afraid we are ahead of you; and it is your fault that you are not ahead of us. I am sure there are poor women suffering here in New York from evils that can be remedied by organization. . . . Now the trinity of organization is protection, education, and co-operation. We shall never do any good as long as it is understood that women will do the work of men, as well as the men, at far lower rates. . . .

["] . . . In regard to the ballot, I tell you, working-men, that we don't want it until we can give you a chance to vote for us.["] (Laughter.) In conclusion, she said she wanted to see the working-women organized from the Atlantic to the Pacific. Capital must be made the servant of labor and not the master. . . .

In February 1870, Mrs. E. L. Daniels and Jennie Collins of the Workingwomen's Association of Massachusetts succeeded in gaining the endorsement of woman suffrage by the New England Labor Reform League, as announced in the *Workingmen's Advocate*, February 5, 1870.

> Resolved, That those to whom the world owes the most, and without whom human society would cease to exist, the working women, are the very class whom present laws and customs doom to the most abject poverty and degradation; that we will aid them in speedy and thorough organization for self-protection, and welcome them to rights, principles and duties equal with men, foremost of which is the right to vote.

While the Workingwomen's Association of Massachusetts was moving to advance woman suffrage as a labor reform, however, the leaders of the DOSC split publicly over this issue. Martha Wallbridge replaced the antisuffrage Emma Lane as national head of the DOSC in April 1870, but the convention compromised on the issues of equal rights and woman suffrage. The only surviving record of the 1870 DOSC convention is quoted on page 109 of John B. Andrews and W. D. P. Bliss, *History of Women in Trade Unions* (1911; New York: Arno Press, 1974).

> Whereas the common idea among employers has been and still is that woman's labor should receive a less remuneration, even though equally valuable and efficient, than is paid men even on the same qualities of work; . . . Therefore be it
> *Resolved by this Grand National Lodge of the Daughters of St. Crispin*, That we demand for our labor the same rate of compensation for equal skill displayed, or the same hours of toil, as is paid other laborers in the same branches of business. . . .
> *Resolved*, That we assure our fellow-citizens that we only desire to so elevate and improve our condition as to better fit us for the discharge of those high social and moral duties which devolve upon every true woman.

Emma Lane, who quickly became an active critic of the vote for workingwomen, clashed with Jennie Collins over the importance of woman suffrage. Collins claimed that all workingwomen wanted the ballot; part of her private letter of March 10, 1870, to Susan B. Anthony was published in *The Revolution* on March 17, 1870.

> . . . The factory girls, as far as I am able to communicate with them,

understand the full value of the ballot. When I advance the argument that forty-eight thousand girls can stop their looms on the first Tuesday in November, and deposit their votes, an organized body will not dare to reduce their wages twelve cents on the dollar [as in the Cocheco, New Hampshire, textile strike of 1869] without consulting them.

Whatever you may see against the working women demanding the ballot, is spoken without the authority of the working women. All classes claiming to be working women, and petitioning against suffrage, or who speak of it indifferently, so do without the authority of *bone fide* [*sic*] working women. I meet and speak with thousands, and I have not as yet heard a dissenting voice, while all tell me unanimously "you utter our sentiments exactly." I consider it my duty to the working women to state this, for I wish no bogus representatives.

Lane spelled out her position, and Collins responded briefly in letters to the *Boston Post*, April 19 and 20, 1870.

To the Editor of the Boston Post:

In your paper of Thursday last containing a report of speeches made at a meeting of the Boston Workingwomen's Association, it is stated that a Mrs. Macdonald, of New York, affirms as a fact that she travelled through twenty-three States, and never found a woman who (when she explained the benefits of the ballot to her), did not desire its possession. . . . Perhaps she is the woman who, by sound argument and common sense combined, can convince the thousands of our workingwomen that they want the ballot. I was myself for a brief time, of the opinion that the ballot might be beneficial to the workingwomen; but, after studying the subject more earnestly and truly than I had ever done before, I changed back to my original ground. When I made the statement (referred to by Mrs. Macdonald), to the effect that the Daughters of St. Crispin, as a class, did not want the ballot, I said that which I know to be true; for I had put the question before a majority of the local organizations, and in a few places I found members in favor of the ballot, but they were a very few, say one out of one hundred and fifty, taking an average organization. I made that assertion when I stood at the head of the order, and spoke from personal knowledge of the facts. I feel free to say that the lady had better go home and ask her own workingwomen whether they wish the ballot. I asked the officers and members of the New York Cap Makers' Union if they wanted the ballot; but not one could I find in that Union of one thousand members who would say that she wanted it or who professed herself unwilling to trust her political welfare to the hands of her father, brother or husband. The New York Umbrella and Parasol Makers' Union of eight hundred members I found upon inquiry, to be of the same mind with the cap makers, and with these a good part of the Typographic Union. These unions are composed of women as well educated as any of the workingwomen I saw in New York. It seems to me that Mrs. Macdonald had better stay at home and convert her own workingwomen to the female suffrage doctrine, instead of coming here to make a personal attack upon such an humble individual as myself. We who speak just what we feel as *bone fide* workingwomen do not insist upon having the ballot, but we do wish the workingmen to go forward in one great phalanx, and we know when they vote for the glorious principles of Labor Reform that they are voting for our own interests as well, and I have faith to believe they will. We do wish those estimable ladies who go around sounding their trumpets for us as regards the ballot would go to their homes, and go to work and try to secure the love and respect of their male relatives, and they would soon become contented. My object in publishing the article in the New York paper upon which the New York ladies animadverted was as follows:—Miss Jennie Collins, in a letter to the Revolution, said that she had conversed with thousands of workingwomen, and had been unable to find among them all a single person who was opposed to female suffrage. This testimony appeared to me extraordinary, since I have heard *bone fide* workingwomen arguing set speeches against female suffrage right in the presence of Miss C., and to those speeches, Miss Collins replied. Moreover, my opportunities for observation being directly opposite to hers, I felt it my duty to state the facts to the public as I understood them.

I am, most respectfully yours,
Mrs. Emmie A. Lane of D.O.S.C.

To the Editor of the Boston Post:
The communication from Mrs. Emmie A. Lane, published in your paper of yesterday, requires no defense or refutation from me. My time is too fully occupied by the advancement of the mighty question of the elevation of woman to reply to what will certainly never injure the cause in the least.

Jennie Collins

Other Lynn women such as "Kate," whose views appeared in the *Little Giant*, October 14, 1871, were more receptive to the idea of suffrage for workingwomen but agreed with Emma Lane that organization was primary.

> Mrs. Lane is for *women's rights* and against *female suffrage*. Many of us, members of the [Lynn Working Women's Associates] Society, go for *female suffrage*, but after all, we live in a free country, and acknowledge that, in matters of side issues, Mrs. Lane has as much right to entertain her opinions, and express them, as we have to entertain and express ours, and without forgetting her fellowship with us. Our society is organized to defend, not the rights of women as *voters*, but the rights of women as *workers*. . . .
>
>   Kate

Arguments over woman suffrage continued to divide members of the DOSC in Lynn as unemployment increased and wages fell during the depression years of the 1870s. In 1874, "Tryphosia," a Lynn stitcher, wrote two letters that appeared in the *Lynn Record* on February 14 and March 7. She commented on a debate in the "People's Column" of the newspaper over the merits of women's rights, including woman suffrage. Class interest, not sex inequality, she argued, was the fundamental and exclusive issue that should concern workingmen and workingwomen.

> Mr. Editor:— . . . I have recently noticed several articles upon the question of woman suffrage. . . . I too am a stitching girl, and I must frankly say that I think I speak the sentiments of a majority of those who are thus engaged when I say that the question that must effect [*sic*] us as a class is fair compensation for our labor, and that I as frankly state we are not now receiving. . . . Now what I wish to know is if we poor stitching-girls are to be made to bear the burthens of the hard times and high taxes? . . .

> Mr. Editor:—I gladly avail myself of your kind invitation to occupy some portion of your space so kindly allotted by you to the presentation by the people of such thoughts as from time to time they may desire to utter upon those questions [in] which they, more than all others, are interested. Society, as you well know, is divided into two classes. Just two: those who do something, and those who do not. . . . those who

use their capabilities and godlike reason for the benefit of the world, who labor in all departments of life, who produce what is of value to themselves and others, have claims which demand recognition, rights which are worthy of defense. . . . No great or good thing has been accomplished except by and through its [labor's] agency. . . . If then this be so . . . is it not clear that all who thus labor, and produce, and originate . . . have a common interest in the respect and reward that should be bestowed on them for the services they thus render to society? Indeed, have they not a right to *demand* that their services shall be duly and properly compensated? I believe they have and that it is a duty they owe themselves to insist upon its recognition, and that the workingmen everywhere should so fully understand their interests as to act upon these principles. . . . Time it is said is money with those who labor; it is really so and, since it is so, they have a right to demand wages at the highest rate for its use. . . . By highest wages I do not mean more than a fair share of the profits of what our labor and talents produce when acting in connection with capital. What I *do* mean is, that *capital* has no right to arrogate to itself more than a just compensation for its use. . . . To do this, we need only to combine *harmoniously* in a union which shall be of and for the people. . . . This union, I repeat, must be for a *specific* purpose, without a single collateral issue, and he or she who should attempt to divert us for a single hour . . . should be regarded as an enemy. . . . To me, it seems a crime against justice that men and women, essentially of like sentiments, interests and condition, should waste the power which they have for noble purposes in contests with each other [over women's rights], where a defeat will only imbitter unfounded prejudices, and success lead to no good or great influence upon the present or future condition. . . .

Tryphosia

The stitcher who signed her letters "Americus" agreed with the antisuffragism of Emma Lane and Tryphosia; others defended the idea of political empowerment and equal rights for women both as workers and as citizens. These debates among the stitchers of Lynn, conducted between 1874 and 1881, revealed divisions among workingwomen over the capacity of women to contribute to labor protest and over the fundamental character of womanhood.

In the *Lynn Record* of January 31, 1874, Americus showed her mastery of satire.

. . . Sally Samantha Smith and I want to vote. I want my rights. I want to chew tobacco and spit on the floor; and the day is not far distant when we can all do it. And *then* we will see who will be the lords of creation. We don't care who stays at home on election day to take care of the children; that is "his" business. Of course the servant won't do it; she votes; the *big girls* won't do it; they'll all "go up to the ward room" to see the fun, same as the big boys do now, and the probability is that he will have to stay by himself. We won't stay at home any more and cook and wash dishes either; we've done it long enough; let "him" do it a little while. We will put on a clean dickey in the morning, and rush off before breakfast we are in such a hurry to "get to our business down town." We'll forget our hurry after walking a few squares and drop into a hotel and get something nice. Then we'll collect a few of our chums and saunter 'round the streets, and lounge in the saloons, and loaf on the corners, and smoke and spit tobacco juice upon the trowsers of the gentlemen who pass; and if we see one who minds his business uncommonly well, we'll tell him he has a nice foot, and that he is a "stunner."

. . . We'll talk slang. You bet [w]e'll snore; this is another great and glorious privilege that is denied to us. When we have our rights, we sh'an't be afraid of burglars nights; we sha'n't have to keep nudging "him" with our elbows, to inquire if he don't hear a noise. It is being kept in bondage so long, that makes us nervous and timid. . . . As I said before, I believe the day is not far distant, when our vote will be recognized, and won't we have a jolly time. We'll make up for all those years that we have been floundering around in heathen darkness. . . .

Americus

Working wives and daughters resident in Lynn tended to regard their political rights as sufficiently represented by the men in their families. On the other hand female heads of families and self-supporting women such as Ella A. Little, a stitcher from New Hampshire and a member of the Lynn DOSC, were more inclined to see the vote as potentially useful to their interests. A letter from Little appeared in the *Lynn Record* on February 28, 1874.

Mr. Editor:— . . . Many has [*sic*] come to a knowledge of the truth, and cast off the garments of prejudice and superstition, and are anxiously looking forward to the great millennial day when woman shall rank with man and her rights be respected. Some men, who considered their judgment far superior to most sages, have talked very much upon poor, weak woman, of inferiority and small intellect, and always refer to the clinging vine . . . and seem perfectly astonished at the idea of women asking for the right of suffrage; and then with a deep sigh, hope really woman will not make herself a nuisance, acting in a way God never intended for her.

. . . [After Eden] man, being endowed with more strength, at once became selfish (a few are occasionally so now-a-day), and woman was compelled to become a slave, to act the part of a servant and drudge to her lord and ruler, man, and to gratify his fantastical whims always, and to be ruled body and soul; and if she dared express any feelings but those of meekness and submission, she was set down at once as an impolitic, bold person, and acting outside her proper sphere, and of course must desist. . . . Woman is but a servant as regards equality. She has no voice in this enlightened land to say that a law shall be enacted, yea or nay.

. . . Some ladies say they have no desire to go to the ballot-box. They have good husbands and pleasant homes, and have all the rights they desire. I admit this may be so in many instances; but you who are favored and surrounded by luxury, and can recline on your velvet cushions and feel wholly indifferent to this important subject, do little know or imagine the sorrows of oppression which other females have to contend with, and the want and woe which daily and yearly stare them in the face, and of the temptations which lurk in the path of those who are obliged to go forth alone to battle with temptation and earn their livelihood, working far beyond their strength for meagre pay. . . .

. . . Woman has had the idea instilled into her head that her highest aim in life is to marry, that she should aspire to nothing higher. . . . Few women can support themselves comfortably at the low prices paid for work, so that many marry for a home when they cannot give their heart. . . . Some have too much sense and principle to do this, and bear the honorary title of "old maid," and are the jest of society. I think these should pride themselves on their good luck, so to speak, and really deserve praise for their good judgment in the matter. . . . I contemplate with joy the future, and look forward to the "good time coming" as not far distant when woman shall have her rights and all professions shall be open to her as to man; when she shall occupy positions which males occupy now, but which rightly belong to her; and hope soon woman's voice shall echo in senate chambers and halls of representatives.

Ella A. Little

Ella Little's vision of women and men cooperating in public action to benefit society contradicted the view that woman's appropriate sphere was restricted to the home, where her good influences shaped and uplifted family life. Little argued that this moral influence should be empowered and harnessed in the interests of reform and labor protest. Another letter from her appeared in the *Lynn Record*, April 4, 1874.

Mr. Editor:— . . . In your paper of March 7, I noticed an article entitled "Woman's Rights," over the signature of "S.M.E." I read the brilliant ideas with much interest, and thought how very happy and contented the writer must feel . . . to fold her hands with perfect composure and indifference, and feel that all is well with her. . . .

. . . Our sister speaks of woman's highest duty as her relation to man—as wife, mother, her home etc. I think woman's duties, like man's, are many and varied. . . . You cannot confine the wave to the inlet; neither can you confine the woman's influence. She goes out into the world; she visits the sick; she stretches forth her hand to help the needy; she sheds tears of pity over the erring. . . . She sees the strong trying to crush the weak—the capitalist contending with the laborer, forgetting too often the words of Holy Writ. "The laborer is worthy of his hire." While contention is in our land, and right and wrong are at war with each other, can noble men and women remain in silence and see the innocent oppressed[?] No; they will use all their influence to right the wrongs and deliver the oppressed. . . .

Mr. Editor, I do not believed in going to the ballot-box, to be "jostled, squeezed and worried generally by a surging mass of political voters," as my sister so beautifully pictures it. Far from it. . . . No doubt some improvement can be made; but if it is too vile for women, it is also for men. I want men and women governed by the same laws of propriety. I believe in every woman being a lady—in her workshop, her kitchen, her parlor; in fact, mingling in the active duties of life, at all times and in all places. . . .

Mr. Editor, I would not have woman forget her duties to herself, her kindred, her God; but I do not see that any woman is acting out of her sphere—is unsexing herself in living to aid humanity. . . . If a woman, or a man, wants to lecture, preach, practise law, become a sculptor, an astronomer, or a music teacher, I have only to say, God bless them! . . . I hope every year the list of female "Drs." may increase. When a woman is doing her duty, the old plea of acting out of her sphere will never apply. She may meet opposition, but that matters not; she must do her duty nevertheless before Heaven. . . .

Ella A. Little

Despite her strong advocacy of labor reform, Americus staunchly upheld the idea of separate spheres for men and women (*Lynn Record*, May 16, 1874).

Mr. Editor:—Will you allow me to shake hands, through the "People's Column," with that "old woman [with the pen-name of Ye Olden Times] who has seen a heap o' trouble in this world"? for it is my opinion that she will see more before she sees less; and if we are ever to clasp hands in the flesh it must be soon, and before she is pounced on by the Abbie Smith [woman suffrage] Brigade. . . .

. . . Heaven help us! if the time has come when we can no longer place confidence in our fathers, our brothers and our husbands. It will be a bitter and humiliating day for me when I take the ballot from the hand that is left to me, to smooth the rough places in life; for that day will bring with it a conviction that the judgment I rely on has failed me, and the arm upon which I lean, is powerless to protect. . . .

. . . If women would have that anxiety for her own that they show for the stranger; if they would talk less and act more; if they would pray more in secret and less in public, there would be fewer divorces, fewer drunkards and many happier homes. Good gracious, what have I done? Set myself up for a target! So much for getting excited. . . .

Americus

Sisterhood as a principle of labor protest fell victim to the depression years of the 1870s. DOSC membership declined, and high levels of unemployment among stitchers undermined strike efforts, despite the tactics of strikers described in the *Lynn Reporter* of February 2, 1876.

And now the lady operatives in Joseph N. Smith's stitching department . . . to the number of fifty or sixty, have left his employ. The trouble arose on Saturday last, occasioned by a cut, as the manufacturer states, of an average of three and a half per cent. In addition to the reduction, an extra button-hole was provided for a style of boot made, for which the same price was demanded. The employer sent up his list to the stitchers, who in return sent a remonstrance [formal protest], on paper, to which the names of all the female operatives were signed in the form of a circle. . . .

The manufacturer claimed that he was paying fifteen per cent more for the same kind of work than any other in Lynn, and considers that they have acted very rashly, for which move they will deeply repent. The signing of the remonstrance in the style it was, he thinks, was a very clever act, inasmuch as he cannot determine the ringleaders in the trouble. . . .

The girls, of course, give altogether a different version of the story, and have established headquarters in a dwelling-house nearly opposite the factory, where they keep a strict watch upon all movements made by other operatives to get work. Thus far they have been very lady-like in their demonstrations, and if a lady comes to seek work with Mr. Smith, they politely invite her into the house and talk the matter over. . . .

During the long, hard depression years, working conditions and wages got worse, and efforts to protest mistreatment decreased. In one incident, according to the *Lynn Record*, September 7, 1878, when stitchers were denied even their customary right "to see what was to be seen" in the street in front of their workroom, only one woman protested.

On Saturday morning last while the procession connected with Coup's circus was passing through Market street, a number of girls and women employed in a stitching room in Bubier's block, flocked to the windows, as is the custom in all the shops when there is excitement on the street, to view the passing pageant; the windows not being large enough to accommodate all, a large number of them went out to look from the street door. In the course of two or three minutes, the lady who has charge of the shop sent for them to return, probably thinking they were not entitled to the privilege of viewing a street parade. The girls, however, believed they had as much right to see what was to be seen as did those who were viewing it from the windows, and hesitated a little before going back. It took but a few minutes for the procession to pass, and the girls started upstairs to resume work, when, to their consternation and surprise, they found the door to the workroom locked! They being dressed in work-aprons . . . and without hats, shawls, capes, or whatever they had worn to the shop, were obliged to spend about an half an hour on the steps before they could effect an entrance. At the end of that time a number of them went into the shop opposite the room where they were employed, and after the elevator had been risen to the level of the door, one of their number crossed and entered. Upon seeing this, the proprietress of the stitching room became enraged and demanded to know what right had she to take the elevator to gain access to a place where she was not wanted. The operator calmly replied she did not wish to have her think she was trying to force herself into the room for the purpose of again resuming work, for such was not the case; she simply wished to obtain that which belonged to her, and that she had a right to claim. After settling with the . . . overbearing woman who runs the shop . . . the young lady left the establishment. The other girls . . . gradually glided back into their positions, and resumed work, none of them seeming to dare demand an explanation of the hard taskmistress who had locked them out.

During a 1876 strike by the Lynn DOSC, Mrs. Ella A. Little Higginson wrote from Chicago to the *Lynn Record*, February 12, 1876, to reiterate her belief in the central role of equal rights in female labor protest.

Editor, Lynn Record:—Seated in my quiet western home this evening, I received a Boston paper containing a brief account of the recent strike of female operatives at the shoe manufactory of Joseph N. Smith. . . . I do not call this a "strike" on the part of the operatives, not at all; simply raising the standard of principle and justice, to one's self, to each other, and to the cause of woman. The operatives, during my four years' stay in Lynn, were subjected to various reductions in prices, which were unjust and tyrannical on the part of bosses and manufacturers. In the hardest and most trying season for working women to earn a bare pittance on which to honorably subsist, the shoe bosses have seen the chance to make reductions favorable for themselves, for well they know in depression and low tide of business, working girls must have work even at small wages. Female operatives have within the past six years been so often subjected to reduction in prices that forbearance has long ago ceased to be a virtue. . . . I have often urged upon the working women of Lynn the importance of forming a union co-operative society to protect them from the schemes and intrigues of designing manufacturers. But the masses have not come to see the importance of this, hence no permanent sure protection. Women as well as men should make living pay, in order to feed, clothe, educate and elevate themselves. . . . I hope this little cloud which has risen to overshadow the operatives at J. N. Smith's, will be the occasion of speedy organization for a permanent society to protect working girls, and give them equal rights with shoe manufacturers. . . .

Ella Little Higginson

In contrast to Ella Higginson's positive statement of womanhood, a letter from Americus in the *Lynn Record*, June 10, 1876, ascribed the failure of the DOSC strike against Smith's shoe shop to defects in woman's nature, exhibited not only by individuals but especially by women in groups.

Messrs. Editors:—The *Record* is an interesting and instructive paper, . . . but there is one subject that it *don't* understand worth a cent, and that is women. . . . you can't . . . [convince them to organize]; nobody can. That is why women are "peculiar," and you don't understand them. And some of your readers may be in the same sublime state of ignorance as yourself, in regard to the sex, and are wondering why on earth they *don't* organize. Perhaps you wouldn't mind my dissecting their mental and moral natures, and explaining to you to the best of my ability, how fearfully and wonderfully they are made. In the first place I wish you to understand that I am treating now of *women*, collectively. Woman is equal to man; knows as much, can accomplish as much, and behaves herself, generally speaking, better. . . . as they increase in number they grow in foolishness, until they reach the number of five thousand. . . . see the strike in the stitching room of J. N. Smith. . . . Had the men in this establishment struck[,] their places would probably have been vacant until now, . . . but the women strike, and they appeal to the honor and sympathy of their sister stitchers, and their sister stitchers respond in this wise:—They rush in and take the chairs and machines of the absent strikers, and say "Ain't we lucky?" "Seems so they struck on purpose so we might get a job." . . . Said one girl to another in my hearing:—"Where is A.B.?" "Oh," replied the other, "she has gone down to J. Smith's shop, and taken C.D's work."

"Why," returned the other, "she was a particular friend of C.D.'s and besides all that she is a church member. I shouldn't think that looked much like "doing as you would be done by." "Oh well," replied the other, "she gets a quarter of a cent more on a pair down there than she had in her old shop!"

That settled it. . . . And this is the way of women when they attempt to start an organization. Separately there is not a lady shoe operative in Lynn but that has a desire to better her condition, but collectively they don't care anything about it. . . . Men can organize, men be united; men can accomplish that which they undertake. Why? Because they don't do up their hair; because they don't wear frills; because they are not wedded to overskirts. . . . For instance, Miss Black is nominated as President of the Crispin order, and every woman immediately asks "who is she?" "where is she?" "what has she got on?" "how does she look?" "is she engaged?" and at last when the lady presents herself they immediately divide into factions, and one party exclaims, "Oh MY! *That* Miss Black! *She* President, and her hair done in a pug, and no crimps; and only three shirrs on her underskirt, and two loops in her overskirt! . . . You talk with the shoe stitchers of Lynn individually, and you will find each one earnest in advocating the Crispin cause . . . but get them into a hall together and not one of the whole lot knows, while she is there, what she is there for. I am able to give no philosophical reason why this is thus. All I know is that it is so, and that women are "peculiar." . . . It is useless and idle to expect this class alone, and unaided by a stronger hand, to ever reach a state of united discipline. I should as soon expect to see a flock of geese marching sedately to the music of the fife and drum.

Americus

[10]

Married Women in the
Shoe Shops: A Debate

The depression of the 1870s, which increased the dependency of individuals on family support, also increased the numbers of married women seeking paid work. Family need strained the concept of sisterhood as a principle of organizing labor protest and added to the intensity of antisuffrage debate within the DOSC. Self-supporting women and wives argued over which group was more deserving of jobs in the shoe shops. Wives seemed especially irate about the employment of even a few women as lasters.

The number of wives in the Lynn work force doubled between 1870 and 1880. Older married women joined new brides in the factories or labored as homeworkers. As a result, the average age of wives who worked in the shops rose from twenty-two years in 1870 to thirty-two years in 1880. Letters exchanged in the local press exposed the conflicts between single women and wives during a time of low wages and high unemployment. Many felt the need to pool their wages for family survival, while others faced the hard necessity of self-support. Correspondence appearing in the *Lynn Record* in 1879 demonstrates that with effective organization difficult during the depression years, divisions among workingwomen became acrimonious.

[February 1, 1879]
   Mr. Editor,—In last week's *Record*, . . . I noticed this: "Working women, why don't you organize?" . . . I grew more and more indignant and resolved to write the *Record* a letter giving some of the reasons why the D.O.S.C.'s membership fails to increase. . . . Why my blood fairly

boils and I get righteously angry when I think of some of the causes which have brought down the price of our labor! But let me tell you: In the first place, the shops are thronged with married women, the greater portion of whom (and these are the ones I censure) have good, comfortable homes, and girls whose fathers are amply able to provide them with all the necessaries and comforts of life, but their inordinate love of dress, and a desire to vie in personal adornments with their more wealthy sisters, takes them into the workrooms. . . . Ask *them* to join the order, and they are horrified at the thought! They don't want any better wages: they have a home, no board to pay, and so long as they can get enough for pin money, they are content. . . .

Our brother workmen can organize, and redress their wrongs; but for us there is no hope, and the bosses know it just as well as we; so they snap their fingers at us, and as each returning season comes round, they give us an extra cutdown in lieu of cutting down the men, knowing full well there are plenty of married women, with well-to-do husbands, and half supported girls who stand ready to work the few short weeks in which work is given out, at any price they can get. . . . Organize! Would that we might, so that our number might become a power to be feared. I could almost weep tears of blood when I think upon our wrongs.

A Stitcher

[February 8, 1879]

Mr. Editor,— . . . I cannot quite agree with "A Stitcher" in thinking that "married women" and "half-supported girls" are the stumbling blocks in the way of organization. The great majority of our girls are not "half supported," neither are the majority of married women employed in our shops blessed with "comfortable homes" and "well to do husbands": if there are a few of this class, they are *very* few compared with the many who are obliged to work for their daily bread. . . . married women have been well represented in the D.O.S.C. organization, and . . . they have always proved zealous and ardent supporters of that order. . . . There are not many women inside our shoe shops today who are not obliged to work. . . .

Americus

[February 15, 1879]

Mr. Editor,— . . . I am a married woman. I have worked in the shops some years, and never but one married woman have I met but what claimed they worked from necessity, not from choice. What sent many of the married women into the shops are the girls who [would] rather work with a crowd of men [as lasters] than in the stitching room with their own sex. They have been the cause of many men being cut down; men with families to maintain. I for one, and I know many more situated in the same way, work to get bread for my children; my husband has been cut down so that in the short time he has work he cannot support us. I wonder what many of the men would have done in the lockout of last winter [1878] if their wives had not worked in the shops. I consider myself a Crispin in principle, but I will never join an order that takes in girl-lasters! "Stitcher" is altogether too hard on married women. I think some married woman of her acquaintance must have come out with a smarter silk or longer train than hers.

Married Stitcher

[February 15, 1879]

Mr. Editor,— . . . I do not believe any woman, married or single, works for the *fun* of it in these times; neither do I believe most married women work in the shop because they are obliged to—that is to provide themselves with the *actual necessaries* of life. To be sure, some of them may have shiftless husbands, but I think the men would make greater exertions if the women were not so eager and willing to take a man's place. If married women had to pay board bills, washing bills, and then had to be denied all the comforts of home, with no one to look to for aid or support, they would be less content to sit quietly down and submit to reduction after reduction, but would be ready to join any honorable scheme which would bring relief.

. . . Were times good, work and money plenty, why, then, if married women wanted to work out and neglect their homes, they could do so for all me. But so long as there are a surplus of laborers, with a scarcity of work, I shall protest against the married woman question, even though I stand alone. . . .

A Stitcher

[February 22, 1879]

Mr. Editor,— . . . Ah! my dear Stitcher. . . . You say: "So long as there are a surplus of laborers, with a scarcity of work," I shall protest against the married women question." And I reply:—So long as there are "a surplus of laborers with a scarcity of work" so long will your protest be of no avail. So long as there are "a surplus of laborers with a scarcity of work" so long will many married men find it impossible to support their families, and when the husband and father cannot provide for his wife and children, it is perfectly natural that the wife and mother should desire to work for her husband and her little ones, and we have no right to deny her that privilege. . . .

My dear child, don't blame married women if the land of the free has become a land of slavery and oppression. Women are not to blame. . . .

Americus

[March 1, 1879]

Mr. Editor,— . . . For years I have been homeless, thrown here and there by circumstances, but have kept my eyes and ears open to all that has been going on around me; and many times I have been deeply pained at the utter selfishness manifested by a certain class of married women in the shops, till I have been thoroughly disgusted with them all. . . .

. . . from statistical reports there is found to be sixty odd thousand more females than males in the state of Massachusetts, and it is safe to say three-fourths of them have to earn their own support. Now these can never have homes of their own unless they make them. No strong arm on which to lean can ever rightfully be theirs. In the face and eyes of this, can it be fair for them to have to compete with married women who have protectors, in the struggle for bread, besides all the other obstacles in their way?

. . . It is no use, "Americus"; since the days of Mother Eve women have been at the bottom of nearly every trouble: and . . . I think a foolish extravagance in dress and love of display on the part of women, has caused many a once honest man to turn thief, and has helped, if did not wholly, bring about this fearful crisis of distress and want. . . .

A Stitcher

[March 8, 1879]

Mr. Editor,— . . . I don't suppose being married changes the nature of a woman very much. . . . I still have a kindly regard for women, and don't know but that I like them as well as I do men, generally speaking. And I, for one, shall never speak disrespectfully of "Mother Eve." She was another married woman that I honor. . . . I always thought Eve was entitled to a little more mercy than she received, in consideration of the poor material out of which she was made. . . .

You say—"Could there be anything more cheering to a tired, weary man, when at night-fall he seeks his home, to find a loving wife, who he knows has carefully looked after his interests all day, and then made everything bright for his home coming?" I guess I don't know what you mean. If a man had no work and no money, and his stock of provisions had dwindled down to a few baked beans on a tin plate, do you mean that his wife ought to stay at home, and eat the beans, and scour the plate up bright for his home coming? You say—"What could be more cheering to a tired, weary man?" I think the proper answer to that question is—beans. . . . Could there be anything more discouraging to a man than to realize the fact that "a surplus of laborers and a scarcity of work" had left him with no means of providing for his family? . . . But as the first duty of the wife is to consult the best interests of her husband, I believe that, with all the discouraging difficulties that surround the workingman today; it is oftentimes the first duty of the wife to leave her home, and take upon herself a part of the burden that weighs so heavily upon the man she loves. . . .

. . . Urge your girls once more to organize, and if they make the reply, "What can a handful of girls do against so many married women?" tell them that "Americus" says they outnumber the married women three to one, and that married women are more willing to organize than they are, and ask them to help prove she is wrong.

Americus

[11]

Labor Protest and the
Nature of Womanhood

In 1880–81 "Americus" debated with another stitcher, "Columbia," the capacity of women to engage in labor protest and the nature of womanhood. The central issue between these two hardy, intelligent, stubborn, and contentious New England women was the use of elevators by women workers in shoe factories. The elevator question became a symbol that focused their lively conflict over the capacity of females to protest grievances. Columbia's arguments demonstrated a positive sense of female gender that was essential to the involvement of workingwomen in protest against injustice. Her feminism contrasted sharply with Americus's belief in the eternal defectiveness of womanhood. The *Lynn Record* published their exchange.

[June 26, 1880]

Editor Record—"Any person in our employ found riding upon this elevator will be promptly discharged. Jones, Smith & Co." . . .

Such are the signs which greet the delighted eyes of poor, hard working, toiling shoe operatives, as tired, and worn out with climbing three or four long flights of stairs, they approach the doors to the elevator well, thinking they may obtain "a lift." . . . in my opinion— though of course the opinion of a humble female vamper would be counted as naught by the majority of our aristocratic shoe manufacturers—the elevator question is carried *too* far altogether. I think it is a downright shame when female operatives (I am not talking about male operatives, they must look out for themselves) are placed in the top story of a four story building that they have not the privilege of riding upon the elevator in the morning, down and up again at noon and down again at night. This is a rather delicate subject for a lady to write about, nevertheless I do not believe in maintaining a stoney silence when I feel that I or my fellow beings are being oppressed. . . . I know myself, from experience and observation, that there is nothing more prolific of lame backs and sundry and diverse forms of ailments, diseases and distempers among our female laboring classes than this same going up and down long, steep flights of stairs four times a day. Somebody may say that the reason that we are denied the use of the elevators is because the elevators themselves are unsafe. . . . our shoe manufacturers prize their own precious little bodies far too highly to needlessly risk them upon any kind of a machine which they consider in the least might [be] dangerous. . . . Then again the overseers of our stitching rooms are granted the free use of the elevators, and I do not think that one lady's body is more precious than another's when it comes to saving the strength of it. Our shoe factories are little despotisms. The members of the firm are the monarchs and the foremen and forewomen are the princes and princesses of the blood and all the other operatives are many, many degrees . . . below these high dignitaries! . . . And now I will close my letter by again saying emphatically that it is a downright shame for the female operatives in shoe factories to be denied the use of the elevator. . . .

Columbia

[July 10, 1880]

My dear Columbia:— . . . You are tired and nervous, and inconsistent—inconsistent *because* you are tired and nervous. I know very well that it will do no good to reason with you in your present state, but still I am not going to let you think that I am in sympathy with your every desire to break your own neck. . . . A flock of girls are very much like a flock of sheep: when one a little more venturesome than the rest starts in a certain direction all the rest immediately follow. . . . All the girls would ride the elevator whether they know how to operate it or not, consequently some of them would be very likely to be killed. . . . I am aware that it is hard for girls to climb to "the top of a four story building" two or three times a day, . . . but these bones and muscles are in as healthy a condition after they have walked down four flights of stairs as they would likely to be if their owners should step upon an elevator that wasn't there. . . . Why, my dear Columbia, there are plenty of things in shoe shops more worthy of your indignation than this elevator matter!

. . . And now, Columbia, do not feel bad because your employer does not want you to distribute yourself in pieces upon the basement floor of his factory. . . . Don't work too hard. Keep as cool as possible this hot weather; preserve your patience and temper at all hazards, and believe me very sincerely your friend,

Americus

[July 24, 1880]

My dear Americus— . . . I have always been noted for my good sound common sense. Therefore, my dear, there is not the slightest danger of my working too hard in this hot weather—except perhaps in the cause of labor. . . . You say *all* the girls would ride on the elevator. Why! my dear child, that's just what I want them to do. I want them *all* to ride upon the elevator. I wasn't writing for myself merely but for all my fellow laborers throughout the city. . . . My dear girl, do you think it would require a very extraordinary amount of moral courage for one of the male employees of the factory, who understands how to operate the elevator, to volunteer to operate it for say fifteen minutes at morning[,] noon and night? I think there are men in our shoe factories who would be willing to do this to accommodate their sister toilers. . . . I tell you, Americus, this plan of mine is a perfectly reasonable and feasible one. . . . You make me think of a maiden aunt I once had. She was a very prudish and precise person indeed. When I was a little girl I was very fond, in my vacation times, of planning entertainments. . . . No matter what I planned, if I ever said, "I'm going to do so and so tomorrow, Auntie," my aunt invariably exclaimed solemnly, "If you live, my dear." . . . But now in conclusion—I really think that our shoe manufacturers would greatly add to the lustre of their reputations if they would devise some means of letting the girls ride upon the elevators. Don't you?

Columbia

[August 14, 1880]

My dear Columbia— . . . There can be no doubt that you have become greatly confused by the din and clatter of the shoe factory. The

Babel of sounds acting upon nerves already weakened by overwork causes you to rush into the *Record* and exclaim—"I want to ride on the elevator, I do! I do! I will break my bones if I want to, I will! I will!" . . . It is my humble opinion that the elevators in our shoe factories are unsafe, and should not be patronized by male or female employees. . . . And if they are perfectly safe I should not think it good policy to allow the female employees to operate them. There is not one girl in twenty who understands the whys and wherefores of any machine. . . . And if anything happens that the ropes don't work just right they are immediately filled with confusion and dismay; and a class of beings like this is not fit to ride on elevators. . . . And now don't let us hear any more about the elevator. If you are determined on suicide there is laudanum, and the rope, and the razor. . . . it is a mystery to me, how, with all these means at hand, you can have the bad taste to want to destroy yourself in the vulgar and public manner that you seem bent upon. In one thing I think we can agree, and that is, in thinking it a shame that the stitching rooms are so generally located in the upper stories of our factories. . . .

Americus

[September 25, 1880]

My dear Americus— . . . You are the first person that ever accused me of expressing my ideas in an unclear manner. Much fault has been found with me, but hitherto, it has always [been] because I have been too plain spoken. . . . This is what I mean:—If it is generally conceded all over the city, by our shoe manufacturers, that the elevators in their factories are unsafe, then I think it is a duty they owe to themselves and their employees to make them *safe*. . . . Now you know that I have repeatedly said that I do not champion nor approve of a promiscuous use of the elevators, but only wish the use of it at certain hours of the day. . . . you intimate that all reforms for the benefit of labor are impractical and imaginative; and as you have yourself written in the cause of labor for a long time, you distinctly declare that you have been writing nonsense all these years. . . . You say you have nothing more to say upon the subject of elevators. Well, I am sorry in one sense, and glad, of course, in another. I like very much to read your letters; but I feel and know, by your having nothing more to say upon this subject, I have converted you to my side of the question. . . .

Columbia

[November 13, 1880]

My dear Columbia— . . . It is of no use for us to persevere unless our judgment assures us that there is a chance to succeed, and I am of the opinion, Columbia, that your perseverance in regard to this elevator question, is labor thrown away. However strongly constructed an elevator may be, it is necessarily subjected to great "wear and tear." . . . Moreover, as I have already remarked, girls are not properly constituted to ride on elevators. If the elevators were all right and perfectly safe, girls in operating them, would find some means of getting mangled. You know very well that a crowd of giggling, chattering girls, are no more fit to ride on an elevator than so many lunatics. Girls are well enough in their place, but in my opinion, that place is not on an elevator. . . . Why [you ask the manufacturers], if the elevators are unsafe contrivances don't [they] fix them? That word "fix" is rather indefinite, and is usually confined to the vocabulary of women. . . . you will probably have to explain . . . that you meant to ask, why, after his elevator was built and in good running order, he didn't tie a string around it, or stick in a hairpin, and thus make it perfectly secure. Farewell, my dear Columbia, for a season and believe me as always, affectionately, your friend.

Americus

[January 15, 1881]

My dear Americus— . . . Now my dear little girl, I presume that you have begun to imagine that you have utterly squelched and "squashed" me . . . that by the power of your arguments, by the force of your logic, and more than these, by the withering sarcasm and extreme "spiceiness" of your style of writing, you have completely annihilated me. Such is not the case. . . .

Now a word more about elevators and I am done. . . . Everything is subject to wear and tear, always has been and always will be.

There was an invention made some time ago which renders it a moral impossibility, should an elevator break, to fall more than one story. Other inventions have been got up to guard the hatchway. I tell you, my dear Americus, that if our shoe manufacturers really desired to allow us to ride on the elevator, they would soon find a way by which we could do so. If the legislators should pass a law compelling all manufacturers to pay five cents a head for every girl who was not allowed to [ride] upon the elevator at the hours of exit and entrance to the factory, the shoe manufacturers of Lynn would soon find a way of making their elevators safe, and they would hustle their girls on and off in a manner truly surprising. . . .

Now we have discussed the elevator question at considerable length; and in the end we find that you still adhere to your original idea that the elevators are unsafe, that they never will be made safe, and that the manufacturers are darling little angels for refusing to allow us to ride upon them; while I still adhere to my original statement that if the elevators are unsafe, then it is the duty of the manufacturers to make them safe, and that they can be made safe with little expense to our poor, impoverished manufacturers. . . .

Now, farewell, Americus, my dear, dear friend, and believe me ever yours sincerely,

Columbia

With this last letter, the correspondence ended. Columbia's undaunted belief in the capacity of women workers like herself to identify and demand changes in the working conditions of Lynn shoe factories rested fundamentally on her positive sense of womanhood and on her faith in the potential of womankind.

[1 2]

The Persistence of Homework

Despite the mechanization and centralization of shoe production in the 1860s, many women in the late nineteenth century continued to work at home on foot-powered sewing machines. Homeworkers in Lynn represented over one-quarter of the female work force in 1875, but their numbers fell by 1885 to less than 5 percent. Women in Marblehead and Haverhill continued to work at home in larger numbers (in depression years, up to 20 percent) well into the 1890s—stitching, pasting, and pressing uppers and beading and decorating the vamps of slippers.

In both Lynn and Haverhill, the largest shoe cities in Essex County, the work force in the shoe industry remained about 30 percent female between 1870 and 1910. Wages for homeworkers were lower than those of factory workers, whose steam-powered machines ran faster. Nevertheless, busy wives and mothers who could not work the long factory day worked at home, especially when the family needed extra money during the economic depressions of the 1870s and 1890s.

The double standard of wages and conditions for factory workers and homeworkers was divisive. Post–Civil War factory operatives in Massachusetts who worked a typical eight- to nine-hour day, six days a week, earned the highest wages paid to female industrial workers in the late nineteenth century. Many factory stitchers supported themselves and others on their earnings. Some could even afford to pay for amusements after work. In contrast, homeworkers without alternatives bent over their foot-powered machines for low wages reduced even further by the custom of furnishing their own thread and other materials.

Some pre–Civil War homeworkers, angered by low wages, had

adopted the custom of "cabbaging" from shoemaking artisans who kept extra leather, thread, and other materials supplied by shoe bosses for the men's use. One such conscience-stricken but otherwise unrepentant stitcher wrote to her former shoe boss in 1870. The *Lynn Reporter* published the letter on March 5, 1870.

Mr. B_____

About fifteen years ago I bound boots for you, and did as others— when there was any silk or cotton left I kept it. [I] then satisfied my conscience by thinking it was no more than right, as you paid us such a miserably low price for your work. But it has worried me, and I send you two dollars, which is probably all that I kept cost you. I do not feel as if I ought to pay interest on that amount, for the reason that you paid so miserably; but I did not want to have it on my mind, for fear it was not strictly honest to do, even if others did. I pray God will forgive me.

Yours respectfully,

_____

By the 1880s northeastern manufacturers were facing serious competition from midwestern shoe factories in Cincinnati, Chicago, and St. Louis. Homeworkers provided an extra work force to be tapped during the busy seasons of production for the spring and the fall trade. During the depression years of the 1890s, employers recruited homeworkers in eastern Massachusetts cities as the cheapest possible labor.

Irena Knowlton, the wife of George K. Knowlton, a small shoe manufacturer in Hamilton, Massachusetts, stitched shoe uppers at home during the 1870s and 1880s. She combined this homework with the many other demanding duties of a housewife: caring for three children, feeding boarders, selling poultry and fruit, sewing, churning, and baking. The diary she kept between 1879 and 1886 is a litany of fatigue and despair by one homeworker overwhelmed with her responsibilities. Excerpts from the Irena Knowlton diary, 1879–80, are quoted (again, with the writer's spelling intact) by permission of the Essex Institute.

Jan. 1, 1879 done some shoes

Jan. 2 done shoes   done some sti[t]ching last night and this morning for Mrs. Patch. . . .

Jan 7 three boarders besides Mr. Coy to dinner   two to tea and stay all night, Baked 4 pies, ironed some   feel so tired set another hen [to lay eggs]. . . .

Feb. 19 done some shoes

Feb. 20 worked on shoes part of the day

Feb. 21 Done some shoes today. . . .

Feb. 27 cut my dress   run the machine needle through my finger. . . .

March 3 Washed   done few shoes   ironed   feel tired   O! Lord how long. . . .

April 2 worked on [daughter] Idella's dress, Charles to dinner some shoes   set hen No. 20   callers. . . .

April 7 done four pr. button boots girls   set hen No. 21   have not felt very well tonight. . . .

May 5 washed   Chartell to dinner   done few shoes. went to bed sick about middle afternoon   O! dear.

May 6 sick all day. . . .

May 8 done few shoes   feel some better but so weak. . . .

May 20 pasted few [uppers] . . . feel a good deal better today   cow gone to pastore

May 21 done some shoes   have felt pretty well today. . . .

May 27 washed   done some shoes   feel so tiered. . . .

Aug 2 went berrying,   done some shoes, [S]cot to breakfast and dinner   George went away today but O dear what a life to live   *God* help me to do my duty   baked 5 pies   *drove cow.* . . .

Sept 8 boarders come   were here for dinner   cut some garments
sewed   some   done few shoes   churned. . . .

Sept 12 done shoes   sewed on buttons. . . .

Sept 20 stitched few button holes. . . .

Nov 14 friday   clearer   done shoes   Same old story. . . .

During the 1880s, one unsuspecting factory stitcher took some work
from a subcontractor to sew at home during the shop's slack time. Her
experience was printed in a trade journal, the *Boot and Shoe Recorder*, on
November 5, 1890.

Some time ago I saw an ad. in the paper for stitchers to take out work
on serge buskins [ladies' high-cut shoes with wool uppers], and not
having much to do, I went to the factory and took 60 pairs. I had to
press all the tops of outsides and linings with a hot iron before I could
stitch them; it took me two days and until 11 o'clock one night before I
got them done. The foreman said they were well done, and paid me 60
cents. I had to find [furnish] thread, etc., and was five cents out of
pocket by the transaction.

A reporter exposed the widespread system of "sweated" homework on
shoes in the *Haverhill Gazette*, February 20, 1892.

. . . The horrors of the degraded life of the sweaters of the clothing
trades of Boston, New York and other great cities have been pictured in
the most realistic terms . . . and even congress ordered a special committee to investigate this evil and recommend some legislation. . . .

All of this is very good and deserves the support of Haverhill shoemakers. . . . But . . . it would be well if the union shoe workers in this
city . . . should investigate the shoe trade of our own city. . . .

Of course the squalor and vicious life that characterizes the crowded
tenements of the metropolis are not to be found in this city, but at the
same time the fact remains that there are women who toil 14 and 15
hours a day over a machine surrounded by wretched poverty, and are
able thus to eke out from 50 to 75 cents a day, on which they try to
support themselves and their families. . . .

The amount of homework done on the Haverhill product is enormous, although little by little it is being drawn into the factory. Not all of it is to be classed as starvation work, for some of the best fitters in the city are those who have household cares and still continue to take out work to get a little pocket money. It is with another class of work . . . auction goods [those sold in bulk by commission houses], that this article has to deal, and the amount of this class of goods manufactured is little imagined.

The goods are expected to sell for next to nothing. . . . To reach this end the [leather] stock must be the cheapest possible . . . and the labor must be cut down to the lowest possible notch. The union stands in the way of this in the factory, and so the manufacturer steps outside and takes advantage of tenement house life. . . .

A few instances of this work were run across by the *Gazette* man . . . [who] entered a room that showed at a glance the poverty and struggle of the occupants. A worn out oil cloth covered half the floor, and a few wooden chairs, a table, an old stove and two stitching machines formed the furnishings of the room.

A pale-faced woman sat at one of the machines busily at work. . . . Two sets of shoes had just been completed. One of these was a case of operas [pumps], on which the woman had had to close three seams and stay them for which work she got one-half cent a pair. . . . she could by working 14 hours per day, do about three 36 pair cases a day, making her total income 54 cents per day, out of which she had to pay 10 cents for thread. . . .

On Locke St, at No. 25, Mrs. A. M. Burns was found, who had been employed in the past but was out of work now. She worked on Oxfords stitching linings at 20 cents per case, doing work which two or three [workers] did in the shop and yet could make but about 55 cents a day. . . .

A couple of parties, who were doing bead work at wages even less than those mentioned above, were also found. . . .

Some of the manufacturers were seen by the *Gazette* man, and admitted that this work was done all over the city. If a manufacturer gets pinched in his figuring on a cheap shoe, his only way out is by getting his fitting done at bedrock prices. . . .

[13]

Lady Knights of Labor

The Daughters of St. Crispin did not survive the depression of the 1870s, but the return of prosperity in the 1880s prompted a new organization of women shoeworkers within the Knights of Labor. A letter from "A Union Girl" to the Lynn *Knight of Labor* on December 12, 1885, expressed the writer's outrage against the shoe manufacturers' refusal to raise wages in the reviving industry. Her graceful use of language reflected social aspirations and a level of literacy uncommon among women industrial workers in the late nineteenth century but characteristic of native-born New England women stitchers.

> Mr. Editor,—We are glad to know that we have a paper through whose columns we may safely claim redress for the wrongs done to us, and that any explanations we may wish to make in regard to existing trouble, will be inserted in its pages instead of being thrust aside, as such documents have been heretofore by some of the locals of this city, leaving the public to draw their own inference, which was wrong to a certain degree; and instead of gaining the sympathy, it had the disapproval of the community generally, just from misrepresentation.
>
> . . . Gentlemen, you [the shoe manufacturers] have driven us to the step we have taken, as you were not content with a fair share of the profits, but want them all, regardless of the consequences. There are some exceptions, as some men have a conscience, whatever business they may be engaged in. The speaker of the other evening, asked us to "return good for evil"; we know this is the example of our Saviour, but he was not a shoemaker; we also concur with him in thinking it is better

to act from principle than authority, yet gentlemen, we become almost desperate when we remember that there are those among us much more capable, naturally, than their employers, and that it is stooping beneath themselves to even accept a position in a filthy shop, at a just remuneration; and, only for cruel fate, would be occupying much more exalted positions than those to whom they are now compelled to submit quietly. Gentlemen, we have an ambition yet that is hard to tame, to dependence in the hour of misfortune. Had we not ought to claim a recompense to warrant us a comfortable living as we toil patiently on?

Well, sisters, I never read of any such spirit in Our Saviour, did you? That only those with money could afford to sit and listen to flowery sermons in the extravagant edifices, and make long prayers for the wayward, whom they have dragged down; then stand ready to kick them; never mind if justice is not ours here, remember there is a just judge awaiting us at the tribunal beyond, and eternity means forever, and some may be surprised at the sentence awaiting them.

A Union Girl

Women in the Knights of Labor used the status of lady stitcher as a defense against public suspicions about the morality of migrant women workers. The genteel character of ladyhood and memories of its positive connotations in the 1860s also appealed to the first generation of factory workers, largely unmarried Yankee women who had entered the shoe shops after the Civil War and had stayed on for a decade or longer. Many had not expected long-term work in factories.

An analysis of the 1880 census of population in Lynn indicates that native-born women of New England background made up 64 percent of the female work force. Another significant cultural group (about 10 percent) was made up of foreign-born stitchers from the Maritime Provinces of Canada, whose English and Scottish cultural and social characteristics and Protestant upbringing were much like those of Yankee New Englanders. Achieving the status of lady stitcher also proved useful to the 20 percent who were American-born daughters of immigrants, Irish and French Canadian; these women joined the Yankees in the shoe shops in increasing numbers in the 1880s. Of the total female work force in 1880, 49 percent were self-supporting boarders or heads of families. The rest were daughters and wives in male-headed families.

The ideal of the lady stitcher served as a bridge to social respectability for female industrial workers, a troubling problem for wage-earning women in late Victorian society. The lady stitcher was entitled to protection against disrespectful and unjust treatment or unwanted contacts within the community. This was useful particularly for those women who had temporarily left their homes and families to work in the shoe shops. During the depression years, however, one shop girl had written angrily to the editor of the *Lynn Record*, June 12, 1875, that lady stitchers were not receiving their due respect.

> Messrs. Editors:—I wish to warn my young lady friends of that class of young men who come to Lynn from Boston on the eight o'clock morning train, and who find no other employment for their time than staring at women all the way like great idiotic, grinning, country school boys. They are a set of indecent hoodlums, and deserve to be kicked from the cars by their male companions. Particularly would I mention one nuisance who is a disgrace to his sex. Of course we have no protection against these half-dozen, ill-mannered boobies and can only say "beware of them."
>
> A Shop Girl

In 1880 a former employee of a Lynn stitching shop filed an assault charge against the forewoman. For the defendant, the accused, and their female witnesses—if not for the lawyers or the judge in the case—the subsequent trial reported in the *Lynn Item*, September 3, 1880, became a contest over which woman had behaved most like a lady. The controversy indicated the importance to women workers of proper standards of conduct in the shoe shops and also illustrated ethnic tensions between New England Yankee and Irish-American women workers.

> On Wednesday, Mrs. Hannah W. Barbour, the proprietress of a stitching shop on Collins street entered a complaint against Sarah McGaghey, for an alleged assault on her, at the stitching shop of T. C. Murphy's shoe factory, Market street, of which Miss McGaghey is forewoman. . . .
>
> It seems that Mrs. Barbour formerly worked for Murphy at stitching, but the work not being satisfactory in one or more instances, he ceased employing her. On Tuesday morning Mrs. Barbour visited the shop, and states that on seeing Miss McGaghey she bid her good-morning, whereupon Miss McGaghey looked at her contemptuously and replied, in answer to a question as to the work, that Mrs. Barbour had better leave the premises or she would pitch her out. Mrs. Barbour

then left Miss McGaghey, and going to Miss Jennie Webster, who was running a machine, entered into conversation with her. Miss McGaghey then came to Mrs. Barbour and again ordered her out.

Angry words ensued between the two, and Mrs. Barbour claims that Miss McGaghey assaulted her by striking her in the face and on the hand, with a bunch of linings. Both then went to the entrance door, and Mrs. Barbour also states that Miss McGaghey attempted to put a threat into execution of pushing her down stairs, at the same time using indelicate language. Mrs. Barbour, to save herself, pushed Miss McGaghey into a corner, whereupon several Irish girls, operatives, rushed to them, and struck Mrs. Barbour. . . .

Miss McGaghey claims that she directed Mrs. Barbour to leave the shop for good and sufficient reasons, and that she did not use any unladylike language. She states that Mrs. Barbour seized her by the throat and throttled her so that she became insensible. One of the operatives who went to the rescue had great difficulty in loosening the grip of Mrs. Barbour. The witnesses for Miss McGaghey testified that Mrs. Barbour was furiously angry, and was not at all chary in the use of profane and indecent language. . . .

The only witnesses for the government were Misses Jennie Webster and Alice Rowe, who testified that they heard no profane or indecent language. . . . Miss Webster states that she heard the expression "liar" used, but could not say who employed it. . . .

Miss Rowe testified that she thought both Miss McGaghey and Mrs. Barbour were in a very "cross" mood. . . .

In summing up, Mrs. Barbour's counsel claimed that the witnesses for Miss McGaghey had compared notes, and to curry favor with her, as their forewoman, were a tribe who had all told their story glibly. . . . Mrs. Barbour was an elderly feeble woman, 51 years old, while her assailant was a young, vigorous woman 27 years old. . . .

The counsel for the defense claimed that Miss McGaghey had not transcended her rights by ordering Mrs. Barbour out of the shop under the facts as testified by the witnesses, and was not guilty of the violent assault that had been charged. At the most it was but a woman's quarrel.

The court adjudged Mrs. Barbour guilty of the assault, and fined her $8 and costs. . . .

It proved hard to reconcile ladylike standards of social behavior—courtesy, civility, and charity—with the militancy required of workingwomen who confronted their employers over wages and working conditions. During one strike a member of the Lady Stitchers' Assembly, Knights of Labor, wrote a public appeal in the *Knight of Labor*, December 19, 1885, to the stitchers of Lynn. For "Union Girl," the characteristics of ladylike behavior, correctly managed as a cultural resource, could be used positively to enhance the self-esteem of female union members in their contests with their employers.

Mr. Editor:—Sisters, we undertook a life work when we enrolled our names on the "Knights of Labor" records; then let us stand firm and unwavering while we know our cause is just. Charity is a much needed trait in one's character, especially at the present time; but we want a well-balanced judgment to know when to exercise this gift and not use it too freely. I am sorry to say it has come to that pass where most employers evince the spirit that the honor is recompense enough for our labor. But that does not buy bread and clothes, and while we are willing to toil patiently on, we must and will not submit to tyranny, as such was never the intention of the Almighty. It is our duty to be courteous and civil to our employers, yet the task would be less irksome if by kindness they would win our voluntary admiration and respect. Sisters, we constitute a large body, so be careful that every member be useful, as in "union is strength."

Don't for one moment forget your obligation and turn traitor in the camp, as this would bring reproach upon the cause, and make "the just suffer for the unjust."

Never try to convey the wrong idea to the public, that because you bear the name of Union Girl, you will be sustained in unladylike and wrong doings, as you know our organization has nothing of the kind in its constitution, and you will bring the censure of the community on the whole for the rash folly of one.

The Knights of Labor Platform is grand and noble in its design, and its aim is to elevate, instead of degrading any of its members.

Outsiders think we are only banded together to fight on the subject of prices, etc., but they are mistaken; our principles and object are peace if we can be allowed the privilege of enjoying them, and the only way for you to become enlightened, is to come and join our ranks.

Union Girl

The native-born Yankees among Essex County stitchers felt themselves the social equals of their employers and valued their republican political heritage. Although increasing numbers of stitchers in the 1880s were daughters of immigrant families, all seemed to benefit from public identification with the social status and self-respect of native-born factory girls. Shoe stitchers in New England factories were often favorably compared with the early factory girls of Lowell and other textile centers, as in an article published in the *Lynn Bee*, February 16, 1886.

The female operatives in the shoe manufactories of Lynn differ materially from the [present day] factory operatives of Lowell, Lawrence and Fall River. In the latter cities the foreign element predominates—almost entirely prevails at the present day. In Lynn comparatively few are employed who are not strictly American, by birth and blood. Once this could have been said of the factory operatives of those cities. A generation ago their factories were largely filled with ambitious and self respecting daughters of New England, who flocked to them for employment that could not be obtained nearer home. . . .

The Lynn female operative occupies an important social position in the community. In the intervals of her employment she sometimes does valuable service in charitable work, and every Sabbath finds her attired in the very latest styles and the most costly fabrics, a constant and devout attendant at church and Sabbath school. . . . There she meets her employer and other employers on a perfect equality, and even sometimes become the leading spirit in movements in which she often exercises authority over their less enthusiastic temperaments.

Most of the shop girls employed in Lynn are permanent residents here, living with their parents. . . . Many, however, are compelled to live in the excellent boarding houses, for which Lynn is noted, and the lively times enjoyed after the day's work is done is [*sic*] the natural consequence of a gathering of youthful spirits released from all care. There is another class of provident female operatives who club together, and hiring a suite of rooms either cook for themselves, taking an occasional meal out, or go regularly to meals at some restaurant. . . .

The comparatively strict discipline common in the factories of Lowell and Fall River is unknown in Lynn. . . . but it has been partially maintained by the self reliant and independent spirit of the operatives themselves, who never hesitate to chaff and torment any self-important overseer who may start out upon the idea of requiring implicit obedience to any code of rules and regulations. . . . The Yankee girl is proverbially a girl of mischievous spirit, and she never hesitates to assert herself . . . whatever be her comparative station in life. . . .

Women active in the Knights of Labor in Massachusetts in the mid-1880s combined a strong gender consciousness as lady stitchers with control of stitching operations. This helped them gain a reasonable wage that would guarantee a decent annual income to self-supporting women. One stitcher, who was described and quoted in the *Shoe and Leather Review*, September 20, 1888, retained the sense of sisterhood acquired during her participation in the Daughters of St. Crispin.

A lady stitcher of Lynn, a maiden lady, most active in organizing her sisters, and who has actively participated in all of the union schemes for twenty years [1868–88], says: "There is a disposition in many quarters most manifest to misrepresent us upon the wage question, but it can have no good results. The printed statement of wages received by a stitching room vamper, top stitcher, or other operative, for a few weeks in a year amounts to nothing. You should take the whole fifty-two weeks in order to fairly and truly average an operatives' pay. In a year's time, since I have been at work, there have been many weeks in a year that I have had nothing to do, and I have earned from $3 to $28 per week. . . . At present I have what a stitcher would call a first-rate job, yet I did not earn more than $7 or $8 per week, take the full year through. I costs me $5 a week to live, so you can readily see the margin I have left for dress and luxuries."

The Lady Stitchers' Assembly of the Knights in Lynn included residents of local families and, in even larger numbers, young migrant boarders. The needs of these young, unmarried, geographically mobile workingwomen in the shoe industry inspired their activities in the Knights. James H. Carr, the assembly's secretary, who represented the stitchers during the arbitration proceedings reported in the *Lynn Bee*, April 18, 1888, described its membership.

Mr. Carr addressed the . . . [State Board of Arbitration] upon the different phases of the questions involved. He referred to the different classes of stitchers, such as those girls who have a home to go to, and parents to look out for them; to married women who were ambitious to assist their husbands for which he did not blame them, but they stood in the places of others who needed the work; of the poor widow who was struggling to bring up her children, but by far he was here to speak for that large class of young women who had no homes here, but lived in rooms and who must have work to earn an honest living. He did not believe in cutting down the wages of the operatives and he did not see the necessity for so doing.

Stitchers in Lynn organized their Knights of Labor assembly to represent the interests of women shoeworkers alone, despite criticism from male Knights. Like artisans in the 1840s and the striking shoemakers in 1860, the Knights sought to organize the moral power of *all* "true" women, including wives and daughters not gainfully employed, to aid in the fight against the evils of industrial capitalism. The Lady Knights in Lynn, insisting instead on a female-controlled assembly that operated like a trade union, successfully resisted appeals—such as one appearing in the *Knight of Labor*, May 15, 1886—to admit all women.

In Lynn, the hot-bed of the Massachusetts Knights of Labor, there are already formed thirty-four assemblies, whose membership embraces nearly every branch of industry within the city limits. The opportunity for ladies and misses to become enrolled in our ranks, however, have never received the attention its importance demands. True, the Lady Stitchers' Assembly embraces more than twenty-seven hundred members, and is in a most flourishing condition, but none other than females employed at some branch of boot and shoemaking are admitted to its folds. The lady clerks, dressmakers, milliners, and other industrious women have frequently expressed a desire to be provided for and when D.A. [District Assembly] 77 shall again decide to continue its work of organizing we hope to see a "mixed" assembly for women here in Lynn. The K. of L. order is one that any one can join with propriety, and that every woman, no matter whether or not she be a wage-earner in the strict sense of the term, could be a member of. Our wives and daughters, mothers and sisters, and every true woman who is interested in the well-being of her sex, should avail herself of the protection of the K. of L. The influence that women wield over men could not be better used than by associating it in this great cause.

As the result of successful political lobbying by the Knights of Labor in 1886, a new Massachusetts State Board of Arbitration began to hear cases involving the wage levels of industrial workers. Some of the early disputes concerned the wages and work conditions of shoe stitchers. In their testimony against Samuel F. Crossman in 1887 and Henry C. Mears in 1888, Lynn stitchers explained the craft customs of their work in the shoe shops. They argued for piece rates instead of weekly pay and for control over how the work was distributed during the slack seasons. These arguments revealed the sense of craft status and the ethic of mutual support and self-respect shared by skilled women workers in the New England shoe industry.

The state board supported the Lynn stitchers' position in the Crossman but not in the Mears case. The Crossman hearing was reported in the *Lynn Reporter*, November 18, 1887.

Mr. Crossman presented his case and stated his object to be to make a change in the manner of conducting his business as to payment for work. He was of the opinion that he could get better work done by paying by the week than by paying by the piece. He runs two shops, one in Lynn and one in Beverly. . . . He thought that 4000 button holes of the good grade of shoes and 5000 of the cheap grade a good fair day's work. He made this proposition to his employees: That he would give them $10 per week for ten months, they to work 9-1/2 hours per day. . . .

Lizzie M. Waite, of Salem, was the first witness and testified: Have worked for Mr. Crossman since a year ago last August. He wished to suspend work during the dull season. She thought that six cents a hundred [Crossman's price] for button holes was enough. Had rather work by the piece than for $10 a week. Had never heard any complaint in regard to work. Had heard fault found with the work in regard to the stitching. The Reece [button hole] machine will lengthen its stitch of its own accord. If Mr. Crossman should offer her $10 per week for ten months, or six cents per hundred, she should accept the six cents per hundred.

To Mr. [George] Carr [Crossman's attorney]—she had rather work by the piece, she had worked in other shops . . . she had earned $16 in six days while working for Crossman. Mr. Keene [another shop owner] found a machinist to repair the machines when they break down. Think this is an advantage. Had earned $531 in forty-nine weeks while in the employ of Crossman.

To James F. Carr [secretary of the Lady Stitchers' Assembly in the Knights of Labor]—Mr. Crossman runs a shop in Beverly. When a machine breaks down you have got to wait until it is repaired. . . .

To Mr. Carr—Mr. Crossman is a good man to work for, and so is Mr. Keene. Had rather work by the piece than by the week; if operators work by the piece, when work is dull all get some of it to do, while when they work by the week some will get the work and others will go without. From November 18, 1886 to November 1887, she had, when there was a rush of work, earned $17 per week for seven weeks. . . .

Miss Eliza Merrow testified—Have worked at Mr. Crossman's shop since a year ago last April. . . .

To chairman—Think that 4000 or 5000 button holes per day is an excessive day's work. Think 4000 would be a fair day's work. Had rather work by the piece, because she would feel freer than if she worked by the week. . . .

To Carr—The girls would like to have steady work at 9-1/2 hours per day at present prices.

Emily Glines testified: Have been at work since a year ago last April in the Beverly shop. . . . In Mr. Crossman's Beverly shop, there were stitchers earning $18 per week and getting only $10 for it. Am considered an expert operator and have earned $20 per week. . . . Vamping is better than buttonholing. Can make more on good work than on cheap. . . .

The issue in the Mears case was the price (wage) paid for various grades of stitching work. Lynn manufacturers and stitching subcontractors wanted to cut prices on third-grade—the cheapest—shoes in order to compete with factories elsewhere in New England. A sense of status and power as skilled workers led Lynn stitchers to reject the initial decision by the State Board of Arbitration in the Mears case by threatening to strike all stitching shops until their grievances were heard. Over the protests of the employers, the state board agreed to reopen the case. Yet it both ignored the stitchers' desire to protect high wages on first-grade work and granted Mears a wage cut on third-grade work in order to attract the production of cheap ladies' button boots back to Massachusetts factories. The hearing was reported in the *Lynn Bee*, April 17, 1888.

[Charles T. Harvey, a stitching subcontractor, testified that] . . . grades are determined by the quality of work put into it: the third grade is all cotton [thread]; second grade is silk [thread in the] vamp and silk buttonholes; the first grade is all silk.

To chairman.—The manufacturers require them to do the work upon these grades; the trade demands it; manufacturers indicate by their tags the grade of the work; don't find any manufacturers who want their best work done in cotton; it is the cheapest grades that are done with cotton; think it advisable to have three grades in shop. . . . his girls do best on an average on the third grade; they average about the same on the third as on first when they have all of this grade of work that they can do. . . .

Theresa Quigley—Have worked for Mr. Mears 16 months staying. To Mr. Carr—Get 50 cts for plain boots and 70 cts for Rochester stay. The pay in all the other shops is 5 to 10 cents higher. At present prices could earn $10, which is the highest; have earned as low as $2. Last year averaged $6 to $7 per week. Judges the quality of the boot by the [leather] stock, . . . Mr. Mears' staying is done with both cotton and silk. It is harder work to run cotton than silk, as the cotton breaks frequently. Rather run silk as far as labor is concerned. . . . A majority of Mr. Walden's work is stitched with cotton; Mr. Durgin's with silk, but the price [contrary to the Mears' proposal] is the same. But there is this difference: One stayer on silk and one on cotton; the one would have the best work while the one on cotton would make the best pay [on a greater volume].

Miss Laddy testified that she was a stayer for Mr. Mears. To Mr. Carr—The wages in this shop are all very low. Have worked for Mr. Jennings. The most she ever earned in Mr. Mears' shop was $9 per week, the prices being the same in both shops, but she could earn $12 to $15 a week in Mr. Jennings. The reason was because Mr. Mears' work has to be done better. Mr. Mears offers now 40 cents. It make no difference whether she uses silk or cotton. . . .

Miss M. J. Clark was a vamper and had worked for Mr. Mears five years. To Mr. Carr—Have worked on all kinds of work. Have done plain vamping with one side turned back for 60 cents per case. Have 75 cents where both sides are turned back. . . . Could do 1-1/4 cases per day. This is as good as the average on the 75 cent work. For overlap vamp and pressed vamp the prices are $1, $1.20 and $1.50 but have seen very little of the $1.50 work. . . .

The difference doing the work is that on a $1.50 boot done with silk, you have to shorten the stitch. Do scalloped vamps. The price is $1.80 per case for two rows in the scallop. It is not so easy to run cotton. . . . Don't think it would be well to grade by the quality of material used in stitching, could tell the quality of the best by the [leather] stock that was in it. . . . Can earn at present wages $15 per week, but my wages have been cut down to $6 per week. My [vamping] work is mainly overlaps.

The further mechanization of stitching operations in the 1880s through the development of double-needle attachments for sewing machines and automatic buttonhole devices began to undermine the skill and experience of Lynn stitchers. Nonetheless, commentary published in the *Boston Herald* on July 17, 1888 (and reprinted in the *Boot and Shoe Recorder*, a leading trade journal of the industry, on August 8, 1888), emphasized the good working conditions and social respectability of stitchers in shoe factories and identified them as "genuine American working women." A reputation for good treatment and good wages would attract other young women to the shoe shops and guarantee shoe manufacturers an ample supply of stitchers at the lowest possible wages.

The Shoe Girls of Lynn

. . . Has it ever occurred to you, careless wearer of . . . boots, how many hands every pair went through before they finally reached you? Well at least thirty; . . . and at least half these hands are women's. Women with just the same womanly instincts and desires that you have; women who are, as a rule, self-respecting, and consequently respect compelling; pretty women and plain women, just about the same average as the women of your own set; quick women and slow women, nervous women and stolid women; those who like a solid hold on the world in the shape of a bank account; careless women and provident women—just like many another whom you know. . . .

It would be ever so much better for the world, and for the world's workers of every degree, if the different women knew each other better. . . .

It is probable that the girls engaged in the industry in this special town may be a fair example of the girls in the same branch of work elsewhere. But it must be confessed at the outset that the girls seen by a visit to the "city of shoes" represent a fine claim on the genuine

A SHOE STITCHER.

A shoe stitcher. From "The Shoe Girls of Lynn," *Boot and Shoe Recorder*, August 8, 1888. Courtesy of Lynn Public Library.

American working women. Take, for instance, this large room, occupying the entire floor of one of the largest, manufactories in the place. There are nearly 200 women at work there, each one with her own appointed task. You certainly never saw a better assemblage of women anywhere. There is nowhere any trace of the sordid appearance that labor is supposed to give. Glance up and down the long line of faces and see what you will find. That woman in black, nearing the middle age, with a refined face framed in bands of golden hair, through which a silver thread strays in and out, might be the wife of a New England clergyman. She has the face and manner and the fine poise that one sees in the women of that class, and one is not disappointed when she speaks to her nearest neighbor to hear a low, cultivated, well modulated voice. Generations of fine breeding must have made her what she is, and neither you nor I would be surprised to learn that she bears a name that was known and respected in colony times, long before we lived under King George and insisted upon breaking away from his stubborn, tyrannical rule. The woman who is taking us about and showing us the different steps of the work might be the principal of a girls' school. She is dignified in manner and carriage; she has a rare intelligence, and will talk with you about the latest book, the outlook of the country's future, and discuss political economy with a keenness that shows she has studied the situation. . . . That girl over there with the alert bright face and the eyeglasses might be a successful newspaper girl. She has the eyes to see affairs, and evidently the mind to appreciate; and if we may judge from the quiet laugh of the girl beside her at something she is saying, the faculty of telling things snappily and well. The lovely girl beyond her, with seashell complexion, dimples playing hide and seek about the rosiest mouth that Cupid ever kissed, and pale brown hair afluff above mischievous brown eyes, would compare madame of Commonwealth avenue, in beauty and grace with your petted girl. . . . That woman there, with rapidly graying hair and a face in which the gravity of middle life has replaced the freshness of youth, and who has worked 20 years for the house which still employs her, might be the house mother in any comfortable country home. The woman sitting next her, who is of the same age and circumstances, might be a neighbor. On every side of you you see the various types of American womanhood, all with earnest faces, and with busy fingers working out for themselves the problem of living. Where do they come from, this army of women? Well, they come from homes all over New England.

Some of them are Lynn girls, living in the shelter and protection of their own homes, the others come from adjoining towns or from the villages and farms of Maine, Vermont, New Hampshire and northern Massachusetts. The large industry of Lynn attracts them, as years ago the factories of Lowell attracted the same class of women and girls. There are probably no manufactories of any kind that in spirit and in verity come so near to the factory days of Lucy Larcom and Harriette Robinson, and the women of that time as certain of the shoe shops of Lynn. . . .

Does it interest you to know how these girls live? Well, very much as other girls do, probably; those who have homes in the city or near it live at these homes, under the protection of their fathers and mothers. . . . There is no "corporation boarding house," as there is usually connected with factories, and each girl chooses her own home. Some are married, their husbands working either in the same shop or at some other employment . . . ; some are women with children who must be cared for; the father has died, and the mother is left to make the fight single-handed not only for herself, but for others dependent on her. Many of these have relations who are glad to keep house for them for the sake of the home which the mother's busy fingers make. Most of the girls take rooms, for which they pay from $1.50 to $3 a week, then board either in some family or at a boarding house, paying on a average $2 or $2.50 a week for board. . . .

As you look at the girls out for their dinner hour, or going home after the day's work is over, you would not associate them with "the shop." Prettily dressed, with the last notion of hairdressing, the latest caprice in the way of wearing their dresses, you would regard them as you do the girls you meet every day in the homes which you visit. . . .

. . . From another establishment that you pass on your way up town comes out a group of girls. In front of them are two others, who have just come out from the counting room. They are the daughter of the proprietor and a friend. You cannot see that they are more ladylike in appearance or behavior, or more fittingly dressed for the street, than the girls in the other group, who are the employes of the house. . . . Girl of leisure and working girl, as they stand side by side, it would puzzle you to tell which was the one and which the other. . . . among all the long list of working women you will find none better circumstanced, more content, more physically strong and attractive, better cared for or more generously dealt with than the shoe girls of Lynn.

Thirteen Lynn stitchers took the train to Boston to inform the editor of the *Boston Herald* that the circumstances of their employment had been distorted in "The Shoe Girls of Lynn." They wanted to make public the grim reality of their working lives and to prevent inexperienced young women from contributing to an already overcrowded labor market in Lynn. The *Herald* editor published his impressions of this contingent on July 29, 1888.

> . . . if these thirteen ladies were representatives of their class of Lynn shoe girls, they certainly bore out the description already given in the *Herald* of them, for they were well and tastefully dressed, ladylike in bearing and demeanor, and their conversation evinced an intelligence and refinement that would do credit to the best of their sex.
>
> . . . They showed their intelligent appreciation of the subject by pointing out the embarrassment which might occur in the event of large numbers of young women being attracted to Lynn with the expectation of earning high wages, when in reality they could only hope for the barest subsistence, and at that would be taking the work from the hands of those who already had too little to do for their own comfort and hope of independence.
>
> . . . There are now said to be 180 manufacturing rooms and 300 stitching rooms [shops] in Lynn, each employing 150 to 200 girls.
>
> ["] . . . A great deal of my time [said one stitcher] has been spent among the poor girls of Lynn connected with the shoe industry, and I know that their lot is not to be envied. Often, after getting a few weeks' pay, they are thrown out on to the world, and all the winter and spring there is any amount of poverty among them. Many at these times have to live on bread and water in order to get along. There is a large class in Lynn of these homeless girls, who, for a great part of the time, undergo such hardships as I have described. . . . Some of them drift off to Boston, which is already overstocked with the unemployed of their class. I say I have had to do with these girls, and I have had them come to me a dozen times in the week for help or advice, telling me they had no money to pay for their room or to pay for food or for a nurse or for medicine. . . . I should say that one third of the girls of Lynn are homeless and subject to these changes of fortune. . . .["]

Women in the Knights of Labor in Lynn who conducted strikes against their employers came to appreciate the potential of woman suffrage in municipal elections, especially if they could influence the behavior of the police force. A female member of the Knights expressed these sentiments in a letter to the editor of the *Knight of Labor*, November 21, 1885.

> I wish I was privileged to cast a vote for those men who are to control the destiny of Lynn for the coming municipal year. If I was thus favored, I would not vote for any man for Mayor who would not openly announce his determination to "rake out" the police department and drop at least one half of the miserable timber found there . . . but particularly would I like to see that old and useless ornament, Captain Thurston—a man long past his usefulness—removed. . . . Let those having the power to elect, have a care this year who they nominate, for with a good strong candidate at the head of the workingman's ticket, backed up with a strong board of aldermen, and clean council nominees, labor can easily win the day. However, I say boys, select the best men nominated and elect them.
>
> Daughter of Labor

Another woman reacted angrily in the *Knight of Labor*, January 2, 1886, to women's lack of political influence in municipal politics.

> *Mr. Editor:* To the shame of the present municipal administration, placed in power by workingmen, a man is now retained in a high position on the police force who did all that was in his power to injure the cause of the poor striking shop girls in the Doak lock-out; who went so far as to rudely seize several of them by the shoulders and push them with his burly form against the wall of the factory. It is a well known fact that this man's sympathy is with the manufacturers, but it is argued that he is an old veteran and must be retained. Away with such an excuse. It is fight for bread and life with the shop girls of Lynn, and no enemy of theirs should be allowed to remain in a position where he can do them injury. If the male organization have not members who are gallant enough to take up the cause of their sisters and see that this old veteran sympathizer of the manufacturers is removed and placed where he can do no more harm to working girls, then let the daughters assembly, K. of L. rise to the emergency and see what they can do. Let them teach old men as well as young, that if they would be policemen, they must treat Lynn working girls respectfully.
>
> Closer-On

Lady Knights discovered that the political power wielded by men of the local Knights' assemblies did not protect their interests as women. For example, because of the personal objection of one politician, the Workingmen's Party (a coalition of Knights and middle-class reformers) in 1885 refused to include on its ticket any of the women nominees eligible for the Lynn School Committee.

Lady Knights faced another problem of underrepresentation within the structure of the Knights of Labor arbitration procedures. No stitchers sat on the Knights' board of arbitration in Lynn, which negotiated wages with the shoe manufacturers. Shoe stitchers were therefore unable to bargain directly for the wage list on stitching in early 1886. Dissatisfied, they rejected the list. The Lynn editor of the *Knight of Labor* tried on February 27, 1886, to persuade them to be patient.

> . . . The new schedule of prices to govern the upper stitching in the Lynn factories from the six months from March 1 to October 1, 1886, as printed in last week's *Knight of Labor*, does not appear to be giving entire satisfaction. This, perhaps, is quite natural when the various grades of works included, and the perplexing number of parts is taken into consideration. The board of arbitration labored long and faithfully in the arrangement of the list, and if some discrepancies are discovered it is not at all to be wondered at. By the new list many portions of stitching have been advanced from 10 to 20 per cent., while, may be, an equally large per cent. of those affected by the change have been slightly reduced. Naturally the faultfinders in the employes' ranks are those who have suffered a reduction by the new order of things, and they are questioning the results attained by the board, claiming as they do, that they have simply "taken from one pocket and given to another." This is not so. The joint board of arbitration have accomplished what they desired, viz., established a uniform list of prices throughout the city. . . . After the new list has been thoroughly tested its defects will appear, and by the time of its expiration it can be arranged by the Stitchers' Union to demand an increase, which, of course, can be far more easily attained than if a hundred different prices were being paid in as many different stitching rooms. Give the new system a fair trial, girls.

The lady stitchers refused, however, and insisted that the list be changed. Very reluctantly but under great pressure, the Knights re-opened negotiations to satisfy the stitchers. Lady Knights continued to push for direct and formal representation of stitchers' interests in local arbitration procedures.

Women shoeworkers were very active at the national conventions of the Knights of Labor to ensure better representation for workingwomen throughout the organization. Forty percent of the female delegates to the important Richmond General Assembly of the Knights of Labor in 1886 were shoe stitchers from Philadelphia, New York, and Massachusetts. Forming a coalition with female textile and garment workers, they persuaded the assembly to authorize a Woman's Department to investigate the condition of women workers. The women at Richmond also sponsored resolutions that endorsed cooperation with temperance organizations and supported woman suffrage. These resolutions, recorded in the Knights of Labor, *Proceedings of the General Assembly* (Richmond, 1886), on page 287, represented the highest point of political activity by female industrial workers in the Knights of Labor.

Report of Committee on Woman's Work.

To the General Master Workman and Members of the General Assembly:

. . . Acting upon the privilege accorded to the committee by the General Assembly, we have formed a permanent organization, the object of which will be to investigate the abuses to which our sex is subjected by unscrupulous employers—to agitate the principles which our Order teaches of equal pay for equal work and the abolition of child-labor. . . . The officers elected are as follows: Mary Hanafin, President [former shoe stitcher of Philadelphia]; Mary O'Reilly, Vice President; Nellie Hardison [shoe stitcher from Lynn], Treasurer; and we recommend that Leonora Barry [hosiery worker from New York] be elected as General Investigator . . . who shall devote all her time to the work. . . . The expenses of the members of the committee . . . [and the] salary and expenses of the General Investigator shall . . . be paid by the General Assembly. . . .

After three years of strenuous effort as full-time director, however, Leonora Barry had become so discouraged by the difficulties of organizing women industrial workers that in 1889 she recommended the dissolution of the Woman's Department. One of the greatest illusions of women workers, she believed, was the prospect of marriage as a solution to their economic needs. Despite the successes of the assemblies of Lady Knights in Essex County and in Philadelphia, Barry concluded that female-controlled organizations were ineffective. Sisterhood as a principle of labor protest disappeared from the Knights of Labor. Barry's report is excerpted from pages 1–2 and 5–6 of Knights of Labor, *Proceedings of the General Assembly, 1889.*

Report of the General Instructor and Director of Woman's Work

To the Officers and Members of the General Assembly:

. . . Brothers and sisters in this work, for three years I have labored for and among you with such ability as I possessed, with what success I constitute you my judges. My work has not been confined solely to women and children, but to all of earth's toilers, as I am of the opinion that the time when we could separate the interests of the toiling masses on sex lines is past. . . . The many and varied channels of industry into which woman has either forced her way or has been forced . . . has opened a line of competition and strife, greater even among the ranks of women-workers than among men, and in which women suffer much more than men. . . . because she is a woman her natural pride and timidity, coupled with the restrictions of social customs, deter her from making that struggle that can be made by men. Second, because there is such a lack of industrial training among our girls, which throws upon the labor market an army of incompetent women who are compelled to work, but who have little or no practical knowledge of any particular trade. . . . If it were possible, I wish that it were not necessary for women to learn any trade, but that of domestic duties, as I believe it was intended that man should be the bread-winner. . . . Every effort has been made to perfect and extend the organization of women, but our efforts have not met with the response that the cause deserves— partly because those who have steady employment, fairly good wages and comfortable homes seem to see nothing in organization outside of self interest and . . . do not feel it incumbent upon themselves to do anything to assist their less fortunate co-workers. . . . a prevailing cause . . . is the hope and expectancy that in the near future marriage will lift them out of the industrial life to the quiet and comfort of a home, foolishly imagining that with marriage their connection with and interest in labor matters end; often finding, however, that their struggle has only begun when they have to go back to the shop and work for two instead of one. . . .

. . . A few words about the Woman's Department. When I took a position at its head I fondly hoped to weld together in organization such a number of women as would be a power for good in the present . . . I was too sanguine . . . and I believe now we should, instead of supporting the Woman's Department, put more women in the field as Lecturers to tell women why they should organize as a part of the industrial hive, rather than because they are women. There can be no separation or distinction of wage-workers on account of sex, and separate departments for their interests is a direct contradiction of this, and also of that part of our declaration which says "we know no sex in the laws of Knighthood." Therefore I recommend the abolition of the Woman's Department . . . thereby making it incumbent upon all to work more earnestly for the general good, rather than for sex, Assembly or trade.

I am willing to serve this Order in any capacity . . . but I cannot stand at the head of something that—owing to the failure of the women to organize more thoroughly—does not exist except in name. . . .

L. M. Barry

Shortly after the Richmond convention, the stitchers of Essex County left the Knights of Labor for a national trade assembly composed entirely of shoeworkers. In this association, organized in 1887, women workers finally obtained formal and direct representation in arbitration proceedings, a concession which, as reported in the *Boston Herald*, June 10, 1887, meant that their voices would be heard in the new organization.

In case the trouble is in an assembly which is made up of female operatives, the local assembly will choose one of the females [rather than the master workman] who will confer with the master workman of the national assembly, and who will have the same position as the member of the executive board from the state in which the trouble had taken place would have, as that member will not be called upon.

[14]

Trade Union Women

Efforts after 1886 by shoeworkers in the Northeast to establish trade unions quickly drew shoe stitchers into these new organizations. In 1891, the stitchers of Haverhill formed a local of the new International Boot and Shoe Workers' Union, an affiliate of the American Federation of Labor. Led by Mary A. Nason, a self-supporting stitcher from Maine, the Haverhill Lady Stitchers' Union heard addresses by Samuel Gompers, president of the AFL; Martha Moore Avery of the Socialist Labor Party; and Mary Kenney of Chicago, the first female organizer for the AFL. A report on the Kenney speech and its reception appeared in the *Haverhill Bulletin*, October 1, 1892.

The announcement that Mrs. Mary Kennedy [*sic*] of Chicago would speak in the Stitchers' Headquarters last evening called out a very appreciative audience of machine operatives and others who listened very attentively to the speaker. . . .

The president [Mary A. Nason] then introduced Miss Mary Kenny [*sic*] who spoke with much earnestness of the benefits of organization and gave an account of her experiences as an organizer and the importance of union and persistent work in order to accomplish the purpose of organization. She graphically described a strike in Chicago against a reduction—the strike lasted 3 months. Finally the firm yielded to the workmen and workwomen.

The reason given by some women for not joining the union is that they do not expect to work long, but expect to be married when they will leave the shop or factory. This is not the way to do [she argued],

A stitching room in Haverhill, c. 1890. Courtesy of Haverhill Public Library.

join the union and by doing so you will help others. In conclusion, the speaker advised the members of the union to work with those who do not belong to the organization and induce them to join. . . .

The meeting was very enthusiastic.

Once established in Haverhill, the International Boot and Shoe Workers' Union conducted an important strike in 1895 which resulted in the formation of a new national federation of shoeworkers, the Boot and Shoe Workers' Union (BSWU), which included members of the Socialist Labor Party and the Knights of Labor assemblies in Lynn. During this strike, reported in the *Haverhill Gazette*, January 23 and February 4, 1895, many young women stitchers experienced for the first time the compelling necessity of collective action to protect their interests as workers.

At Chick's factory there are many girls who make only $3 and $4 a week. A vamper gets only 35 cents for vamping 60 pairs of boots. Overlaps are paid at the rate of 55 cents for 60 pairs in the Chick factory. Formerly the price in this factory was 65 cents, but this kind of work was cut down along with other kinds of work to the present price. This is work requiring expert skill, and if any of the work is not done according to rule, the work is thrown back on the hands of the operatives, and if spoiled they have to pay for it.

To the Editor of the Gazette:

So much has been said about the manufacturers being willing to treat with their help individually that perhaps an instance of individual treatment of the wage question may be of interest. Last June in the stitching room in which I was at work a cut-down was proposed. I knew that the price paid was less than was paid for similar work in other factories and remonstrated, and was assured by the superintendent that my employer was willing to pay what others did. I at once secured the figures from two other factories and proved that they were paying from 20 to 100 per cent more than we were getting, presenting the figures to the superintendent. The result was only that the cut was prevented, but the promise made to me that the wages should be the same as in other factories was forgotten. It was at the end of the sales. I, as an individual, was at the mercy of the manufacturer and was forced to continue to work at low wages, until as a crew, backed by the union, we struck. The plea of individual agreement sounds well, but the individual is always offered Hobson's choice: "Accept my proposition or get out."

A Striker

The stitchers, many of them either self-supporting or female heads of

Chick Brothers' shoe factory, c. 1895, Haverhill. Courtesy of Haverhill Public Library.

families, organized regional support for the Haverhill strike, most successfully among the stitchers of Lynn. These gender-conscious activities introduced the principle of sisterhood, developed by the DOSC and the Lady Knights of Labor, into trade unionism. The *Boston Globe,* January 18, 1895, reported this cooperation.

. . . The sex could hardly be a factor of so much consideration in any strike outside a boot and shoe community. The women are almost all stitchers. . . .

If the employers would fill the ranks of the strikers they must import women, which is a much more difficult matter than to import men.

Factory women, like all their sisters, have the domestic instinct, which leads them to establish themselves and make some kind of a home wherever they work, and they are not inclined to break up these homes and move so readily or for such small inducements as men. . . .

The secretary of one of the women's [shop crew] organizations . . . said . . . : "I can't tell what we shall do if we come to actual destitution. I don't think there is a girl among the strikers who would give in under such circumstances, because she lacked the personal courage, but you know that many of us have parents or other relatives solely dependent on us, and we might not have the heart to see them suffer."

The ladies stitchers' union—apologies are made for "ladies" by its officers who put up with the term in deference to the wishes of some of the pretty girl operatives—then [in 1892] numbered only 28 and the members had hard work to keep the organization alive during the past three years. . . .

Many of the striking girls make their homes in lodging houses. . . . Not a few of them are daughters of farmers who live over the New Hampshire line, and can go home if matters grow worse.

Of this number [150] there were only two [in the shop crew] who appeared to be more than 40 years old. All except a small percentage were probably under 25. . . . Indeed the strike seems to be a movement on the part of young women. The president's chair was occupied by a girl who could not have been much more than 20, and the secretary was not much older. . . . The "shop's crew" meeting offer one diversion. These gatherings are always incidental to a strike whenever there is good organization. . . . They all addressed each other as "sisters," and referred to the different crews as "the Chick Bros," "the Winchells, no. 1," etc. . . . Miss Mary Nason, who is at the head of the Haverhill working women, is the center of advice and information. Miss Nason is a socialist and a friend of Martha Moore Avery. She was one of the first strikers, but being an accomplished worker, she secured employment with only a few days idleness.

Crucial to the effectiveness of sisterhood in the Haverhill strike was the stitchers' ability to count on the refusal of workingwomen in other cities, especially Lynn, to stitch shoes for Haverhill manufacturers. One

Stitching room at the Durgin shoe factory, Haverhill, c. 1892. Courtesy of Baker Library, Harvard Business School.

Lynn stitcher underscored the importance of gender solidarity in the *Lynn Item*, January 15, 1895.

> Messrs. Editors:—I must take the liberty to say what I think of the Lynn girls that are doing the Haverhill work. I think they are mean cowards. They cannot come to me and say "We don't know where the work comes from," for they all know it. . . . All know they are scabbing, and that if they do it[,] it is a disgrace. . . .

Shoeworkers leaving a Lynn factory, 1895. Photograph by Frances Benjamin Johnson. Courtesy of Library of Congress.

Don't you see that they [the Haverhill manufacturers] can't do anything if you don't help them[?] . . . Do you want to stop the stitchers in Haverhill from gaining their strike?

Don't you see that you are killing the prices in Lynn? . . . I wish I could put some of my principles into you. . . . Now girls, stop doing that work. It is not possible that you have fathers or brothers, or they would stop you, I am sure.

We girls work for a contractor, and if any of that work should come in our stitching room we would make short work of it, but there is no fear of having any. We work for a man.

A Lynn Vamper

Membership in the Lynn stitchers' assembly increased by 700 during the 1895 strike in Haverhill. Lynn stitchers held meetings to protest the presence of Haverhill work that showed up in Lynn shops and threatened to strike any local shop where such goods were handled. They also refused to accept tempting offers of work as strikebreakers, according to the *Lynn Item* of January 18, 1895.

The Haverhill manufacturers, whose employees are now on strike against the contract labor system in that city, are making desperate efforts to secure help elsewhere in order to fill the strikers' places. An agent for a leading Haverhill shoe firm has been in Lynn this week straining every nerve to hire help to be sent there. After a few days peregrinating around the city he succeeded in hiring quarters on Munroe street, where he hung out a shingle "closers-on and turners wanted."

As might be expected he had a large number of applicants and everything went along smoothly until he announced to the unsuspecting seekers after employment that he required them to go to Haverhill and take the places of stitchers there. . . .

He offered good wages and all expenses paid to Haverhill, to any who would engage to go there. Some lady stitchers, whose husbands are at present working in the Thomson-Houston [electric] factories in West Lynn, were offered positions in the Haverhill stitching rooms, and also told that their husbands would be given jobs in the making rooms there. . . .

The man did not succeed in hiring anyone, as far as known, as most of the applicants declined to accept his liberal terms, as soon as they found out they were wanted to take the strikers places. . . .

The labor leaders are very busy these days looking after the stitching rooms where they have a suspicion of Haverhill work being done. One of them said today, that, although it was hard to detect Haverhill work being done in Lynn, as it was being sent here from other towns and cities in different names, nevertheless he was of the opinion that no Haverhill work was being done in this city at present. . . .

A Lynn vamper, 1895. Photograph by Frances Benjamin Johnson. Courtesy of Library of Congress.

In addition to organizing regional support among shoe stitchers, the Haverhill strike committee in 1895 developed cross-class ties with reform-minded Frances Willard, president of the Woman's Christian Temperance Union. Willard and her companions, Lady Henry Somerset and Amy Hicks, prominent in the English temperance and labor movements, came to Haverhill. Their presence gave the women strikers the support and moral respectability of politically active and socially prominent women. The *Haverhill Gazette*, January 2, 1895, described a large public gathering on the night of January 1 following a successful march led by striking shoe stitchers. Female speakers argued that womanhood must take on new meanings for women workers: strength, courage, determination, and independence of mind.

Miss Frances Willard was applauded when she stepped forward. She said:

Dear Brothers and Sisters: I come tonight from Boston to pay the tribute of good-will and sympathy for those who are standing up for their rights. I thank God that you had the grit and grace and gumption to help yourselves. . . .

When I was invited this morning to speak to you, I said I did not believe I quite dared to. But I lifted up my heart to God, and as I gazed at a picture of my mother for advice, there came a tender voice which said: "My daughter, go to Haverhill. Tell them that as they are, so are you. Give them an elder sister's blessing." So I came, with hope in my heart that sometime it may be written that the women of Haverhill, aided by the men, set God's great ball rolling for a wider outlook for the honest, holy sons of toil. . . .

Lady Henry Somerset was given a hearty greeting. She declared that the labor question must spread the world over. . . .

A wider freedom is coming to the women of America than has ever been dreamed of. The power to resist our great enemy of capital must come from the women as well as from the men. It is just as foolish for women not to organize as it is for them to confine their efforts to the four walls of their own homes. . . .

Mrs. Hicks said: As today is the beginning of a new year, so this is the beginning of a new era. Today we see it is woman who holds the fort. Around them must centre the interests and welfare of the men. You are standing in the full pride of your womanhood in defense of the right to live. . . .

. . . Too long has it been held that woman has no right to enter these movements. So much the worse for the movements. Politics is the place for woman. We don't want a woman placed on a pedestal while thousands are living a life not worth living. I appeal to you to remain true to the cause you have entered upon . . .

Mar[y] E. [*sic*] Nason, the local leader of the women, was applauded loudly as she was introduced. She said:

I told you yesterday was the proudest day of my life because I regained faith in the women. The events of yesterday raised the women of Haverhill 100 per cent, not only in my estimation, but in the estimation of everybody on earth. This struggle is of vital importance. . . . You will meet with discouragement, but you are right and you are sure to win. Will any one say it is not respectable for women to organize after listening to these advocates? . . .

Miss Willard was introduced for closing words, and said, . . . : If you will make a "ring around rosy" you can be the solid nucleus of that which will give justice to the manhood that is under the lash in Haverhill as you are. There is nothing attractive about weakness in either man or woman. Men need women with a mind of [their] own.

It is only by being independent and good and brave that you can achieve what you want. The thought of my heart is that out of these organizations will come a pure, a white life for two. . . . As you have breathed and rejoiced so have I. All humanity is mine and mine is yours. May God bless this labor movement, and may every good man and woman help with hand and purse and prayer.

"I am surprised at the appearance of these young women," declared Lady Somerset, after the meeting. "They are well dressed, some of them elegantly, and their conduct is a credit to them. In my country young women of their station and occupation spend their money in saloons, and they do not compare with these in looks and bearing."

Frank Foster, editor of the Massachusetts AFL publication, *Labor Leader*, pointed up the new qualities of womanly strength and determination in his celebratory poem "The Union Girls of Haverhill," published on January 26, 1895. He invoked as inspiration to Yankee women the heroic females Barbara Frietchie and Grace Darling.

> . . . The "newer woman," no longer suppliant[,] meek—
> The moment's fancy or the hour's delight—

But full equipped, abreast with those who seek
 For those who toil the measure of their right.

Pentucket's streets have seen their columns march,
 Through storm and sleet, upon the entrenched foe—
What though above them towered no triumph arch
 The foul injunction armed to lay them low?

Barbara Freitches [*sic*] here fast held the UNION flag.
 Grace Darlings braved the fierce industrial sea;
Their firm demand. "Take off the contract gag,
 For union stitchers must and shall be free!"

One indication of feminist concerns during the 1895 strike was the demand of the Haverhill stitchers, published in the *Boston Advertiser*, January 15, 1895, for equal pay with a tiny number of men who stitched uppers in factories but routinely received higher piece rates. Women workers also criticized as a threat to self-supporting women the presence in the stitching rooms of married women whose wages went to their families.

 Miss Mary E. [*sic*] Nason, the leader of the Haverhill women . . . : "What we demand," she said, "is equal pay and equal hours for both sexes. We believe in the changing of the school age to 18 years, and we demand legislation that will prohibit married women from working in competition with [their] sisters. Against the contract system [used by Haverhill shoe bosses to prevent unions] we will struggle till death or victory rewards us. . . ."

During the depression years of the 1890s, the issue of marital status continued to divide women workers. Haverhill strikers who discussed the pitfalls of marriage also advocated equal treatment of men and women, in costs as well as wages. The union's proposal to charge 50 cents for men and 20 cents for women as the admission fee to benefits held to support the strike became part of a discussion reported in the *Boston Herald*, January 21, 1895.

 " . . . I've always said I'd never get married," said one member of a group discussing the matter at the stitchers' headquarters, and who had evidently been true to her determination. "No, never till I can see my way clear to a better home than I have now, and one I wouldn't be compelled to leave. I always say when one's got all she can do to support herself, there's not much fun in taking another to support. I've seen too much of that."

"You must remember the women here have to work whether they are married or not," put in another. "I have to do it."

"And do you suppose I would work if my husband could earn enough to support me?" put in another. "Well, I guess not. I like home too much for that. . . ."

"That isn't right," was the indignant retort. "I don't see why they want to charge less [for admission to strike benefits] for women than for men. Why don't they make it the same for both? We can pay as much as they can."

"Yes," put in another, "if we ever intend to become independent and get equal rights, we might as well begin right away."

As the strike continued for several months, the Haverhill stitchers changed their name from the old Knights of Labor Lady Stitchers' Union to the Women Stitchers' Union, a move supported by Mary Nason to emphasize their class position as factory workers. Stitchers found, however, that their new militancy in the strike, judged by their employers to be unladylike conduct, won them rougher treatment. The *Haverhill Gazette*, January 22, 1895, reported one example.

About 80 of the women stitchers went to the factory of the Gale Shoe Co., yesterday afternoon to present their [work] coupons and to get things they had left behind at the time of the strike, and were not a little angered at the treatment they received.

According to their statement, Mr. Herbert Gale refused to allow them to go up stairs to get their things saying that they would be "thrown out the window" to them, and also ordered them to get out of the factory quickly or he would "kick the whole crowd out."

One serious risk to workingwomen was that abandoning ladylike conduct might provoke public suspicion regarding the sexual morality of migrant female workers. In an unfortunate and much publicized statement during the Haverhill strike, T. T. Pomeroy, the leader of the strike committee, unwisely linked the low wages paid to female shoeworkers during the depression years with the causes of prostitution. By stating further that on Merrimack Street, the main thoroughfare of Haverhill, 300 women were living in rooms "paid for by men," he implied that low wages for stitching had driven these women to sin. The sensationalized reaction to Pomeroy's statement in the New England press illustrated the recurrent problem of moral respectability for female industrial workers, especially for stitchers who had left their homes and families to live and work in shoe cities. Community sympathizers and the striking women themselves defended their moral reputations in the *Haverhill Gazette*, January 21 and 23, 1895.

> The story of the curse of low wages told in the *Boston Herald* . . . has stirred up a considerable tempest. . . . there were many facts in the article, but at the same time it is to be remembered that the great majority of the female operatives of Haverhill are pure girls.
>
> The facts in the case are uncomfortable ones to face, and yet so far from being a disgrace to the working women of Haverhill, it is an honor to the 2500 and over who fill the stitching and packing rooms that, in spite of the low wages, which do not appear to be denied, the widest statement is that 300 have yielded to temptation. . . .
>
> Chairman [Oliver] Hubbard of the overseers of the poor, thought that nowhere could a better class of girls be found than those employed in the shoe shops. The girls are not one-half as bad as the men who talk about them, and while a few have gone astray, that has always been due to some man.
>
> Rev. Calvin M. Clarke [of the Centre Congregational Church] said: "The women of this town are more free from sin than those of any city of its size in the world. I know personally of no girls living in sin. The girls are above the average of girls who are compelled to work. They are careful of the company they keep and of how they show themselves on the street. They are from strict Presbyterian or Congregational homes, as a rule, and are carefully trained to live in the right way. I am surprised that a paper should attack them. As to the Irish girls, although I do not come in contact with them through my pastoral duties, I know their type well, for in the days before I went into the ministry I saw a great deal of them in connection with the business that I was then engaged in, and I can say that they are a pure set of girls. While they may show themselves on the street in large numbers on Saturday nights, that is not a sign of their immorality, but merely indicates, as

with all the other nationalities, that they are in search of relaxation and do not have to get up early the next morning. . . ."

Rev. Fr. O'Doherty [of St. Joseph's Church] said: "We have only five young ladies living on Merrimack street. I can vouch for the moral standing of each of these. I have 450 young ladies in my Sodality. More than 250 of that number have been members for 16 years, and the others, who have joined since, have come in like the first, as soon as they have reached their 15th year. I have not had one expelled on account of immorality. I would have known had there been. As to the charge that has been made that on Merrimack street between the bridge and Railroad square there are living 300 girls in rooms, the rent of which is paid by men, there is no truth in it. . . . As to the good character of our shoe employees, for the men are as good as the women, I think the best thing I can say is to call to your attention the fact that where else could you see a strike last over three weeks and not a striker arrested in that time? . . ."

. . . James F. Carey . . . apparently voiced the union sentiment.

"I think," said he, "that there are men on our side who feel so strongly on this matter and who want to drive it home to the public, which they know can only be awakened from its lethargy by something startling, that they exaggerate in making their statements. But I contend that low wages are unquestionably conducive to immorality, and that if even only a single girl is driven to sell her virtue by low wages it is the duty of every fair-minded man to demand that the wages be high enough to prevent the recurrence of such a case. . . . .

"Under these circumstances, I think that it is greatly to the credit of our girls that, in the face of all they have to bear, they remain virtuous."

To the Editor of the Gazette:

Dear Sir—Will you kindly allow me a little space in your paper to express my sentiments as regarding the character of the working girls and to publicly thank Chairman Hubbard, Rev. C. M. Clark and Fr. O'Doherty and the others that spoke so nobly in our defense morally? While we do have a hard time to live, dress well and pay our bills unless we get good wages, still I think it very cruel and unjust to assert that so many live in such ways. Now the one that knew 300 girls that had their expenses paid by men—God forgive me if I judge him wrong—but he must be either a philanthropist or a busybody, in my mind, to know so much of the private affairs of 300 girls. I hope he is the former, and any

"Labor" man that asserts such things is but injuring his own cause, for surely a man that can support himself and a separate home for a mistress could surely support a wife, for it does not seem to refer to wealthy men as providing for them. Now the women came out [on strike] to help the men. This has been said repeatedly, and they have tramped through mud and snow to help in this cause, so, shoemakers, I appeal to you one and all, don't let their fair fame be tarnished. If you know of some that cannot see how they live on such small wages give them the benefit of the doubt and "cast not the stone," rather pay a compliment to a woman's wit for living on such small wages and soundly denounce a system that obliges them to wear out their wits for such an end. I can tell you a few instances as examples.

One girl hired a room on Merrimack street, for six months in the year she made from $7 to $8.50 [per week], the other six she made from $2 to $5 and she did thus, took her dinners at the 5 cents dining room, having in the good season a 20-cent dinner, tea or coffee included, in the dull time a 10 or 15-cent dinner, dispensing with the warm cup of drink and got her other meals at her room, costing less than $2 per week, and she always looked neat and happy; then, another on the same street, helped out her day's wages by sewing nights. Another did writing evenings, and another that earned small wages had a small, cheap room, and to avoid the expense of heating it used to go out every evening to meeting or to the reading room, and sometimes to call on a more fortunate friend. All this is very unhealthful, and I think should touch the heart of the public as much and more than tales of immorality, though of course, there are those that fall from paths of virtue among the poor, but among the rich also. Now, sisters, stand firm for the right and we will win. Brothers, be united for your rights and brave in defending those of your wives, daughters, sisters and sweethearts.

L. C. Bell

Support from upper-class and reform-minded women in Boston reinforced the moral respectability of the striking women of Haverhill. With the help of AFL labor activist Mary Kenney O'Sullivan, temperance leader Frances Willard, Massachusetts factory inspector Mrs. Charles G. Ames, Josephine Shaw Lowell of the New York Consumers' League, and others interested in the trade union movement, the Haverhill stitchers were able to raise money for their strike fund from contacts with upper-class Yankee men and women in Boston's Back Bay. A cross-class sisterhood proved important to organizing the kind of public support cited in the *Haverhill Gazette*, January 26, 1895, and the *Boston Globe*, February 16, 1895.

> . . . Within the past few days Miss Nason has been called upon to address private meetings of wealthy and influential people on the Back Bay, and in nearly every instance at the conclusion of her remarks the people addressed have placed checks for handsome amounts in her hands, the money to be given to the women on strike.

> Another meeting of the wealthy citizens of Boston interested in the settlement of the Haverhill strike took place last evening at the residence of Miss Annette Rogers, 5 Joy Street [Beacon Hill].
> The meeting was attended by between 30 and 40 persons, about evenly divided between men and women. . . .
> A rule adopted at the first meeting a week ago, not to give out a word of information to the press, was rigidly adhered to last night, although one man who was present stated positively that no representatives of the strikers were present. . . .
> It is said that the sentiment of the women, which was quite freely expressed, was not of a particularly compromising spirit, and was inclined to be more strongly in the support of the strikers than some of the men were willing to consider.

The Haverhill stitchers' insistence on equal treatment as union members and equal pay for equal work inspired the efforts of Mary Nason, after the 1895 strike ended, to organize all stitchers in the new BSWU federation into autonomous women's locals. As one of the first women to sit on the general executive board of a trade union federation, she represented the interests of her sister workers in the BSWU. A June 1896 announcement (published on page 4 of the *Monthly Reports*, April 1895–June 1899) which centralized important policy decisions in the hands of Massachusetts members of the board, enhanced her position as the only female member.

> No strike or lock-out shall be declared without the consent of the General Executive Board which has authorized the three General Officers, John F. Tobin, Horace A. Eaton, and A. Charles Howe and

MRS. MARY E. NASON,
Secretary Ladies' Stitchers' Union.

Mrs. Mary A. Nason, Secretary, Ladies' Stitchers' Union, Haverhill. From *Boston Post*, January 8, 1895. Courtesy of the Trustees of the Boston Public Library.

Brother John H. Murray and Sister Mary A. Nason to act as an emergency committee with the same powers as the board to act upon cases requiring prompt action.

The new leadership of the BSWU, however, especially President John Tobin of Rochester, New York, quickly disappointed many women activists. At the second national BSWU convention in June 1896, John H. Murray of Marlborough, Massachusetts, attacked Nason's influential position on the executive board. She and her work were defended by other delegates, as reflected in the *Report of Proceedings of the Second Convention of the Boot and Shoe Workers' Union* (Boston, 1896), pages 110–111.

Mulligan, [Local No.] 35, moved an amendment to the amendment that the number of the Executive Board members from Massachusetts be three. . . .

Murray, 10, favored, stating that he believed it was necessary that the number of Executive Board members for Massachusetts should be increased as, in his opinion, the work could not be properly done because the number was too small, there being only two members in Massachusetts—himself and Sister Nason—and she, being a woman, was not called upon to adjust differences.

T. J. Costello, 17, stated that, in his opinion, Sister Nason was one of the most valuable members of the Board, and that she had been of the greatest assistance in organizing the 200 female members of Local Union No. 17 of Stoneham.

Murray, 10, stated that he had no desire or intention to belittle the services of Sister Nason, that she was thought very highly of, and received the votes of the members of the Local Unions in the city [Marlborough] which he in part represented.

Murray's proposed amendment did not carry. Nevertheless, as a result of opposition both to her views and to her powerful position, the sole woman was gone from the board by 1897. In a national referendum, Nason—little known outside of New England—failed to be reelected. Tobin and Murray proceeded to reorganize the women shoeworkers in Rochester, New York, and Marlborough, Massachusetts, into mixed locals of both men and women. Thus, Nason's policy of sisterhood as the basis of labor activity through autonomous locals controlled by women was abandoned by the BSWU.

The 1902 convention of the BSWU, as reported in Boot and Shoe Workers' Union, *Proceedings of the Fifth Convention* (Detroit, 1902), page

42, agreed to organize the female consumers of ladies' shoes and boots into pressure groups to insist that these goods bear the union label. These "label leagues" were designed to involve sympathetic women reformers and middle-class consumers in persuading manufacturers to sign BSWU contracts with shoeworkers. Cross-class support between middle-class and trade union women had been useful during the 1895 Haverhill strike which had led to the creation of the BSWU. Now, although it had abandoned autonomous women's locals, the union attempted to utilize cross-class coalitions among women for its own purposes in a nationwide organizational drive.

> Committee recommends that the General Executive Board employ a lady organizer to organize ladies' label leagues to promote Union Stamp interests and organize stitchers.
>
> Sister [Emma] Steghagen allowed the floor. Spoke in relation to the good results coming in from ladies' label leagues. Believed in encouraging the leagues as much as possible. Stated that they did great good in Chicago in increasing the demand for Union Stamp shoes, and believed that the suggestion of the Committee would be calculated to increase the number of ladies' label leagues thereby getting the women [consumers] interested in our cause, which would undoubtedly be one of the most important and valuable suggestions to this Convention.

Shoeworkers Emma Steghagen and Mary Anderson of Chicago later served as executive board members in the BSWU. After 1903 they used their position at the top level of the union's bureaucracy to join with middle-class women in the Women's Trade Union League to fight for special protective legislation for women workers and for woman suffrage.

Middle-class women reformers in the late nineteenth and early twentieth centuries studied the lives of female industrial workers and often observed them at first hand as settlement house workers or social statisticians. Some even disguised themselves as working girls to gather evidence in support of factory reform. In 1901 Marie Van Vorst, who called herself "Bell Ballard" from France, took a job in a shoe shop in Lynn. Although she found the work exhausting and disagreeable, she went away strongly impressed by the strong ties of womanhood that united the female shoeworkers she met. She also noted the importance of personal appearance and stylish dress to those who tried to maintain the status of the lady stitcher. Her experiences were published in Mrs. John Van Vorst and Marie Van Vorst, *The Woman Who Toils, Being the Experience of Two Ladies as Factory Girls* (New York, 1903). These excerpts are taken from pages 172–214.

One bitter December morning in 1901 I left Boston for Lynn, Mass. . . . Out of the town proper in a quiet side street I saw a little wooden tenement set back from the road.

"Furnished Room to Let," read the sign in the window. A sweet-faced woman responded to the bell I had rung. One glance at me and she said:

"Ve only got a 'sheep room.'"

At the compliment I was ill-pleased and told her I was looking for a *cheap* room: I had come to Lynn to work. Oh! that was all right. That was the kind of people she received. . . .

The room was $1.25 a week. Could I pay her in advance? I did so, of course. . . . On the landing below I made arrangements with the tenant for board at ten cents a meal. Madame Courier was also a French Canadian, a mammoth creature with engaging manners.

"Mademoiselle Ballard has work?"

"Not yet."

"Well, if you don't get a job my husband will speak for you. I have here three other young ladies who work in the shops, they'll speak for you! . . ."

I was determined before nightfall to be at work in a Lynn shoe-shop. . . . the largest building, one of the most important shops in Lynn [Parsons'], was my goal. . . .

Through the big building and the shipping-room, where cases of shoes were being crated for the market, I went, at length really within a factory's walls. From the first to the fifth floor I went in an elevator, a freight elevator; there are no others of course. . . . I reached the fifth floor and entered into pandemonium. The work room was in full working swing. At least five hundred machines were in operation and the noise was deafening.

I made my way to a high desk where a woman stood writing. I knew her for the forelady by her "air"; nothing else distinguished her from the employees. . . .

She didn't even look at me, but called—shrieked, rather—above the machine din to her colleagues:

"Got anything for a green hand?" . . .

"Ever worked in a shoe-shop before?"

"No ma'am."

"I'll have you learn *pressin'*; we need a *presser*. Go take your things off, then get right down over there.". . .

My object was gained. I had been in Lynn two hours and a half and was a working-woman.

On my left the seat was vacant; on my right Maggie McGowan smiled at me, although, poor thing, she had small cause to welcome the green hand who demanded her time and patience. She was to "learn me pressin'," and she did. . . .

Before me was outspread a pile of bits of leather foxings, back straps, vamps, etc. Dipping my brush in the glue, I gummed all the extreme outer edges. When the "case" had been gummed, the first bits were dry, then the fingers turned down the gummed edges of the leather into fine little seams; these seams are then plaited with the awl and the ruffled hem flattened with the hammer—this is "pressing." The case goes from the presser to the seaming machine. . . .

Meanwhile my teacher, patient-faced, lightning-fingered, sat close to me, reeking perspiration, tired with the ordeal of instructing a green horn. With no sign of exhausted patience, however, she gummed my vamps with the ill-smelling glue. . . .

The cold struck sharp as a knife as I came out of the factory. . . . Into the kitchen I was the last comer. . . . My place was at the table's end, before the Irish stew.

"Miss Ballard!" The landlady put her arm about my waist and introduced me. . . . There were four women besides myself and four men. . . .

At my left sat a well-dressed man who would pass anywhere for a business man of certain distinction. He was a common operator. Next to him was a bridal couple, very young and good looking; then came the sisters, Mika and Nannette, their brother, a packer at the shop, then Mademoiselle Frances, expert hand at fourteen dollars a week. . . .

Although I was evidently an object of interest, although countless questions were put to me, let me say that curiosity was markedly absent. Their attitude was humane, courteous, sympathetic, agreeable. . . .

Great surprise was evinced that I had so soon found a job. . . .

"It's wonderful you got a job right off! Ain't she in luck! why, most has to get spoken of weeks in advance—introduced by friends too!"

Mika said: "My name's been up two months at my sister's shop. The landlady told us about your coming, Miss Ballard. We was going to speak for you to our foreladies."

Here my huge hostess, who during my stay stood close to my side as though she thought I needed her motherliness, put her hand on my shoulder.

"Yes, *mon enfant*, we didn't want you to get discouraged in a strange place. *Ici nous sommes toute une famille.*"

"All one family?" Oh no, no, kind creature, hospitable receiver of a stranger, not all one family! I belong to the class of the woman who, one day by chance out of her carriage, did she happen to sit by your side in a cable car, would pull her dress from the contact of your clothes, heavy with tenement odours; draw back as you crushed your huge form down too close to her; turn no look of sisterhood to your face. . . .

In Lynn, unless she boards at home, a girl's living costs her at best $3.75 a week. If she be of the average her month's earnings are $32. . . .

A word for the swells of the trade, for swells exist. One of my companions at 28 Viger Street made $14 a week. Her expenses were $4; she therefore had at her disposition about $40 a month. She had no family—*every cent of her surplus she spent on her clothes.*

"I like to look down and see myself dressed nice," she said; "it makes me feel good. I don't like myself in poor clothes."

She *was* well-dressed—her furs good, her hat charming. We walked to work side by side, she the lady of us. Of course she belongs to the [Boot and Shoe Workers'] Union. . . . She is only tired out, thin, undeveloped, pale, that's all. She is almost a capitalist and extremely well dressed. . . .

In Viger Street, I was more simply clad than my companions. My aspect called forth only sisterhood and kindness.

Fellowship from first to last, fellowship from their eyes to mine, a spark kindled never to be extinguished. The morning I left my tenement lodging Mika took my hand at the door.

"Goodbye." Her eyes actually filled. "I'm awfully sorry you're going. If the world don't treat you good come back to us."

I must qualify a little. One member of the working class there was on whom my cheap clothes had a chilling effect—the spoiled creature of the traveling rich, a Pullman car porter on the train from Boston to New York! Although I called him first and purposely gave him my order in time, he viewed me askance and served me the last of all. As I watched my companions in their furs and handsome attire eat, whilst I sat and waited, my woolen gloves folded in my lap, I wondered if any one of the favoured was as hungry, as famished as the presser from Parsons'. . . .

[15]

The Crisis of Sisterhood

Lynn shoeworkers who had backed the Haverhill strike in 1895 received support in return during a major strike in 1903. This confrontation pitted the nineteenth-century traditions of local autonomy and militancy in the Crispin and Knights of Labor movements against the conservative unionism of John Tobin, president of the BSWU. Lynn stitchers joined with the Knights of Labor cutters in 1903 to demonstrate their opposition as skilled workers to the oppressive policies of the BSWU by going out on strike against union contract shops. In the *Lynn Item* of February 24, 1903, one testimony to the skill and experience of Lynn stitchers came from a forewoman.

> Messrs. Editors—Through the columns of your valuable paper we have heard from both the manufacturers and the stitchers, but as yet I have failed to see any opinions expressed by the forewomen—a class well qualified to judge of the merits of the present state of affairs, and to that class I belong. For the past 20 years I have had charge of help in Lynn and other cities and therefore feel that I know whereof I speak, when I tell the stitchers in this city, or any other city, that they are not obliged to pay $13 a year [in union dues] for the privilege of being honest bread-winners. For the past three years good stitchers have been at a premium in Lynn, and are also at the present time. . . . With the cutters' side of the question I have nothing to say, only as a free-born American working woman it seems to me an outrage . . . to be threatened by any order . . . for the privilege of earning their daily bread. . . .

The skilled Lynn stitchers—the best on earth—God bless them. I have had charge of help in Maine, New York and Boston, but give me two teams of the real Lynn help and we would turn out more and better shoes than five teams of any other. . . . Now girls, a last word to you:— Have your own local, make it fraternal in every way. Remember that your employer's interest is also yours. Have your work perfect; it will help to sell the shoe ahead of the [union's] stamp. . . . Yours with sympathy.

A Forewoman.

Many Lynn stitchers in the Lady Stitchers' Assembly of the Knights of Labor, which had represented them since 1884, did not agree that their interests as workers were identical to those of their employers. They had successfully opposed the bureaucratic and unrepresentative character of the BSWU locals, whose contracts they saw as benefitting the shoe manufacturers. Others, more cautious of hostile confrontations with their employers, hoped for a union that would both represent their interests and work in harmony with the manufacturers. Their views appeared in the *Lynn Item*.

[February 10, 1903]

"Messrs Editors:—I became a member of that organization [the BSWU] when it was in its infancy in this city and was in it for two years. There was not a week during that time when I earned over $5 and there were others who earned but little more. If we did not have the 25 cents ready for the collectors they would be very indignant. There were a great many weeks I deprived myself of the necessities of life to pay an unfair tax of 25 cents for the privilege of the firm to use a label or stamp of organized labor, supposed labor to be under righteous conditions.

Now, when they were going to have a meeting, they would pass a circular to announce it, with a promise of ice cream and cake for the lady members, who would attend. Probably a few girls would attend the meeting. But instead of ice cream and cake which were promised, beer was served to the men and nothing to the ladies. . . .

Mr. Tobin and his agents receive their salary [during the dull seasons] just the same, do they not? Does it make any difference to them whether the shoe business is dull two months in the year? What is it to them, if we have a mother or some other member of the family sick at home, and we must stay home to take care of the sick one? What is it to them, when we are eight weeks in arrears [in dues] that we must pay $2 for a fine before we can go to work in one of their stamp factories? What is it to them if our machines break down, as they very often do, and we are two or three days earning little or nothing? What is it to them when two girls are hired to do the work that one could do easily? . . . we [have] become the dupes of shoe manufacturers.

Stitcher

[March 5, 1903]

Messrs. Editors:— . . . I am employed in one of the busiest shops in our city; which has not as yet had to resort to the use of the B. and S.W.U. stamp, having always been able thus far to sell its goods on its own merits. Our interest is our employer's interest to be sure, and we would most gladly welcome any union for the good of both. . . . I fail to see the advantage of placing ourselves in bondage and paying $13 a year for what protection the B. and S.W.U. offers us. . . . While we would gladly lend a helping hand to all our fellow workmen, is it to be in our interest to have a [stitching] school [in Boston], as proposed by the B. and S.W.U., to produce an army of recruits to take our places at any time? Our employers could take advantage at the slightest provocation. . . . Humanity cannot long be trampled in the dust. Let us not forget that our forefathers fought for our liberty once. Let us all unite to retain it.

A Stitcher

[March 14, 1903]

Messrs. Editors:—A movement is proposed to conciliate the striking stitchers. Until now the women have been of the very least importance to the B. and S.W.U. except to donate their 25 cents weekly. There never has been anything done to better their conditions. . . . I think it would be easier to start anew. Our labor is the most valuable possession we have, as we cannot live without it, and it should be protected. We realize that unions have come to stay, and I think it would be well to have a union in which we could unite under one head, but that head must have something in it: something for the working people as well as the manufacturers. . . .

If a stamp is required for the success of our employers, they should have it by all means, but let it be founded on good union principles that shall combine honor, justice and prosperity for the good of all and be worthy of the patronage of all union people. . . .

Lynn Stitcher

The strong sense of sisterhood among the women shoeworkers of Lynn stretched across the region, and even the nation. As a cultural resource, it proved useful to warn others against ruthless recruiters, whether for western factories in 1879 or for strikebound shops during the 1903 strike in Lynn. These statements appeared in the *Vindicator*, January 4, 1879, and the *Lynn Item*, February 14, 1903.

Dear Sir:—We, the late employees of the Wentworth Boot and Shoe Company, at West Berkeley, California, take the privilege of making known to you the following facts, asking the publication of them in the *Vindicator*, for the benefit of the working girls of Lynn, and elsewhere, some of whom, we learn, are about ready to follow the advice of Horace Greeley and "go West." The prevailing opinion in the East is that wages are much better than there, but it is not so, which we have found out by experience. Some of us have been here nearly three years and have been so badly victimized that we submit the following to warn those who are on the verge of being allured to the "golden" state with big promises. At current prices [wages] here, with plenty of work, we are unable to make more than expenses, and there are not more than four or five months in the year that we have work enough. . . .

Miss Howe, late of Chicago, has just arrived here, and brings a price list with her, offering to take entire charge of the aforesaid stitching department at full one-third less than the starvation prices that we are receiving and Mr. J. M. Wentworth proposes furnishing girls from Lynn to do the work. We do not make the statement out of fear that we shall lose our situation with the above-named firm for our notice is given to quit their employ. . . . We care not who fills our places, but hope that no more girls will be allured three thousand miles from their homes by false statement. This is not the voice only of two poor working girls, employed by the firm, in malice or envy, but on the contrary, it is the voice of *all* the girls in their employ—all of whom have given their notice to quit work, and who now deem it their duty to make known the true state of affairs here, so that those who may contemplate a trip across the country to better their condition by work, may not be deceived.

The above is drawn in its mildest form, without *bias or prejudice*, and approved by the forewoman and all of the girls.

Very respectfully yours,
Mattie J. Cook
Hannah F. Brown

The stitchers who are out on strike [in 1903] in the union stamp factories are remaining loyal in their struggle for what they believe to be their just rights. . . .

Recently a young woman was lured to Lynn from Farmington, Me., by a promise of a good position in a leading factory here. After going to the shop in question she reported to the stitchers what she had experienced, and not being willing to stand out against members of her own sex she refused to take one of their places. . . .

In 1903, President Tobin of the BSWU became the target of the strikers' anger when he named rebellious women in a petition for a court injunction against disorderly conduct by strikers. His decision provoked expressions of sisterly outrage by stitchers over such attacks on their respectability. The term "lady stitcher" as a badge of respectable womanhood remained a part of labor nomenclature in Lynn until 1912, when the Lady Stitchers' Assembly was absorbed into the United Shoeworkers' Union. Angry stitchers were quoted in the *Boston Globe*, January 25, 1903.

The stitchers are very indignant with the instigators of the injunction proceedings who have used the name of one of their number who, they claim, is not physically able to be out of doors and much less to create disturbances, even if she wanted to.

Miss Katherine McClellan is another who has been served with the injunction papers. She feels very much grieved about it.

"I am innocent of the charge, for I have yet for the first time to even go around where the crowds assemble in the evenings and mornings. I do not like the insinuation that the charge implies, that I am rowdyish, unladylike and riotous. I am not that sort and I deeply resent the whole proceedings," she said.

Miss Mary E. Peabody is another striking stitcher who belongs to the injunction contingent. She said with some degree of warmth, "I am mad clear through. I am mad for several reasons. First, because I am

Shoe dresser, Lynn. Photograph by Frances Benjamin Johnson. Courtesy of Library of Congress.

innocent and I believe in having 'the game as well as the name.' That is the main reason why I am sorry, for if I had known that this was coming I would have 'had the deed as well as the credit.' The only thing I am sorry for is that I did not take some part in the riots."

Stitchers in Lynn and Haverhill, in coalition with like-minded male shoeworkers, fought to maintain their traditions of local control and autonomy for women workers against efforts by the BSWU leadership to force them into the mixed locals. One of the rebels, Mrs. Jeanette Hamilton of the Lady Stitchers' Assembly, told the *Lynn Item*, January 27, 1903, that the BSWU ignored the needs of many women workers by undermining female control of their locals.

No matter what the earnings [in the union stamp factory], we must pay our dues to the union. There was one instance a few weeks ago and where a woman earned 87 cents for the week, but she had to give 25 of that to union. Another girl in the factory some weeks ago earned $1. She pays that amount for her room and works in a restaurant for her meals. When Agent Chesley [of the BSWU] came for the dues the girl said she did not want to change the bill, and finally she borrowed a quarter, and the agent waited until she brought it to him. . . .

In regards to our not carrying our grievances to the union, we wish to register a protest against this statement. At one time we were cut down. The vamping department and a committee of six women of whom I was one, went to the union office and there laid the matter before the officers. They told us to return the next night and they would see what right the firm had to cut us down without an agreement. When we arrived at the hall the next night, we were told that the others had gone to Boston. We tried several times to have the price adjusted, but always without success.

There are other things about the union we wish to speak about. At one time there was an election and when the ballots were brought around to the girls they were marked with crosses against certain names. I was told when a ballot was handed me—"Those are the people that we want you to vote for." I kept the ballot and refused to vote.

At the next meeting I demanded an explanation of why a marked ballot was given me to vote and the answer was that the heads of the union had done this "for the good of the organization."

Since being compelled to join this union, . . . there has been no raise in wages, but cut downs instead and there is hardly a person who is not heartily disgusted with the whole affair.

The policies of the BSWU divided the women shoeworkers of Essex County between a small minority of stitchers loyal to the national union during the 1903 strike and the majority of women workers in Lynn and Haverhill who supported local autonomy. As loyalists tried to break the strike of those women who rejected the leadership of John Tobin and the BSWU, sisterhood became the victim of numerous angry confrontations, which were described in the *Lynn Item*.

[February 11, 1903]
Woman against Woman in the Shoe Strike
During the evening a number of men and women, strike breakers [BSWU members from Cincinnati and other cities] and their escorts, were made targets for eggs, said to be fairly fresh, and many of which were thrown by women. . . . Many of the women strike breakers . . . quit work much sooner than was expected and were able to make their way to their homes without interference. The striking stitchers appeared to have no animosity against the women who first came out on strike and returned to work later in the union stamp factories . . . as their efforts were directed entirely against the women brought to Lynn to take their places by the Boot and Shoe Workers' Union. The women who were in wait for the stitchers when the latter left the factories, carried hand bags in which eggs were stowed away ready for instant use. . . .

[February 16, 1903]
. . . One indignant Boot and Shoe Worker stated Saturday evening that the actions of the men who assaulted the women stitchers was a disgrace to the city and would not be tolerated by the members of his union. He said when a decent woman cannot walk the streets without danger of being rotten-egged, it is about time for something to be done. . . .
The Boot and Shoe Workers' Union has had considerable trouble with the stitchers brought to this city, on account of the egg assaults that have taken place on the streets, consequently it has been decided to put an end to this state of things once and for all by fitting up . . . [a] factory in Boston with up-to-date stitching machinery, where several

hundred women stitchers will be employed and stitching work will be done for the Lynn manufacturers and, for the union stamp manufacturers in any other city that may have trouble.

[February 24, 1903]
Several egg throwings occurred last week, but were kept very quiet. In one of these an attack was made upon the Cuthbert sisters, two girls who are at work in the D. A. Donovan [BSWU stamp] factory. They were attacked on Summer street and had their faces scratched and hair pulled, causing them considerable discomfiture. . . .

[February 27, 1903]
Men masquerading as women, rather than women themselves, seem . . . to be the ones most industriously engaged at present in throwing eggs at stitchers brought by the Boot and Shoe Workers' Union to work in the Lynn union stamp factories. . . . [One Lynn woman denied that such disguises were unfair:] "it just serves those women right for coming here to take the places of good Lynn girls. . . ."

[March 13, 1903]
Members of the Lady Stitchers Assembly 2618, Knights of Labor declare that if any men have been around the city in women's clothing just to throw eggs at strike breakers they have had no encouragement from stitchers now out on strike. . . . To think of men masquerading as women without detection is absurd. Men cannot dress to look like women by just putting on an old dress, and as far as running away, why, a man in a woman's dress could not run at all.

[March 14, 1903]
An innovation in the strike is the spraying of asafoetida on the clothing of strike-breaking stitchers. Besides doing damage to their clothes, it emits a much more disagreeable odor than even decayed eggs. Its German name is *teufelsdreck*, meaning devil's dung.

For a number of days past girls coming to the headquarters of the B. and S.W.U. at Lasters' Hall have complained of an odor coming from their clothing. . . . The introduction of this ill-smelling liquid causes much inconvenience and annoyance to those on whom it has been sprayed or thrown.

For the past two evenings women returning to their homes out of town were unconsciously saturated with the stuff while they were in the Boston and Maine Railroad station waiting for a train. . . . In a crowd it is an easy matter to spray asafoetida, and consequently, no one was seen. . . .

The victims did not discover their condition until they were on the train. One of them, a young woman from Beverly, received such a dose that her clothing smelled so strong that people left the seats close by her, while it is reported the young woman burst into tears. . . .

One of the imported stitchers had a long white coat ruined . . . by having it spattered with ink. The attack came from the back. . . .

As another tactic to replace striking stitchers, the BSWU sent immigrant men and boys from shoe shops in the Boston area to work in the stitching rooms of union factories in Lynn. This significant action began to alter the sexual division of labor that had characterized Essex County shoe production for a century. The introduction of men into stitching rooms under union auspices slowly undermined women's control of the stitching process on which sisterhood and female-controlled locals had been built.

During the years that followed, the growing scarcity of skilled stitchers influenced shoe manufacturers to recruit immigrant men from southern and eastern Europe, where male workers were trained in needle skills on leather goods and garments. Greek, Italian, Jewish, and eastern Mediterranean men began to take jobs formerly held by Yankee women and native-born daughters of immigrants in Essex County shoe shops. During the busy seasons, men could work longer hours than women, for whom special protective legislation sponsored by concerned middle-class reformers had decreed shorter workdays. Many of the native-born American women who had been attracted to shoe stitching began to move into clerical and retail occupations. In 1900 only 2 percent of all stitching jobs in Lynn were male; by 1910 the proportion had jumped to 20 percent. As the sexual division of labor changed, the nineteenth-century domination of stitching by women gave way to a heterosexual work force.

The 1903 strike nearly destroyed the BSWU in Essex County, but the union made one final attempt to organize Lynn stitchers by sponsoring a local chapter of the Women's Trade Union Label League in alliance with local woman suffrage groups. As reported in the *Lynn Item*, Stuart Reid, national organizer for the AFL, came to Lynn in 1903 to promote the league's efforts to create consumer demand for the union label on cigars, garments, hats, and shoes.

[September 28, 1903]

The committee of 15 . . . to take steps to introduce union made goods in Lynn and create a demand for the same, submitted a report . . . that steps had been taken to form a branch of the Women's Trade Union Label League in Lynn. It was announced that a mass meeting of women, for the purpose of forming the proposed branch of the league will be held in Lasters' Hall. . . .

The committee reported having a conference with members of the Women's Suffrage Club, who promised to give all aid possible to further the sale of union goods in Lynn. . . .

[September 29, 1903]

There was a good attendance of men and women at the meeting in Lynn. A temporary organization was perfected with Miss Ellen F. Wetherell, Chairman, Miss Mamie Donovan [of the BSWU], Secretary, and Miss Mary Doyle, Treasurer. The meeting was held under the auspices of the committee of 15 members of the Central Labor Union [AFL], recently appointed to push the sale of union-made goods in Lynn. . . .

Miss Ellen F. Wetherell . . . introduced Edward Cohen, member of the International Cigarmakers' Union, who made an excellent address in favor of the increase of union-made goods. . . . He had in mind the solution of the labor problem by bringing the men and women together on an equal footing, not only in the workshops, but also at the polls. The women should see to it that the union label appeared on everything they wore, and as far as possible on everything they ate, for the union label was an emblem of purity. . . . If they demanded the union stamp on all shoes, the present trouble in the city [the conflict between the BSWU and the Knights of Labor] would soon be settled. . . . The rank and file of the other side was not opposed to honest labor, and it was only a few leaders who were fostering the trouble. . . .

Mrs. A. S. Carr, President of the Lynn Equal Rights Club, made an address that made a deep impression on the women present, for whom her remarks were directly intended. She believed that they should all take an interest in the suffrage question, as they all had to work for a living. She was in favor of the object of the meeting. . . .

[October 6, 1903]

. . . The meeting [of the Women's Trade Union Label League] was remarkable for the fierce attack made [by John Cowper of the Central Labor Union] on the Knights of Labor in general and the Cutters' Assembly . . . of this city in particular. . . . Stuart Reid, National Organizer for the A.F. of L. made one of his best speeches since coming to Lynn, addressed directly to the women present, in which he made mention of the wonderful drawing power of women, and told of an incident in his own career, many years ago, when he tramped five miles over a mountain to see one woman, and believed there was no man living he would go so far to see.

[Reid said] the women had it in their power to compel the store-keepers of Lynn to keep union-made [BSWU] goods for sale. . . .

The Lady Stitchers' Assembly of the Knights in Lynn immediately organized to oppose the effort of the BSWU's label league, although they accepted the general strategy of boycotts against other goods not bearing union labels. The *Lynn Item*, October 6, 1903, described their activities.

. . . The [stitchers'] union . . . entered on a "new departure," that of deciding to combat the influence of the new Women's Trade Union Label League, established in Lynn, Monday evening, and will show to the merchants of Lynn that it will not be for their interests to handle shoes with the union stamp of the Boot and Shoe Workers' Union. . . . the talk about union-made goods of all kinds was thinly veiled for the purpose of deceiving the public and making the people believe that the league is honest in its efforts in pushing the sale of all union-made goods. A committee was appointed at the meeting that will act with a committee of [the] Cutters' Assembly . . . in circulating a monster petition for signatures among the working people of Lynn, who will pledge themselves not to purchase any shoes bearing the union stamp of the Boot and Shoe Workers' Union. . . .

It is the intention to circulate this petition in the factories and obtain thousands of signatures that will be presented to the Lynn Merchants' Association, . . . so that taken all in all another very merry labor war between the parties may be looked for almost immediately. . . . The joint committee will, however, only make their fight against shoes bearing the union stamp of the Boot and Shoe Workers' Union. . . .

After an openly sarcastic attack on the Knights in Lynn by Stuart Reid on behalf of the BSWU, the stitchers responded in kind in the *Lynn Item*, October 15, 1903.

Messrs. Editors—We implore you to intercede for us and put to Stuart Reid, through the medium of Lynn's most popular paper, this query:—

"Were you ever in Lynn with your hat off?" Our evening's enjoyment is marred by the ever present picture of the man-from-nowhere-with-his-hat-on. The columns of our *Item* are monopolized by his senseless prattle and show an utter ignorance of the cause he expounds. The warmth of our last summer has been intolerable, so in mercy's name spare the stitchers of Lynn his volcanic eruptions.

We all understand that the stitchers are the keynote to the present situation, and although one man tries to "club" us in, and another to "blow" us in, we will remain outside, and proudly proclaim ourselves bone fide Knights of Labor, with both eyes open to the wiley tactics of the B. and S.W.U. and the A.F. of L., also, and emphatically state we are done with them, now and forever.

. . . We ask . . . [Reid] to inquire of the first street boy he meets to explain the present controversy, and he will be possessed of a more comprehensive view of the situation than he now has.

In conclusion, we wish to impress upon him that the cutters and stitchers are fighting the obnoxious B. and S.W.U. stamp and no other. There has been no backing down by the stitchers. . . . Once more we ask this man to refrain from any more advice to the stitchers, as we will not recognize in any way this man-from-nowhere-with-his-hat-on.

K. of L. Stitchers.

The Women's Trade Union Label League of Boston made no progress among the shoeworkers of Lynn and Haverhill. Anger against disloyal sisters in 1903 had created irreparable divisions between the stitchers who still belonged to the Knights and the BSWU women in the AFL. Women shoeworkers in Essex County had abandoned a common sense of sisterhood as a unifying bond for national organization.

In addition to sponsoring the label league in Lynn, the leaders of the BSWU voted to punish two Haverhill sisters, May Mack and Mrs. Alice McMenamon, members who had supported the Lynn strike in 1903. On January 12, 1904, the general executive board denied their claims

for sick benefits and adopted a policy that subsequently penalized all
women BSWU members by refusing to accept miscarriages as legitimate
illnesses. The action is recorded in the Minutes of the General Executive Board, Actions and Decisions, 1895–1906, Papers of the Boot and
Shoe Workers' Union, Wisconsin State Historical Society. Excerpts are
quoted courtesy of the United Food and Commercial Workers International Union, AFL-CIO & CLC.

Secretary Baine [of the General Executive Board] submitted the
following letter from Local Executive Board #287 [Haverhill], setting
forth their reasons for disallowing both of these claims:
The cause of sickness was typhoid fever, and inside of three
weeks, she was able to be out and attend the academy of music one
night, Monday, October 12th, when it rained hard. When Sister
[Alice] McMenamon was asked in regard to her attending the
Academy of Music, she said that [May Mack] was well wrapped up
and took the [street]car at the Door. The Executive Board . . .
notified the Committee that as long as [May Mack] was able to go
out nights, especially in the rain, that no claims would be approved.
. . . There had for some time past been a disposition on the part of
the members in Haverhill to secure all of the sick claim money possible
from the General Organization. . . . The members seem to show a
disposition to get even with the General Union by endorsing anybody's
claim whether justifiable or not. . . . In the case of Mrs. Alice
McMenamon, the Constitution provides that in case of Confinement
[childbirth], members shall not receive [sick] benefits for three weeks
prior, nor for three weeks after such confinement. . . . Delegate Mc-
Clean on behalf of the two sisters who had appealed, stated that it was
not true that May Mack had visited any theater, and that she had been
under the Doctor's care and unable to work for some time after the
claim had been filed. In the case of Mrs. Alice McMenamon, he stated
the miscarriage had been brought on by sickness [bronchitis] and for
that reason, believed that she should receive benefits. . . . Delegate
Lowell moved that the decision of the General Secretary, wherein he
decided that a case of miscarriage comes under the same law covering
confinement [ineligible for sick benefits], be endorsed by the Board.
Carried unanimously.

At its November 1903 convention, the AFL reorganized the label leagues into the national Women's Trade Union League (WTUL), the most important effort by the AFL in the early twentieth century to advance the interests of workingwomen. Among the officers of the WTUL organization in Boston were supporters of the BSWU: Mamie Donovan and Mary Kenney O'Sullivan. The refusal of many Essex County stitchers to support the BSWU was a tragic loss to the AFL and to the Boston chapter of the WTUL. Women shoeworkers in the nineteenth century possessed the longest tradition of interest in women's rights and the most effective record of labor protest among female industrial workers. Without their heritage of female autonomy and power and their commitment to feminism and equal rights, the Boston WTUL failed to represent the interests of many Massachusetts workingwomen.

Nonetheless, the traditions of skill, experience, womanly strength, and self-organization left by nineteenth-century New England women shoeworkers offered a political heritage to the new immigrant workers, male and female, coming into the shoe industry. The challenge to twentieth-century workingwomen in New England shoe cities lay in reworking this heritage into new grounds for class action.

With the resurgence of feminism in the 1960s and 1970s and the increasing number of women in the late twentieth-century work force, especially self-supporting women and female heads of families, feminism has again become an issue for women in the labor movement. In 1974 the Coalition of Labor Union Women (CLUW), which represents women in the AFL-CIO, began work to recruit the millions of unorganized women workers. They endorsed the Equal Rights Amendment, supported the pro-choice position on abortion rights, and joined politically with middle-class feminists to push for an expansion of women's rights. The organizations and militancy of clerical, service, and hospital workers in the 1970s and early 1980s represent the current involvement of workingwomen in protecting their interests and bettering their conditions. The successful 1989 unionization of the mostly female clerical staff at Harvard University is a recent victory in this organizational effort.

The legacy of nineteenth-century women shoeworkers includes a warning to contemporary women workers: balancing the complex interests of gender and class requires a cautious approach to male-controlled organizations or cross-class coalitions with middle-class women. The positive core of that legacy emphasizes the importance of collective action, the potential in sisterhood, the need for autonomy and power for women within the labor movement, and the urgency of political action to redefine women's place in society. It is eloquently expressed in the words of the Lynn striker in 1871:

We will not submit to being crowded; we will not be enslaved. We are freeborn American women: and when they attempt to tell us what they will do, we will rise in our might, and . . . [our] voices will tell them what we will do.

Selected Bibliography

Baron, Ava. "Women and the Making of the American Working Class: A Study of the Proletarianization of Printers." *Review of Radical Political Economics* 14 (Fall 1982): 23–42.

——, ed. *Work Engendered: Toward a New History of Men, Women, and Work.* Ithaca: Cornell University Press, 1991.

Baxandall, Rosalyn, Elizabeth Ewen, and Linda Gordon. "The Working Class Has Two Sexes." *Monthly Review*, July/Aug. 1976, pp. 1–9.

Buhle, Mari Jo. *Women and American Socialism, 1870–1920.* Urbana: University of Illinois Press, 1981.

Cantor, Milton, and Bruce Laurie, eds. *Class, Sex, and the Woman Worker.* Westport, Conn.: Greenwood Press, 1977.

Cooper, Patricia. *Men, Women, and Work Culture in American Cigar Factories, 1900–1919.* Urbana: University of Illinois Press, 1987.

Davis, Margery. *Woman's Place Is at the Typewriter.* Philadelphia: Temple University Press, 1982.

Diner, Hasia. *Erin's Daughters: Irish Immigrant Women in the Nineteenth Century.* Baltimore: Johns Hopkins University Press, 1983.

Dublin, Thomas. *Women at Work: The Transformation of Work and Community in Lowell, Massachusetts, 1826–1860.* New York: Columbia University Press, 1979.

Dye, Nancy Shrom. *As Equals and as Sisters: Feminism, Unionism, and the Women's Trade Union League of New York.* Columbia: University of Missouri Press, 1980.

Eisenstein, Sarah. *Give Us Bread but Give Us Roses: Working Women's Consciousness in the United States, 1890 to the First World War.* London: Routledge & Kegan Paul, 1983.

Foner, Philip S. *Women and the American Labor Movement: From Colonial Times to the Eve of World War I.* New York: Free Press, 1979.

Frisch, Michael H., and Daniel Walkowitz. *Working-Class America: Essays on*

Labor, Community, and American Society. Urbana: University of Illinois Press, 1983.

Groneman, Carol, and Mary Beth Norton, eds. *"To Toil the Livelong Day": American Women at Work*. Ithaca: Cornell University Press, 1987.

Hall, Jacquelyn Dowd, et al. *Like a Family: The Making of a Southern Cotton Mill World*. Chapel Hill: University of North Carolina Press, 1987.

Janiewski, Dolores E. *Sisterhood Denied: Race, Gender, and Class in a New South Community*. Philadelphia: Temple University Press, 1985.

Jensen, Joan M., and Sue Davidson, eds. *A Needle, A Bobbin, A Strike: Women Needleworkers in America*. Philadelphia: Temple University Press, 1984.

Jones, Jacqueline. *Labor of Love, Labor of Sorrow: Black Women, Work, and the Family from Slavery to the Present*. New York: Basic Books, 1985.

Kennedy, Susan E. *If All We Did Was to Weep at Home: A History of White Working-Class Women in America*. Bloomington: Indiana University Press, 1979.

Kessler-Harris, Alice. *Out to Work: A History of Wage-Earning Women in the United States*. New York: Oxford University Press, 1982.

Kleinberg, Susan J. *The Shadow of the Mills: Working-Class Families in Pittsburgh, 1870–1907*. Pittsburgh: University of Pittsburgh Press, 1989.

Levine, Susan. *Labor's True Woman: Carpet Weavers, Industrialization, and Labor Reform in the Gilded Age*. Philadelphia: Temple University Press, 1984.

McGaw, Judith A. *Most Wonderful Machine: Mechanization and Social Change in Berkshire Paper Making, 1801–1885*. Princeton: Princeton University Press, 1987.

Milkman, Ruth. *Women, Work, and Protest: A Century of Women's Labor History*. Boston: Routledge & Kegan Paul, 1985.

Peiss, Kathy. *Cheap Amusements: Working Women and Leisure in Turn-of-the-Century New York*. Philadelphia: Temple University Press, 1986.

Stansell, Christine. *City of Women: Sex and Class in New York, 1789–1860*. New York: Knopf, 1986.

Turbin, Carole. "Reconceptualizing Family, Work, and Labor Organizing: Working Women in Troy, 1860–1890." *Review of Radical Political Economics* 16 (Spring 1984): 1–16.

——. *Working Women of Collar City: Gender, Class, and Community in Troy, New York, 1864–1886*. Urbana: University of Illinois Press, 1991.

Walkowitz, Daniel. *Worker City, Company Town: Iron and Cotton-Worker Protest in Troy and Cohoes, New York, 1855–1884*. Urbana: University of Illinois Press, 1978.

Yans-McLaughlin, Virginia. *Family and Community: Italian Immigrants in Buffalo, 1880–1930*. Ithaca: Cornell University Press, 1977.

Index

Library of Congress Cataloging-in-Publication Data

Blewett, Mary H.
  We will rise in our might: workingwomen's voices from nineteenth-
century New England / Mary H. Blewett.
      p.   cm. — (Documents in American social history)
  Includes bibliographical references and index.
  ISBN 0-8014-2246-9 (cloth: alk. paper). —ISBN 0-8014-9537-7
(pbk.: alk. paper)
    1. Women—Employment—Massachusetts—History—19th
century.   2. Shoemakers—Massachusetts—History—19th
century.   3. Women—Massachusetts—Social
conditions.   I. Title.   II. Series.
HD6073.B72U63   1991
331.4'88531'009744—dc20

                                                      91-55077